Empowering Women in Work in Developing Countries

Empowering Women in Work in Developing Countries

Maarten van Klaveren
University of Amsterdam – Amsterdam Institute of Advanced Labour Studies (AIAS), the Netherlands

and

Kea Tijdens
University of Amsterdam – Amsterdam Institute of Advanced Labour Studies (AIAS), the Netherlands

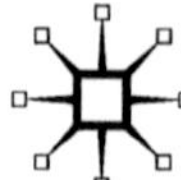

First published 2012 by
PALGRAVE MACMILLAN

Palgrave Macmillan in the UK is an imprint of Macmillan Publishers Limited, registered in England, company number 785998, of Houndmills, Basingstoke, Hampshire RG21 6XS.

Palgrave Macmillan in the US is a division of St Martin's Press LLC, 175 Fifth Avenue, New York, NY 10010.

Palgrave Macmillan is the global academic imprint of the above companies and has companies and representatives throughout the world.

Palgrave® and Macmillan® are registered trademarks in the United States, the United Kingdom, Europe and other countries.

ISBN: 978–0–230–36935–1

This book is printed on paper suitable for recycling and made from fully managed and sustained forest sources. Logging, pulping and manufacturing processes are expected to conform to the environmental regulations of the country of origin.

A catalogue record for this book is available from the British Library.

A catalog record for this book is available from the Library of Congress.

10 9 8 7 6 5 4 3 2 1
21 20 19 18 17 16 15 14 13 12

Printed and bound in the United States of America

Contents

Tables

Figures

Boxes

Preface

Sometimes, inspired by an outstanding experience, researchers take up a challenge without fully understanding its implications. This was the case when the authors, associated with the Amsterdam Institute for Advanced Labour Studies (AIAS) of the University of Amsterdam, after contributing to the large Decisions for Life (DFL) project, in May 2011, attended the final day of the International Young Women's Conference in Amsterdam. That conference was a major event in the DFL project which by then had been underway for nearly three years in 14 developing countries. The vibrant atmosphere of that day's debates, together with the in-depth and convincing nature of the working group reporting, made us decide to produce a proposal for a book on this project aimed at empowering young women in work in developing countries. When Palgrave accepted our proposal and we went on, we became aware of the daunting task that we had taken on. In the first place we felt the need to underpin the situation of the target group, girls and young women aged 15–29, in life and in work with statistical data. This forced us to update information that we had gathered in the years before. Second, we aimed at providing the reader with a flavour of what went on at the DFL project, allowing views on the barriers and challenges young women meet in everyday practice in finding balance between the various spheres of life. In pursuing these objectives, we hope to have done justice to the massive efforts of the three pillars of the DFL project: the many young female participants; the paid and lay officials of the involved trade unions, affiliated with the ITUC and UNI global union umbrellas; and the international and regional *WageIndicator* teams. The rapid growth of the DFL project in just three years would definitely have been impossible without the *WageIndicator* teams and their *WageIndicator* websites.

We are very grateful to all who contributed to this book and the DFL project as its basis. We are particularly indebted to our former AIAS colleague Melanie Hughie-Williams, for her research assistance covering many issues, and our current colleague Nuria Ramos-Martin, for her contributions on labour law. Of course, all remaining text errors are ours. Special thanks are due to the staff of the ITUC Equality Department. As in all other *WageIndicator*-based projects, we are greatly indebted to the colleagues of the *WageIndicator* organization, especially to Paulien Osse, director of the Wage Indicator Foundation (WIF). Last but not least we are grateful to the Netherlands Ministry of Foreign Affairs, whose grant enabled the Decisions for Life project and its extension.

Acknowledgements

The authors would like to thank Paulien Osse, director of Wage Indicator Foundation, Amsterdam, Netherlands, for permission to include the citations of the Decisions for Life project reports, posted at the *WageIndicator* website.

1
Introduction

Introducing the Decisions for Life project

From 9 through 11 May 2011, more than 100 women from 23 countries gathered at an International Young Women's Conference to discuss the next stage of a campaign to empower young women workers around the world. The conference was held in Amsterdam, in the framework of the Decisions for Life) campaign, and organized jointly by the International Trade Union Confederation (ITUC), the UNI Global Union, the Wage Indicator Foundation (WIF) and the University of Amsterdam (see Box 1.1). The authors of this volume are associated with this university.

The DFL campaign started with the DFL project, covering trade union and web activities in 14 developing countries: Brazil, India and Indonesia; the CIS (Commonwealth of Independent States) countries Azerbaijan, Belarus, Kazakhstan and Ukraine; and the southern African countries Angola, Botswana, Malawi, Mozambique, South Africa, Zambia and Zimbabwe. The project was awarded a substantial grant from the Netherlands Ministry of Foreign Affairs as part of its strategy to support the UN Millennium Development Goal 3 (MDG3), "Promote Gender Equality and Empower Women". DFL focused in particular on one of the four MDG3 priority areas as identified by the ministry: promoting formal employment and equal opportunity at the labour market.

The DFL project ran from June 2008 until December 2011. It aimed to raise awareness amongst young women about their employment opportunities and career possibilities, about family building and about work-family balance – in short, it aimed to empower young women and show them that they have choices in life. The project's point of departure was that the lifetime decisions adolescent girls and young women face will determine not only their individual futures but also the future of society: their choices are key to the demographic and workforce development of the nation. The project targeted women in the service industries because these industries employ the majority of working women in the 15–29 age group and because these industries are expanding in (almost) all 14 countries. The project focused on eight occupational groups in commerce (salespersons/cashiers in retail), finance (secretaries, bookkeepers), call centres and IT/BPO (call centre operators, IT programmers) and tourism (hotel housekeepers and receptionists, travel agents).

The Decisions for Life project followed a two-pronged awareness-raising strategy. The national trade unions developed campaigning activities through meetings and training sessions in 12 of 14 countries. These activities were facilitated by online information through the respective national *WageIndicator* websites, particularly on statutory minimum wages and on rights of women and labour. Female organizers of the unions affiliated with ITUC and UNI – increasingly those from other unions too – played major roles. As a result, at the end of the three conference days in 2011, the participants unanimously adopted a declaration in which they demanded that ITUC and UNI, as well as their affiliates and the *WageIndicator*, expand Decisions for Life and mainstream the methods used in the project.

Box 1.1 Tabisa

The International Young Women's Conference was dedicated to the memory of Tabisa Sigaba, a young South African woman and a DFL campaign leader and full-time shop steward from SACCAWU (South African Commercial, Catering and Allied Workers Union). In 2010 Tabisa passed away suddenly because of a tragic car accident. She came up with the idea to organize an international conference with young women. The event in Amsterdam was held in memory of her passionate commitment to the empowerment of young women workers.

In the Decisions for Life project, the University of Amsterdam, in particular its Amsterdam Institute for Advanced Labour Studies (AIAS), was responsible for drafting a gender analysis of work and employment for all 14 countries involved. These inventories served the campaigns and the websites. Although Botswana and Malawi were not included in the trade union and web activities, these countries are included in this book. In total, 14 country reports were published as AIAS working papers (Van Klaveren et al. 2009a–g; 2010a–g). This book builds on these reports as well as on DFL project reporting, *WageIndicator* survey data and recent literature.

Impact of the Decisions for Life project

The trade union activities deployed in the Decisions for Life project have considerable impact. The national union campaigns under the DFL umbrella reached out directly to the nearly 100,000 girls and young women who attended meetings or were talked to in streets and public places. For Mozambique, South Africa, Zambia and Zimbabwe alone, an evaluation report stated that the DFL trade union activities had reached over 21,000 beneficiaries between 2009 and 2011. This resulted in an increase in union membership of the target group and an increase of women's participation in union decision-making bodies ranging from 1 to 40 per cent. The *WageIndicator* websites reported five million web visitors to the websites in the 14 countries in 2010 and 2011. Brazil and India reported 850,000 and 680,000 web visitors, respectively. In 2010 the midterm DFL project evaluation meeting of 40 representatives from southern Africa and Brazil presented a snapshot of their experiences. They considered the achievements up till then as unique in their trade union history: allowing them to put working women's problems and needs on the union agenda, triggering new union policies and leading to solutions. Already in November 2009, the COSATU (Congress of South African Trade Unions) confederation in South Africa decided to integrate the DFL aims in its programme for the next three years. Since then, the DFL project has been filtering down through all COSATU affiliates, as illustrated in Box 1.2.

Box 1.2 Decisions for Life in South Africa

"In terms of the effect the Decisions for Life project has had on the trade union organization as such, it supports the need to rejuvenate the leadership. Young female trade union activists have picked up the relevance of the Decisions for Life aims soon after their introduction and used them to widen working girls' horizons, open up their minds and give them a more optimistic outlook on working life. And while doing so they have explored their own capacities to direct a union and to recruit new members, which are very much needed." (Theodora Steele, organizing secretary COSATU, DFL midterm meeting, Maputo, 22–6 March 2010)

"It is important, [it] comes at an opportune time for the trade union and it is a good tool. "Because times have changed. During the anti-apartheid struggle it was quite normal for working people to join the unions, it was the

> sensible thing to do. But in today's South Africa unions are in membership need, in particular of young recruits, and especially in the services sector where female employment predominates. But young working girls are not interested, they don't even know the unions exist, or they think it is something for older people. They don't automatically come to the unions any more. Yet, the Decisions for Life project somehow is changing that." (Patricia Nyman, national gender coordinator, South African Commercial, Catering and Allied Workers Union (SACCAWU), Maputo, 22–6 March 2010)

On the last day of the International Young Women's Conference, the participants unanimously adopted a declaration in which they demanded that the ITUC and UNI, jointly with their affiliates and the *WageIndicator*, expand Decisions for Life to other countries and fully support, integrate and mainstream DFL methods. The declaration then stressed demands to be made in the organizational and facilitating sphere. Of the five ways specified, these three stand out: (1) building a modern trade unionism which is inclusive for young women and includes a young woman–centred approach reflected in trade union policies, actions, structures and in the composition of its membership and leadership at all levels; (2) helping to build spaces where young women feel safe to meet and talk and receive education which assists them to make decisions in life; and (3) providing to young women vital labour market information about wages, salaries, law in national *WageIndicator* websites, plus in-print, radio and television discussion, including union media resources and social networks, to encourage young women to use the *WageIndicator* instruments. The reactions to this declaration of the ITUC staff members in the conference room were highly positive; clearly the worldwide union umbrella is committed to integrate DFL methods and best practices in its policies and activities (cf. the Decisions for Life website).

The target group

In the 14 countries, the DFL project targeted adolescent women in the 15–29 age group and working in commercial services. This seemingly clear definition of the target group hides a heterogeneous group, including school-attending girls of 15, late adolescents (the 16–19 group), adolescents of 20 and over, and women with a partner and children. This age group is in several stages of the transition into adulthood, whereby entry into adulthood is mostly retreat into the domestic sphere. The transition differs greatly based on gender. Compared with the younger years, it is at this age when gender roles intensify and increasingly shape day-to-day experience. Temin and Levine (2009, 11) emphasize that successful health programmes must accommodate gender-related needs, including the need for confidentiality and an awareness of girls' unique vulnerabilities. We add that this also applies to programmes and campaigns focusing on education and employment. In all these activities adolescents cannot just be treated as adults. What is more, this age group is currently also part of the first generations to come of age in a world facing a complex constellation of challenges, ranging negatively from HIV/AIDS to, mostly positively, mobile phones and the Internet (cf. Donahue 2010). Although the world they are growing up in is built on choices made by adults, the women in the 15–29 group will make their own decisions concerning their future. This book addresses the challenges facing this group.

Against this backdrop, we aim to provide a lively but also – as far as possible within existing limits – statistically underpinned overview of the perspectives of our target group. In 192 countries around the globe, approximately 860 million girls and young women in the 15–29 group are living (authors' calculations based on ILO EAPEP database, ILO 2011b). In the 14 countries at stake, DFL reached out to 11.8 million girls and young women working in urban areas in commercial services; that is, to about 1.4 per cent of all females in this age cohort in the world, including wage earners as well as self-employed or contributing family workers. The countries contributing the largest numbers of targeted girls and young women were Brazil (4.3 million), Indonesia (2.5 million), India (2.4 million) and South Africa (1.4 million). We also calculated that in the next five years in the DFL countries 4.6 to 5.7 million girls and young women (depending on economic conditions) would enter into commercial services employment (calculations based on ILO 2011b and national statistics).

The figures assembled make clear that neither agriculture nor manufacturing is leading in providing female employment; the service sector at large is the current mainstay of female labour. In eight of 13 DFL countries – including South Africa (84%), Brazil (73%) and Ukraine (63%; data for Angola is lacking) – the share of services at large (including government services) in total female employment is over 50 per cent. Indonesia (45%) makes up a middle category of its own, whereas with 26 per cent India displays a substantially lower score. The share of females employed in the service sector in the mainly agricultural southern African countries is even lower: Mozambique has just 10 per cent, Malawi 9 per cent, Zambia 18 per cent. The share of females employed in commercial services (including domestic workers) shows similar variation across countries: with 55 per cent it is largest in

South Africa, followed by 46 per cent in Brazil, 39 per cent in Botswana, 35 per cent in Indonesia, 30 per cent in Kazakhstan, 28 per cent in Azerbaijan, 18 per cent in India, until only 9 per cent in Mozambique and less than 7 per cent in Malawi (sources: Figure 4.2).

The MDGs and empowerment

The Millennium Development Goals (MDGs) are eight international development goals that all 193 UN member states and at least 23 international organizations have agreed to achieve by the year 2015. One of the eight is MDG3, aiming to promote gender equality and empower women. How progress to this rather vague goal was to be measured is specified. MDG3 aimed to eliminate gender disparity in primary and secondary education preferably by 2005 but at all levels by 2015. The 2005 goal was not met, and this book will discuss the chance that it will be met by 2015 for our 14 countries. MDG3 additionally aimed at increasing the share of women in wage employment in the non-agricultural sector and the proportion of seats held by women in national parliaments. A second MDG is also important for women; namely, MDG5, which is aimed at improving maternal health. Progress on these two important MDGs is mixed. According to UN reporting in 2011, in the ten years since 2000 in the developing countries, primary education progress for girls has shown significant improvement towards gender parity, and the share of women in non-agricultural paid employment increased to almost 40 per cent in 2009, though progress has slowed in recent years. Finally, the maternal mortality ratio dropped significantly, to 290 maternal deaths per 100,000 live births, but here the MDG target is still far off (UN 2011).

The World Bank's *World Development Report 2012*, on gender equality and development, strongly holds that closing the persistent gender gaps in education and health matters (World Bank 2011b, 2–3). According to this report, it matters because gender equality is a core development objective in its own right and because greater gender equality can enhance productivity, improve development outcomes for the next generation and make institutions more representative. Based on these and similar arguments, the conclusion is inevitable that women's empowerment is critical to reaching the MDGs. Our vision on empowerment builds on connotations derived from the *World Development Report 2012* and other international reporting, as well as on grassroots experience. Our vision on grassroots empowerment has in substantial part been shaped by experiences from the DFL project. The basic message was and is that, first of all, girls and young women have to invest in themselves and in the project. Thus, empowerment cannot only be regarded in terms of the results of (young) women's activities in the DFL context undertaken in and jointly with trade unions; empowerment should also be seen in terms of the activities themselves. Of course, outcomes matter, whether they concern higher participation in employment, higher wages or broader life choices regarding education, jobs and family life. But the variety of activities and experiences in a project like DFL matters, too; clearly the DFL project exposed quite well that such activities and experiences are instrumental for many women to gain self-confidence and self-esteem and to show that they are "active agents that navigate social, economic, and political life" (Neumayer and De Soysa 2011, 1066). The implication is that empowerment basically is a dynamic process of change whereby "those who have been denied the ability to make choices acquire such an ability" (Kabeer 1999, cited in Mahmud et al. 2012, 611).

Discovering the target group

It obviously took some time until the international community, policymakers, researchers and trade union and other activists alike discovered our target group in its broad sense – adolescent girls and young women in the 15–29 age group. In an early stage of the DFL project, it became clear that dedicated programmes and projects focused on empowering that target group had been quite limited in number and largely also in scope. Reporting from the UN "machinery" delivered a wealth of evidence from both field research and mostly UN-supported surveys on health, education and employment issues but rarely focused on problems, needs and aspirations of the target group. In the early 2000s some projects, like Meeting the Development and Participation Rights of Adolescent Girls, covering 12 countries (UNFPA/WHO/UNICEF 2003), started up, but they remained limited and isolated. In many countries major sectors in society, including health and education, have to a considerable extent neglected the needs and interests of adolescent girls. As far as we can see, the needs and interests of the next cohort, young women in the 20–9 age group, have been only slightly better served.

The international community has also largely overlooked adolescent girls. Concerning health, for instance, the report "Start with a Girl – A New Agenda for Global Health", points out that of 19 indicators for the health-related MDGs, only four pertain to young people, and only one is specific to girls (Temin and Levine 2009, 10). Such neglect has obviously had practical consequences. The foreword of the final report of the same project frankly states: "Yet today, only a tiny fraction of international aid dollars is spent – and spent effectively – on needs specific to adolescent girls [. ...] The girl effect is the missing and transformative force needed to achieve the Millennium Development Goals, with the unique power to break the intergenerational cycle of poverty" (Levine et al. 2008, xi).

In the course of the 2000s, rapid changes could be observed, including impressive outcomes in terms of intervention programmes linked with research and high-level publications. Here we mention those that seem most important. First, the "Because I Am a Girl" project, initiated by Plan International, a global children's charity fund working with the world's poorest children so they can move from a life of poverty to a future with opportunity. The campaign aims to support four million girls to stay in education and fulfil their potential. The plan does so by raising financial and other forms of support. Part of the plan's campaign was the fascinating "Real Choice, Real Lives" cohort study (Plan International/Plan UK 2007, 2010; Plan International 2011). A second project of importance, already signalled above, was the "Adolescent Girls Initiative" of the Center for Global Development (Washington, DC) and supported by the Nike Foundation and the Bill and Melinda Gates Foundation. It aimed at implementing a comprehensive health agenda for adolescent girls, including eliminating marriage for girls younger than 18, focusing on HIV prevention and making secondary school completion a priority (Katz 2008; Morrison and Sabarwal 2008; Levine et al. 2008; Greene et al. 2009; Lloyd 2009; Temin and Levine 2009). The third project concerns the Adolescent Data Guides, a UN research and data collection project which aims to provide decision makers at all levels – governments, nongovernmental organizations (NGOs) and advocacy groups – with data on the situation of adolescent boys and young women in the 10–24 group. This project covers a large number of countries and draws principally on data from the national Demographic and Health Surveys (DHS; website UNFPA). Fourth, there is the DFL project, based on the wider *WageIndicator* project. Central to this project is labour market transparency, as will be explained in the next section.

The *WageIndicator* project: labour market transparency

Economic labour market theories assume that individual workers have perfect information and that they know how much other workers are earning and what prevailing market wages are. In a job search, knowledge of current wages helps workers make informed decisions, particularly in cases of job search in another region. In wage negotiations trade unions' knowledge of wage information for similar jobs in other companies has the potential to prevent unfairness or exploitation. Employers can enjoy similar advantages by making wage determination fairer and more transparent. Having reliable and transparent data is the key to launching collective bargaining and ensuring productive and effective social dialogue. For several reasons, however, employers' and workers' information about wages is not perfect. First, mouth-to-mouth communication, a major mode of exchanging wage information, bears several risks: of exaggerating or even falsifying information, of reaching out to only small populations and of leaving workers with little or no information concerning job decisions in the wider region. Second, collective bargaining and collective agreements are not spread widely. Third, as will be discussed in Chapter 8, minimum wage information is not well disseminated. Fourth, job vacancy advertisements, if they mention wages at all, present only starting wages. Though in a few industrialized countries websites provide salary information, it is seldom free of charge and is often targeted at higher job levels. In many developing countries, where no labour market information at all is available, room is left for the *WageIndicator* to fill the gap.

With the Internet opening immense possibilities for increased labour market transparency, the independent, non-profit WageIndicator Foundation (WIF) has addressed the challenge. It has done so by using the Internet to spread information about wages and benefits for occupations at all levels and thus making it far more widely available and readily accessible than it has ever been. As Jelle Visser, professor of industrial relations at the University of Amsterdam, stated at the third *WageIndicator* conference in April 2008: "A *WageIndicator* website may serve as a Lighthouse: providing signals to users about the wage norm or standard rate for particular jobs, or about pay gaps." The mission statement of the WIF reads: "Share and compare wage information. Contribute to a transparent labour market. Provide free, accurate wage data through salary checks on national websites. Collect wage data through web surveys."

In 2000 the *WageIndicator* project started as a paper-and-pencil survey for establishing a website with salary information for women's occupations in the Netherlands. A year later, the website, once launched, was instantly successful. Soon information about men's occupations was included, and the number of web pages in the site increased to cover a wide range of labour-related topics. The number of web visitors grew constantly. In 2003 WIF was established under Netherlands law and based in Amsterdam. The foundation expanded its operations to other European countries from 2004 on, and it included countries outside Europe from 2006 on. In 2012 the foundation was operating national websites in over 65 countries on five continents. It had regional branches in Ahmadabad, Bratislava, Buenos Aires, Cape Town/Maputo and Minsk.

All *WageIndicator* websites post job-related content, such as labour law information, minimum wage information, tips for interview talks and a free and crowd-pulling feature called Salary Check, presenting average wages for various occupations. It also lists earnings of VIPs to attract web visitors. Additionally, web operations include search engine optimization, web marketing, publicity and answering visitors' email. Countries are clustered by region, each region with its own web manager. Coalitions with job vacancy sites, media groups and publishing houses with a strong Internet presence contribute to the sites' large numbers of visitors. The sites are consulted by employees, students, job seekers, individuals with a job on the side and the like for information gathering, job mobility decisions, annual performance talks, occupational choices or other reasons. Increasingly, social media are used to reach out to targeted groups. In return for the free information provided, web visitors are asked to voluntarily complete a web survey on work and wages. Between 1 and 5 per cent do so. The web survey takes approximately 10 to 15 minutes to complete and has a prize incentive. Each web survey, in the appropriate national language(s) and adapted to peculiarities of its country, is continuously posted and is anonymous. The survey contains questions about wages, education, occupation, industry, socio-demographics and the like (Tijdens et al. 2010). In the ten years since the start of the first survey, more than a million web visitors have added valid information about their weekly or monthly wages to the *WageIndicator* wages database (see Box 1.3). This database is used for the computations underlying the Salary Check.

In countries with high Internet access rates, web visitors are to a large extent representative of the population at large, but in countries with low access rates web visitors are predominantly young and well educated. This leads to a bias towards young and educated individuals in the web survey data. To counterbalance this bias, the WIF increasingly conducts face-to-face surveys in countries with poor Internet access. In 2010 and 2011 such surveys were conducted in Indonesia and Zambia, among other countries. In the next chapters, data from both the *WageIndicator* web survey and the face-to-face surveys will be used.

Box 1.3 Mozajarplata, Belarus

"In the spring of 2009 I lost my job. It was absolutely unexpected for me and I didn't know what to do to find a better job. The situation was worsened by the economic crisis. And I really needed a new job as my wedding was planned for September. I didn't want to start to build a family being unemployed and unsure of the future. ... It was necessary to organise a self PR campaign. I read the articles about how to get an interview, how to respond to the recruiters' questions, what to dress to wear and how to distinguish myself from other candidates. My technique was to create a self-presentation in PowerPoint. And it worked – I got the job I wanted! Where did I learn these important tips? The answer is simple – on website Mozajarplata.by. And I still visit it and read it with interest. Our family celebrates the first anniversary of our wedding, and I think I'll start visiting the section on mothers' rights and child benefits soon." (Marina, 25, Belarus, Decisions for Life project website)

Characteristics of the 14 countries

ITUC, UNI and WIF, partners in the Decisions for Life project, with their choice of 14 countries "condemned" the authors to the study of these countries, including comparisons in quite a few fields. One can identify two clusters, the seven southern African countries (Angola, Botswana, Malawi, Mozambique, South Africa, Zambia and Zimbabwe) and the four CIS countries (Azerbaijan, Belarus, Kazakhstan and Ukraine), as having more characteristics in common but also major differences, with Brazil, India and Indonesia, not least because of their immense populations and diversity, standing alone in many ways. In total, in 2010 the population of the 14 countries numbered 1.885 billion, over one-quarter of the world's population, divided as follows: over 145 million inhabitants in the African countries, 81 million in the CIS countries, 195 million in Brazil, 220 million in Indonesia and 1.225 billion in India. The DFL country with by far the smallest population is, with 2.2 million, Botswana (UNICEF country statistics). In the course of this book, comparisons focusing on health, education and employment issues will reveal characteristics of the 14 countries.

Figures concerning standard of living, measured by per capita gross national income (GNI over 2010, in constant 2008 PPP US dollars), indicate that the development levels of the 14 vary widely. Of the 13 countries with adequate data (Zimbabwe is missing), the GNI per capita was lowest in Mozambique (US$854 per year), followed by Malawi (US$911) and Zambia (US$1,359), and highest in Botswana (US$13,204), Belarus (US$12,926) and Brazil (US$10,607). South Africa's figure (US$9,821) was close to Brazil's, while the levels of Indonesia (US$3,957) and India (US$3,337) were in the same league (UNDP 2010c). Two reservations are needed here. First, since some of these figures hide large internal income inequalities, they may give a too rosy impression of the living standards of large parts of the population in, especially, Botswana, Brazil and South Africa.

A second reservation is that higher income levels do not necessarily translate into higher living standards; the relative purchasing power of earnings has to be taken into account. As an illustration, a highly uniform product available everywhere in the same quality – a Big Mac sandwich – is used as a comparison. The combination of Big Mac prices as collected by *The Economist* in July 2010 and wage figures derived from the *WageIndicator* survey in 2010 (converted into US$) allows an impression to be given of the value of wages across countries. For example, according to this exercise a manual worker from Brazil could on average afford 0.6 Big Macs per hour of work, whereas his or her colleague in the UK on average gained 3.5 Big Macs in that hour and a Dutch colleague 2.7 Big Macs. Similarly, an Indonesian manager could on average afford 1.1 Big Macs, but the manager's British counterpart could afford 4.8 (Guzi 2011).

Of course, a country's progress or an individual's well-being cannot be measured by money alone. On the basis of this assumption, over two decades ago leading development thinkers worked out the Human Development Index (HDI) for the UN Development Programme (UNDP) and its annual *Human Development Reports*. Over the years, the HDI has received much public attention. It is a composite measure of achievements in three basic dimensions of human development: a long and healthy life (life expectancy), access to education (years of schooling) and a decent standard of living (per capita GNI). For ease of comparison, the average value of achievements in the HDI is put on a scale of 0 to 1, greater being better. Through the HDI it is possible to roughly trace the vicissitudes of countries on the path of human development over the course of more than 30 years, as shown in Figure 1.1 for the 14 DFL countries.

By focusing on 2011, the figure pictures the current large differences across these countries. The underlying data clarify that the 2011 HDI values vary widely: 0.322 for Mozambique (ranking 184th of 187 countries), 0.376 for Zimbabwe (worldwide rank 173), then up to 0.745 for Kazakhstan (rank 68) and 0.756 for Belarus (rank 65). Among

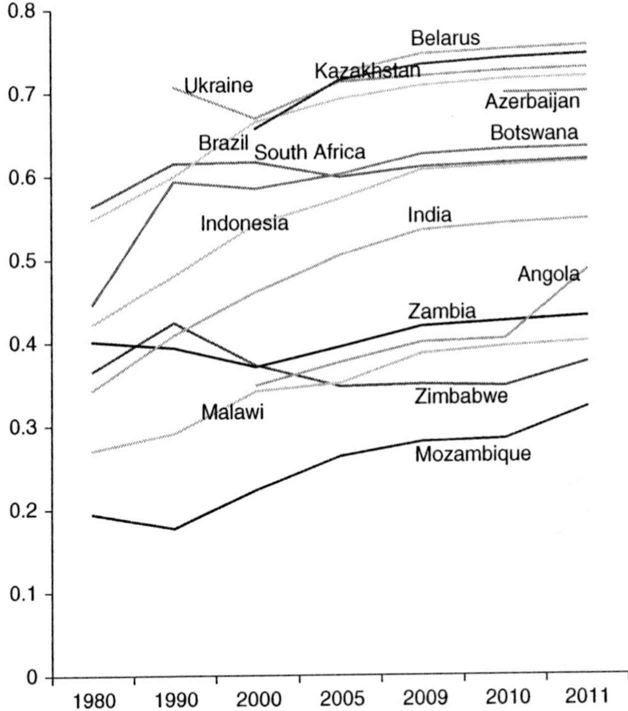

Figure 1.1 Development of the Human Development Index (HDI), 1980–2010, on a scale of 0 to 1

Source: UNDP 2010a, T. 2.

the largest DFL countries, Brazil's HDI ranks highest (0.718, rank 84), followed by Indonesia (0.617, no. 124) and India (0.547, no. 134). Over time, the HDIs of most countries show continuous progress, in line with progress around the world from an average HDI of 0.594 in 1990 to 0.682 in 2011 (UNDP 2011). Four out of 14 countries were exceptions here; their HDI values decreased during five or more years: Zimbabwe between 1990 and 2010, Zambia and Ukraine in the 1990s and South Africa from 2000 to 2005. The positions of the 14 countries have not changed much, except for the relative rise of Botswana and the fall of Zimbabwe and, albeit to a lesser extent, South Africa. In comparing most recent developments (i.e., 2005–11 with 2000–5), progress has speeded up in eight of the 12 countries for which data is available (they are lacking for Azerbaijan and Belarus), has continued with the same speed in two countries (Brazil and India) and has slowed in two countries (Kazakhstan and Ukraine).

Human development and inequalities

Measuring progress along the HDI has many limitations. In conformity with the *Human Development Reports*, where work and employment have hardly found a place (cf. Alkire 2010, 14), the index does not at all cover employment, including compliance with labour rights. Neither have human and women's rights been integrated, aspects closely connected with empowerment of people and with political freedom and participation (cf. Ranis et al. 2006). Though addressing these aspects in one index presents practical and methodological problems, the lack of indications on human, labour and women's rights implies serious limitations in characterizing countries with the HDI's help. In a basic way, the challenge to compare countries according to "rights'" yardsticks is borne by Chapter 7.

The UNDP has recently met two other criticisms of the HDI; namely, that the index did not look at inequalities within countries and that it captured the gender dimension only weakly. To start with the inequality issue, there were and are good grounds to provide more insight on internal inequalities in income and asset distributions. First, as Wilkinson and Pickett (2009) have shown for 23 high-income countries and the US states, income inequality is strongly associated with shorter life expectancy, higher infant mortality, more depression – in brief, with shorter and unhealthier lives. The most unequal countries do worse on almost every quality-of-life indicator; put otherwise, the more equal the society, the better its performance on these indicators. Although these authors hesitate at drawing the same conclusions for developing countries, it is unlikely that these would not also apply to this country category (cf. VandeMoortele 2011, 17). Second, there is a growing consensus that developing countries with initially relatively equal distributions of income and assets tend to grow faster than countries with high initial inequality (Van der Hoeven 2010). Conversely, growth paths that enlarge inequality and, for that matter, poverty may well meet major problems in providing decent employment opportunities for women in particular (cf. Heintz 2006).

The 2010 *Human Development Report* introduced the inequality-adjusted HDI (IHDI), a measure of the human development level that accounts for inequality. When there is inequality in the distribution of health, education and income, the HDI of an average person in a society declines and is less than the aggregate HDI; the lower the IHDI (and the greater the difference between it and the HDI), the greater the inequality. In 2011 the average worldwide loss in HDI due to internal inequalities was 23 per cent. By then the largest overall loss due to inequalities in the 14 DFL countries was 32 per cent in Malawi, followed by five countries (Mozambique, Zambia, Zimbabwe, Brazil and India) with losses in the 28 to 30 per cent range. The CIS countries lost relatively little in HDI value due to inequalities, and Belarus (8%) and Ukraine (9%) showed the smallest losses (UNDP 2011). The recent *Human Development Reports* also present subdivisions of the losses in HDI due to within-country inequalities in life expectancy, education and income. Chapter 2 will treat the outcomes for "our" countries in health, and Chapter 3 in education. Here, note the outcome presented in the 2011 edition: that in the last two decades worsening income inequality has offset large improvements in health and education inequality on a global scale. Though according to the UNDP researchers, the largest increases in income inequality took place in Europe, North America and central Asia, they also refer to income becoming more concentrated among top earners in China, India and South Africa (UNDP 2011, 28–30).

Concerning the gender issue, in 2010 the UNDP launched the Gender Inequality Index (GII). The GII approach is consistent with that for inequality sketched above; it compares women and men and considers only inequalities between them at the country level. Three dimensions are measured through five indicators: women's reproductive health, through maternal mortality and adolescent fertility; empowerment, through the ratio of female to male representatives in parliament; female educational attainment (secondary level and above); and labour market (female labour force participation, including the unemployed). The GII increases when disadvantages across dimensions are associated – that is, the more correlated the disparities between genders, the higher the index. According to the UNDP (2010, 90), overlapping disadvantages are an important aspect of gender inequality, and capturing them is a major advantage of the GII. Room for criticism here, notably on the narrow operationalization of "empowerment" may be present, but the researchers in question here refer to data (cf. Gaye et al. 2010).

The 2011 *Human Development Report* reveals that the largest losses due to gender inequality are in sub-Saharan Africa, followed by South Asia and the Arab states. In sub-Saharan Africa the biggest losses arise from gender disparities in education and from high maternal mortality and adolescent fertility rates. In South Asia women lag behind men in each dimension of the GII, especially education, national parliamentary representation and labour force participation. On the lower ends of both scales, a close relation shows up between HDI and GII: all the low HDI countries have high GII values (UNDP 2011, 61). Indeed, Malawi, Mozambique, Zambia and Zimbabwe, low in HDI ranking, have high scores on gender inequality. However, for countries higher on the HDI ladder, this correlation becomes weaker. Botswana, Brazil and India have higher GII scores than comports with their HDI ranking. For example, on gender equality Brazil ranks 78th of 145 countries, against its HDI ranking of 84th (of 187) (UNDP 2011, tables 2 and 4). The conclusion to be drawn is that, measured by UNDP yardsticks, in the last three countries gender equality lags behind general societal progress.

The 14 countries in the 2000s

Since 2007 the world has been in the grip of an economic and financial crisis. Already in the course of that year, unmistakable signs of a slowdown of economic activity appeared, and the collapse in 2008 of parts of the US and UK banking systems aggravated negative trends in production, trade and investment. Worldwide foreign direct investment (FDI), for example, fell progressively by 16 per cent in 2008 and 37 per cent in 2009 (UNCTAD 2010). Yet, in 2010 FDI flows recovered by 5 per cent, and UNCTAD expects these flows to continue their recovery and regain their pre-crisis level by 2011. The trade and development organization at the same time states that "the post-crisis business environment is still beset by uncertainties" (UNCTAD 2011c, xii). It goes on to sum up a number of "risk factors", of which quite a few involve the actual restructuring going on in global power relations pertaining, most significantly, to the emergence of the BRICs – originally Brazil, Russia, India and China, with more recently South Africa added to form the BRICS acronym. The BRICS have become (or become home to) major international traders and foreign investors. UNCTAD (2011c), characterizing the emerging economies as "the new FDI powerhouses", noted that developing and transitional economies accounted in 2010 for 29 per cent of global FDI outflows. In this context its other reporting points at the major investments and loans of China in sub-Saharan Africa (UNCTAD 2011b). In 2010 total investment had not fully recovered globally and was about three percentage points below its pre-crisis level (ILO/IILS 2012, 82).

The worldwide recovery in 2010 and 2011 had a "two-speed character", with the gross domestic product (GDP) per capita of the developing countries jointly growing at 7.4 and an estimated 6.3 per cent, as opposed to the by far lower rates for the developed countries – 2.5 and 1.8 per cent in 2010 and 2011. More specifically, the GDP growth figures for Brazil were 7.5 and 4.0 per cent, respectively, and for India even 8.8 and 8.1 per cent. According to UNCTAD (2011b, 2011c), the BRICS' sustained growth was caused by the recovery of commodity prices, governments' fiscal stimulus packages and an increase in domestic demand fuelled by wage increases. At the same time there remained the divide between the large developing countries and the low-income countries with smaller economies, a divide based on agriculture and highly vulnerable to natural disasters and food and fuel pricing. Since mid-2007 rapidly rising food prices have led to food uproars in a number of these countries. For example, in Mozambique, covering its wheat needs by importing two-thirds (Patel 2010), in September 2010 the government's cutting of food subsidies led to violent riots in the capital, Maputo. The large developing economies, notably India, Indonesia and Brazil, could more easily compensate for lost export demand with domestic stimulus policies and trade protection (UNCTAD 2011b).

To focus on employment, the International Labour Organization (ILO) concludes that the global recovery that started in 2009 has been short-lived and shallow and that a large employment gap remains; that is, global job creation is weak. The organization states that globally, nearly 27 million new job seekers have been added to the already high unemployment figure of almost 171 million prior to the crisis; this gap is expected to widen further as new labour market entrants struggle to find gainful employment. Against the ILO projection of 400 million new entrants over the next ten years, the current situation is called desperate for the world's youth: all over the world 75 million young people in the 15–24 age bracket are unemployed, five million more than in 2007. The situation is even worse than official unemployment statistics suggest; as discouraged young people leave the labour market, labour force participation is declining in many countries (ILO 2012). Earlier, the ILO concluded that especially in developing countries, where little or no social safety nets exist, the unemployment rate does not capture the full extent of difficulties young people face (ILO 2010b). In light of these facts and figures, the ILO's warnings are clear: "A continuation of current trends risks further undermining the already dim prospects and aspirations of the world's youth, sowing the seeds for continued social unrest and further weakening global economic prospects"; and "[i]n this light, the increase in social unrest in many countries and regions around the world is of little surprise" (ILO 2012, 31, 33).

Globally, job quality is also under pressure. Where new jobs are being created, they tend to leave new labour market entrants with a lower job quality, including less job security, than older generations had. For example, where new jobs were created between 2007 and 2010, survey data for 20 countries (including Belarus, Kazakhstan, South Africa and Ukraine) show that they were spread over the wage spectrum, with about half of them paying in the lowest 40 per cent range. Non-standard and vulnerable jobs were created in the lower more than in the higher ranks (ILO/IILS 2012, 11, based on *WageIndicator* data). Using a "vulnerable employment indicator' developed by the ILO, it has been calculated than since 2009, 23 million more workers worldwide are in vulnerable employment, with informal work arrangements, without adequate social protection and often working for low pay and under difficult conditions. In 2011 the share of women in vulnerable employment (50.5%) exceeded the corresponding share for men worldwide (48.2%). Women are far more likely than men to be in vulnerable employment in sub-Saharan Africa (85% versus 70%). In that region vulnerable employment expanded, accounting for nearly 70 per cent of all employment growth since 2007 (ILO 2012, 42–3).

Against this backdrop of worldwide and regional trends, it is obvious that many countries encounter massive problems absorbing young newcomers into the labour market. Most of the 14 DFL countries do so as well. Partly the strong macroeconomic growth figures were misleading, largely based as they were on expanding mining and related capital-intensive activities that, due to their enclave-based character, had little effect on employment and enlarged inequalities in the country as a whole (ILO 2011b). Angola is a case in point. In part other, specific national conditions played roles, as in South Africa the legacy of the apartheid era in many fields combined with the underperformance of investment and the low rate of private savings (Eyraud 2009).

Concerning employment creation, over the last decade in particular, Brazil, South Africa, Malawi and Angola underperformed. Calculated over the period 2000–10 (see Figure 1.2), lower average employment than population growth was found in these countries, the largest gap being in Brazil (an employment decrease of 0.1% versus 1.2% population growth) and Malawi (1.5% average employment growth versus

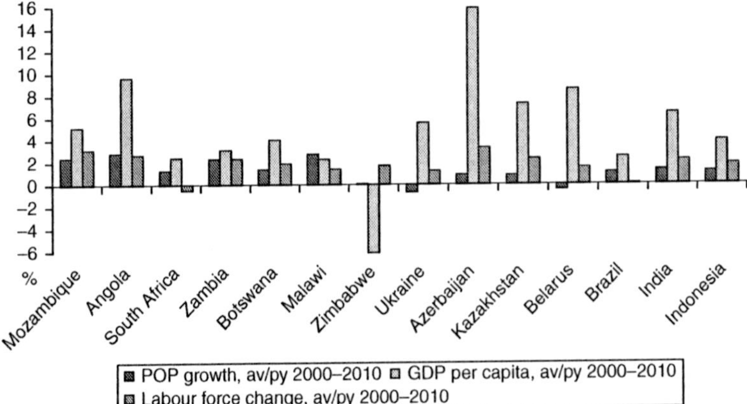

Figure 1.2 Average yearly percentage change, 2000–10, with respect to population, GDP and labour force

Source: For population growth and GDP change, World Bank 2011b; for labour force change, ILO Laborsta database.

2.8% population growth), followed by South Africa (0.7% employment growth but 1.3% population increase) and Angola (2.7% versus 2.9%). With 1.85 per cent per year, the unweighted employment growth averaged for the 14 countries was only slightly ahead of population growth, averaging an unweighted 1.3 per cent. In the years 2008–10 the gap was even smaller, with 1.45 per cent average employment growth over 1.2 per cent average population increase. Through these recent years three countries demonstrated lower average employment than population growth rates: again South Africa and this time also India and Zimbabwe. South Africa's performance is particularly worrisome, with on average 3 per cent fall in employment versus 0.8 per cent population growth (see Box 1.4). Yet the recent outcomes for India also indicate a situation of near-jobless growth. The country's high GDP per capita growth rates (6.3% average, 2008–10) cannot mask a confrontation with (preliminary) figures indicating minimal employment growth: 0.2 per cent yearly, against 1.4 per cent population growth (2000–10 and 2008–10; authors' calculations, based on World Bank 2011b [population] and ILO 2011b, ILO Laborsta database and national Labour Force Surveys [employment]).

In many reports international organizations in recent years have warned governments in developing countries not to fly blindly on economic growth results. One example out of many: in southern

Africa, governments were warned in the *2011 Economic Report on Africa*, by the UN Economic Commission for Africa and the African Union, that the relatively high growth figures were not being translated into needed jobs. The problems encountered by southern African administrations may develop in a similar vein in India. Undoubtedly, many in that country's huge cohort of about 135 million young women and 145 million young men in the 15–29 age group aspire to finding a decent job. Indian government officials have expressed confidence that the huge cohorts of young people and children will be good for the economy, but demographers and social scientists are sceptical about India's capacity to fulfil the new generation's aspirations (UNFPA 2011, 12). If their scepticism proves justified, ideals of empowerment and decent jobs may degenerate into a harsh fight for jobs tout court, and human dignity and decency may well be far off.

Box 1.4 Youth (un)employment in South Africa

South Africa may serve to illustrate the urgent problems concerning job creation for young people. The fundamental problem was and is that after the fall of apartheid South African economic growth has been marked by near joblessness. After Mandela's inauguration as president, the new government quickly found that South Africa's economy was in dire straits, with a record budget deficit, hardly any foreign exchange reserves, immense unemployment and huge inequalities. The *Human Development Report 1996* indicated that if white South Africa was treated as a separate country, its standard of living in 1994 would rank 24th in the world, while black South Africa on the same basis would rank 123rd. Since then, South Africa has faced tremendous challenges on the poverty-inequality-unemployment front, due in part to the legacy of apartheid (cf. Chibba 2011, 79).

Between 1995 and 2000 slow GDP growth in South Africa went along with small employment growth. A process of pro-poor (or shared) growth did not take off (Hoogeveen and Özler 2005, 13). After 2000, in spite of a more radical economic strategy of the government, these trends continued, and structural weaknesses in the South African economy remained. Between 2000 and 2011 total employment grew quite modestly: 7.4 per cent, or just 0.7 per cent per year. Female employment grew even less: 4.3 per cent, or less than 0.4 per cent yearly (SSA 2009b, 2011). Projected against annual population growth of 1.3 per cent, the outcome is immense unemployment and economic inactivity, particularly among the young. In mid-2011 over 1.3 million of the 10.4 million South Africans in the 15–24 age group were officially unemployed, and at least another 2.3 million of them fell in the category of homemaker, ill or disabled, or discouraged work seeker (authors' calculations, based on SSA 2011).

Outline of this book

Chapter 2 looks at the demography and family formation, health and related inequalities in the 14 DFL countries, issues touching upon basic perspectives in girls' and young women's lives. After a brief introduction, fertility, life expectancy, child mortality, the adolescent fertility rate, early marriage and motherhood and similar issues are examined. The focus then shifts to health risks relevant to young people, including HIV/AIDS, sexual and gender-based violence (SGBV) and orphanage concerns due to the AIDS pandemic. As health is closely related to inequality and poverty, this chapter ends with a discussion of mobility out of poverty.

Chapter 3 focuses on education and its importance and on skills of young women. The chapter discusses literacy and inequalities in education. It presents pictures of the enrolment of girls in primary and secondary education, both including country overviews. The importance of vocational training for labour market opportunities is sketched, followed by a section on tertiary education. The chapter ends by reviewing female skill levels. All in all, what is seen is an impressive development of female participation in education, lifting the skill levels of women in many countries, in some of which they even outperform men.

Chapter 4 is dedicated to employment issues touching young women, starting with discussion of women's labour force participation. The focus then shifts to formal and informal employment – an important distinction in the 14 countries. Why do some countries notice a decrease in informal employment, whereas others do not? Next, unemployment and underemployment, the transition from school to work and child labour are covered. Migration comes to the fore again. A chapter about employment cannot be written without going into the distribution of women workers over various industries and occupations and into the female share in them. The Decisions for Life project targeted eight occupations in the services sector, and the chapter ends with a description of these occupations.

Chapter 5 treats another important labour market feature of young women; namely, their wages and working conditions. With wage rankings across industries in the 14 countries at stake, there follows a discussion of the gender pay gap. The focus then shifts to job quality, particularly to working hours, sexual harassment and violence in the workplace and combining work and family life. For young women in employment, compliance with labour legislation and collective bargaining arrangements is essential, but it is at the same time in nearly all countries the Achilles' heel. The problem is addressed at the end of the chapter.

Chapter 6 provides an industry outlook on female employment in the 14 countries. Its introduction presents arguments why such an outlook is important for understanding women's work. Employment structures and prospects for the main economic sectors – agriculture, manufacturing and services – are analysed. Concerning services, after a short section on services at large, the bulk of the space is devoted to analysing employment prospects in the three sub-sectors of commercial services: the wholesale and retail trades, tourism and call centres – the core of interest for the target group of the DFL project. Finally, we briefly go into prospects in two adjacent industries, health, along with public administration and defence.

Chapter 7, describing the institutional framework important for young women's perspectives on work, discusses governance and labour market institutions in the 14 countries and the strategies and activities for empowering women, including women's and labour rights. Labour relations and union organization are discussed, including the position of women in trade unions. Communication and new media, including social media, are of growing importance for empowering women. Therefore, perspectives for using the Internet by and on behalf of girls and young women are examined. The use of print media, TV, radio, mobile phones, mobile Internet, broadband, and the Internet generally, including the important issue of Internet freedom, is looked at.

A main part of the DFL project was the launching of websites with work-related information in the 14 countries involved. The pages providing information on the statutory minimum wages turned out to be among the most popular. Thus, Chapter 8, the final chapter, focuses on information dissemination as it concerns the statutory minimum wage. The level of these wages, their potential to reduce women's vulnerability to low pay, their employment effects, and their effects on income distribution are discussed.

2
Demography, Health and Inequality: Basic Perspectives in the Life of Young Women

Introduction

In this chapter the demography, family formation, health and related inequalities in the 14 DFL countries come to the fore. These issues touch upon the basic perspectives in life of girls and young women. As with other researchers (e.g., Levine et al. 2008, 2), our starting point is the contention that girls' opportunities and prospects are fundamentally shaped by those closest to them. Recent years have seen the publication of a growing, sometimes overwhelming body of evidence on health and adolescents, and as mentioned in the first chapter, various new initiatives have clarified and improved the situation of adolescent girls and young women. Thanks to these initiatives and the statistical basis provided by the UN machinery, this chapter can examine fertility, life expectancy, child mortality, the adolescent fertility rate, early marriage and motherhood (see Box 2.1) and similar issues for the 14 countries. The focus then shifts to health risks relevant to young people, including HIV/AIDS, sexual and gender-based violence (SGBV) and orphanhood due to the AIDS pandemic. As health is closely related to inequality and poverty, this chapter ends with a discussion of mobility out of poverty.

> *Box 2.1* Family in South Africa
>
> "Whatever the reasons, in South Africa most girls when they start working after school are mothers already, single mothers, teenage mothers. The

father may still be around, but usually the couple does not live in the same household. Men are kept at an arm's length, also because sexual harassment and child abuse lurk around the corner. The new family pattern emerging is that of a three-generation extended family, with grandma looking after the child of the young working mother, who brings in the money to support the household. It is under such family conditions that these responsible young working women have to create a balance with their working lives." (Theodora Steele, organizing secretary COSATU, SA trade union confederation, DFL mid-term meeting, Maputo, 22–26 March 2010)

Fertility

The most commonly used measure of fertility is the total fertility rate (TFR), the number of children a woman would have over her childbearing years if, at each age, she experienced the number of births per 1,000 women specific to that age group. Between 1950 and 2010 the TFR in the world was halved, from around 5 children to around 2.5 (UNDESA 2010). Of course, fertility rates influence future population size, as well as the ratio between the old and the young in a country, and fertility rates influence current family and community size and thereby a country's economy. High fertility forces families and communities to consume savings, thereby depleting national-level capital formation and investment rates (cf. Robison and Crenshaw 2010) – though families and individuals have, from their perspective, good reasons for taking opposing views. For many rural poor the notion of family planning seems irrelevant. In large parts of Mozambique and other poor rural areas where life is expected to be short, many children die at birth, food is insecure, and one cannot count on the government for a basic income, farmer families – mostly the men as prime decision makers – create their own social security system by having many children. As Mozambican researchers express it, "Having too many children was for a long time, and still is today, the main form of social protection for most of the population" (UNFPA 2011, 55). This section discusses the TFRs for the 14 countries (see Table 2.1).

A preliminary remark: concerning TFRs for individual countries, the available sources – various UN organizations, the World Bank, the *CIA World Factbook* – show considerable differences. We stick to figures derived from the UN database, sometimes corrected by national figures where these seemed more appropriate. Four of our 14 countries – Zambia, Malawi, Angola and Mozambique, in this order – are still among those with the highest birth rates, though in the last two decades TFRs have

Table 2.1 Total fertility rate (TFR) and adolescent fertility rate (AFR), 2009

	TFR	AFR
Mozambique	4.7	162
Angola	5.1	139
South Africa	2.4	49
Zambia	6.3	144
Botswana	2.6	49
Malawi	6.0	114
Zimbabwe	3.1	60
Ukraine	1.5	22
Azerbaijan	2.2	33
Kazakhstan	2.5	28
Belarus	1.5	22
Brazil	1.8	76
India	2.5	82
Indonesia	2.2	44

Note: Total fertility rate (births per woman of current generation aged 15–49); adolescent fertility rate (yearly births per 1,000 girls aged 15–19)

Source: World Bank 2011a.

decreased in Angola and Mozambique. By 1990 in Angola, women in the 15–49 age group gave birth to on average 7.2 children; in 2000 this was still 6.5, but the 2000s saw a rapid decrease to an average of 5.1. Mozambique earlier witnessed a strong fall in TFR, from 6.2 in 1990 to 4.9, slowing down to 4.7 in 2009. In the 1990s Malawi also saw a rapid decrease in its TFR, from 7.0 to 5.3, but the 2000s brought a fluctuating pattern, settling at 6.0 in 2009. On balance Zambia showed a smaller initial decrease, from 6.5 in 1990 to 6.0 in 2000, but then the figure rose to 6.3 in 2009. The Zambian increase in the 2000s has been due to a rise in the TFR in rural areas that experts did not expect: from 6.9 children in 2001–2 to the extremely high level of 7.5 in 2007, while the fertility rate in urban areas remained at 4.3 (CSO 2007a). The fall in South Africa's TFR mainly took place in the 1990s, from 3.7 in 1990 to 2.6 in 2000, followed by a slower decrease to 2.4 in 2009. By contrast, Botswana's TFR showed a massive fall: from a level over 6 in the 1980s to 3.8 in 2000 and 2.6 in 2009. Zimbabwe's fertility rate developed in a highly irregular way, obviously influenced by fluctuations in political and economic perspectives. After a rapid decline from 3.3 in 2000, a rise from 2007 on led to a TFR of 3.1 in 2009.

The large DFL countries showed massive decreases in their initially high fertility rates. From a long-term perspective Brazil is without a doubt the most spectacular case: its TFR dropped from 6.3 in 1960 to 2.4 in 2000 and 1.8 in 2009 (Berquó and Cavenaghi 2005; see Box 2.2 for background). In India the TFR has also considerably decreased, from 4.0 in 1990 to 3.3 in 2000 and an estimated 2.5 in 2009 – with levels varying across states from 1.9 in the south to 3.5 in the three populous central Indian states (Moore et al. 2009). Indonesia demonstrates a similar drop, albeit from a lower level and slowing in the 2000s: from 3.1 in 1990 to 2.6 in 2000 and 2.2 in 2009 (BPS 2009). Azerbaijan's birth rate development since 1990 equals Indonesia's, but Kazakhstan's TFR shows a deviating pattern: a fall from 2.8 in 1990 to 2.0 in 2000, then a rise to 2.5 in 2009.

Box 2.2 Brazil's birth control

Brazil's massive and rapid demographic shift has astonished social scientists. The fertility rate decline initially occurred in the absence of any official policy in favour of controlling birth rates. Under the Lula da Silva administration and supported by government initiatives on behalf of the poor, large-scale birth control developed bottom up, with women in the growing middle classes taking much of the initiative. Weeks after Pope Benedict XVI denounced government-backed birth control in a visit to Brazil, the Lula administration unveiled a programme to provide cheap birth control pills at 10,000 drug stores across Latin America's largest nation. President Lula said the plan would give poor Brazilians "the same right that the wealthy have, to plan the number of children they want." Brazil already hands out millions of free condoms and birth control pills at government-run pharmacies. But many poor people in the nation of 190 million do not go to those pharmacies, so Lula's administration decided to also offer the pills at drastically reduced prices at 3,500 private drug stores (Dinka 2007). Demographers say the fertility rate is declining due to the country's real income growth, the rapidly rising educational level of Brazil's women and urbanization, but they also point to the influence of the hugely popular soap series on TV and their portrayal of small, glamorous families. Suzana Cavenaghi, a Brazilian demographer, emphasizes that Brazilian women have embraced family planning any way they can. "They have more to say about their reproductive lives than the men. Men interfere less in their lives than [they] would in other countries" (Forero 2012).

Falling fertility rates are perceived quite differently in Belarus and Ukraine. The authorities of both countries regard fertility as "too low" (UNDESA 2011a). That does not surprise, because both countries have been characterized as being in demographic crisis: falling fertility rates in combination with increasing mortality rates and (in Ukraine) high emigration rates have resulted in serious depopulation. Between 2000 and 2010 Belarus witnessed a population decrease on average of 0.4 per cent yearly, in Europe surpassed only by the 0.7 per cent decrease rate of Ukraine. In the first five years after the collapse of the Soviet Union, the birth rate of Belarus, already low, fell by almost 30 per cent, to recover only marginally (Richardson et al. 2008). In Ukraine the decrease started earlier, with the TFR falling continuously from 1982 to 2001, when an all-time low of 1.1 was reached. As with Belarus, the Ukrainian TFR saw some recovery in the 2000s, both countries ending up at an estimated level of 1.5 in 2009. Between 1990 and 2011 the Ukrainian population decreased by nearly 12 per cent, and the population of Belarus by 6.5 per cent (websites Statistics Ukraine and NSC Republic of Belarus).

Life expectancy

For individual women and men life expectancy is essential to formation of their perspectives, not only individually but also in the family context. Causes of death fall commonly into three groups: from nutritional, maternal and perinatal conditions; from non-communicable diseases; and from injuries. Life expectancy expresses many inequalities. In countries with high agricultural productivity, sufficient public health provisions, low child mortality, few diseases and the absence of violence and war, the population will on average live longer – and the other way around in the absence of those conditions. Life expectancy also varies widely within countries, across social and occupational divisions (cf. Wilkinson and Pickett 2009). Thus, the UNDP made the right choice when constructing its inequality-adjusted HDI (IHDI), to choose a life-expectancy index for the health part. That index showed that in 2011 inequality losses due to variation in life expectancy worldwide approached 19 per cent. The largest health inequalities were found in African countries: 46 per cent in Angola and 40 to 42 per cent in Zambia, Mozambique and Malawi. With both having 28 per cent losses, the figures confirm that South Africa and India have high health inequalities, too. The lowest rates of health inequalities were calculated for Belarus (7%), Ukraine (11%) and Brazil (14%) (UNDP 2012). However, the last three figures have to be projected against widespread – albeit not quite unequally distributed – health problems prevailing in these countries.

In all countries women tend to live longer than men, as will be discussed here for a selection of our 14 countries. Table 2.2 shows that women's life expectancy in the southern African countries ranges from

Table 2.2 Life expectancy at birth of females, 2009

Country	Years	Country	Years
Mozambique	51	Ukraine	74
Angola	53	Azerbaijan	70
South Africa	55	Kazakhstan	70
Zambia	50	Belarus	76
Botswana	62	Brazil	77
Malawi	51	India	66
Zimbabwe	50	Indonesia	71

Source: WHO 2011.

50 years in Zambia to 62 in Botswana; in India it is 66. In the remaining countries female life expectancy varies, from 70 up to 77 in Brazil (cf. the global average expectancy of 71 years for women [WHO 2011]).

In the second half of the twentieth century, life expectancy worldwide increased due to improvements in living conditions and nutrition, advances in medicine and medical treatments and international health campaigns. Improvements in public health and expanded immunization programmes caused lower mortality due to infectious and parasitic diseases (UNDESA 2010; WHO 2011). Calculations of Acemoglu and Johnson (2009) indicate that the increase in life expectancy led to a significant increase in population; birth rates did not decline sufficiently to compensate for the increase in life expectancy. In developing countries increases in the proportion of women receiving prenatal care and birth delivery attendance by skilled health personnel have contributed to their life expectancy, whereas the adoption of unhealthy behaviours, such as drinking and smoking, is of relatively little consequence. As a result, female life expectancy at birth has increased by 20 to 25 years in the past five decades. Women now outlive men in every region of the world and in all country groups by income level (World Bank 2011b). In the southern African countries, however, the rise of HIV/AIDS-related mortality since the 1980s has had a devastating impact, resulting in sharp drops in life expectancy. In South Africa life expectancy for women had increased to 65 years and for men to 57 years by the early 1990s, but within a decade the figure declined approximately ten years. By the late 2000s in that country, life expectancy at birth for men had started showing signs of recovery, but for women the declining trend continued (UNDESA 2010, 20).

Following the collapse of communist regimes in CIS countries, life expectancy at birth during the late 1980s and early 1990s decreased.

Especially male life expectancy fell, and the gap with the female rate became immense. Though after the 2000s there was a recovery ranging up to five years for both men and women (UNDESA 2010), the current gender gaps are among the world's largest. The average female's life expectancy in 2009 in Ukraine and Belarus was 12 years higher than the male's; it was 11 years in Kazakhstan. Azerbaijan was the exception, with a regular four-year difference (WHO 2011). Notably in Ukraine men's continuous low life expectancy is symptomatic of what has been called a health crisis. A World Bank report (2009a) labelled this health crisis "an avoidable tragedy". In detailing Ukraine's high mortality rates, the report shows them largely driven by mortality among working-age males. Compared with the other eastern European countries, ischemic heart disease (IHD), HIV/AIDS, poisoning, environmental pollution, violence and nutritional deficits caused by poor diet contributed more significantly to mortality. Ukrainian men had the second-highest mortality from alcohol abuse among men in Europe, women the fourth-highest rate.

Girls and boys: the statistics

At birth there is a worldwide surplus of boys to girls. According to UN estimates, the sex ratio at birth (the ratio of male to female births) reveals growing disadvantages for women. The ratio (discussed in the next section) has increased globally from a stable 1.05 in the early 1970s to a recent peak of 1.07 (UNDP 2011, 76). However, the sex ratio does not apply equally to all age groups; the so-called "gender spiral" points to more boys and men in the younger age groups and more women in the older age groups. In 2010 the world population counted 102 males for every 100 females. The male surplus is not a general pattern, and across countries large differences can be noticed. Ukraine counted 86 males for every 100 females; Belarus, 87 males; Kazakhstan, 91 males, Zimbabwe, 94; Mozambique, 95; Azerbaijan, 96; Brazil, Angola and South Africa, 97; Malawi, 99. In Zambia, Botswana and Indonesia the numbers of men and women were at par, and India reveals a male surplus, with 107 males for 100 females (UNDESA 2010).

Considering population size and gender composition as relevant, critical for the development of a country is population growth. Researchers will encounter major statistical difficulties in calculating population growth in most developing countries, including numbers of boys and girls. For Angola and Mozambique in particular, which till nearly 2010 had large numbers of refugees returning after their civil wars ended, population counting remains extremely difficult and of necessity inaccurate. For example, mid-2011 estimates of the population size of Angola varied between 18.0 and 19.8 million. The problems start literally with birth registration. A 2001 survey found that only 29 per cent of Angolan children younger than five had civil registration documents (UN System in Angola 2002, 40). Though these may be extreme situations, the lack of effective birth registration systems is much more widespread. According to WHO statistics, over the period 2000–9 in India, civil registration coverage of births (children less than five registered at the moment of the survey) was 41 per cent; in Indonesia it was 53 per cent (WHO 2011). UNICEF reports that about half the children in the urban areas of sub-Saharan Africa and South Asia are unregistered. As the UN Children's Fund stresses, the invisibility resulting from the lack of a birth certificate or an official identity paper vastly increases a child's vulnerability to exploitation of all kinds, including being forced into child marriage (UNICEF 2012, 13). The lack of formal recognition also deprives many girls and young women of opportunities to find a job or to travel or study abroad.

Female feticide

The worldwide surplus of boys to girls is most visible in India, prompting the UNDP to speak about the "missing women", referring to mortality patterns and sex ratios at birth that disadvantage women (UNDP 2010a). The country's extremely skewed sex ratio at birth is currently estimated at 1.12 male per 1.00 female. A strong preference for sons is the most plausible explanation for India's high sex ratio at birth: it results in sex-selective abortion, with prenatal detection of the sex of the foetus leading to increased abortions of female foetuses (see Box 2.3). It has to be noted that female feticide practices are not limited to India. It is also practiced in China and, among our 14 countries, Kazakhstan. In the latter, in 2006 over six in ten females surveyed said they were aware of sex-selective abortion practices, though less than three in ten considered such practices acceptable. Kazakh obstetricians expressed their concern to researchers that four in ten women who came to them wanting to discontinue pregnancy did so because they were bearing a girl (ADB 2005; Cosby et al. 2007). A World Bank team has estimated the excess female deaths at birth at over 1.4 million worldwide in 2008. One can add an estimated 600,000 missing girls under the age of five. According to the World Bank (2011b, 15), higher female mortality during infancy and early childhood cannot be explained by a preference for sons alone, although discrimination against girls may contribute to it. It would be a result not so much of discrimination as of poor institutions that force households to choose among many bad options, particularly regarding water and sanitation. Anyway, the "missing women" issue is one of the most telling, indicating that many girls that survive, both from poor and from urban middle-class backgrounds, have to go through a difficult and prejudiced start in life.

Box 2.3 The "missing women" of India

In 1992 Nobel laureate Amartya Sen argued that at the time there were 41 million "missing women" in India: girls and women who died prematurely due to, as he called it, mistreatment. In the past two decades the male population bias seems to have intensified as sex-selective abortion (female feticide), helped by prenatal sex determination techniques such as ultrasound technology, has become more widely used to avoid female births. These practices, as government health officers admit, have increased in educated and urban sections of society, where son preference persists even among educated women. The estimate is that each year nearly half a million female foetuses are destroyed. Older practices regulating the numbers of a family's female children include, besides female infanticide at birth, underreporting of female births, abandonment or out-adoption of girls and selective neglect of girl children, leading to higher death rates among them during infancy. These practices are still common in rural areas throughout India. For example, when children are ill, Indian fathers are more likely to pay for treatment for sons than for daughters (Sen 2003; Jha et al. 2006; UNDESA 2010; OHCHR et al. 2011).

For some years efforts to combat feticide have gone on in India, including a programme by the Health and Family Welfare Ministry to target and apprehend those who carry out female feticide. Just after the start of the present century, the Gujarat state government launched a Save the Girl Child campaign, supported by numerous NGOs all over India; in 2008 the central government made it a national campaign (US Dept of State 2011f).

Child mortality

MDG4 aims at reducing child mortality. Apart from the grief caused by the loss of a child, many of the health problems that women and men face in adulthood have their origin in childhood; therefore, it is important for children to have a healthy start. Worldwide, mortality under age five dropped from 109 deaths per 1,000 live births (1980–5) to 71 deaths per 1,000 live births (2005–10). These improvements have been explained by factors such as increased immunization coverage, higher caloric intake, use of oral rehydration therapies during episodes of diarrhoea, use of insecticide-treated mosquito nets, better access to insecticides, more effective therapies and treatments, as well as improved water and sanitation. Despite intensified efforts at reduction, Africa remains the region with the highest child mortality (UNDESA 2010).

We use the statistics concerning the under-five mortality (the probability of dying between by age five per 1,000 live births) as an illustration. Figure 2.1 presents these mortality rates for 11 of 14 countries, with a breakdown by urban and rural. It reveals high inequalities across countries and partly between urban and rural areas as well. The under-five mortality rates in Mozambique and Malawi are among the world's highest; in both countries the disparities within these rates are quite large, as are those between urban and rural areas (WHO 2011; Republic of Mozambique 2010, 56). In both countries malaria is a huge health risk, with children under five and pregnant women among the groups most vulnerable to this disease. Mozambique has, with 132 to 221 per 100,000 of the population, the world's second-highest cause-specific mortality rate due to malaria. The disease is one of the country's main causes of premature births and low weight at birth (Republic of Mozambique 2010; WHO 2011). In Malawi malaria is the most common reported cause of morbidity and mortality, responsible for about 40 per cent of the hospitalization of under-five children (WHO, Malawi country website). By contrast,

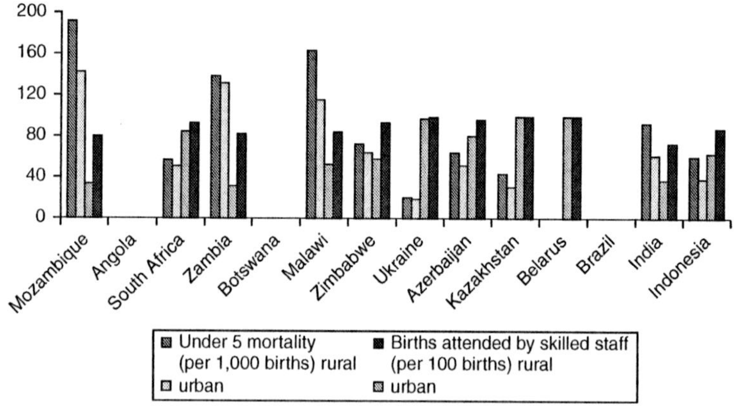

Figure 2.1 Mortality rates of children under 5 per 1,000 births and births attended by skilled health staff per 100 births, by urban and rural areas

Note: No data are available for Angola, Botswana and Brazil.

Source: WHO 2011: Mozambique, 2003; South Africa, 2003; Zambia, 2007; Malawi, 2004; Zimbabwe, 2005–6; Ukraine, 2007; Azerbaijan, 2006; Kazakhstan, 2006; Belarus, 2005; India, 2005–6.

Kazakhstan has extremely low under-five mortality rates, pointing to good prenatal care, birth delivery attendance and nutrition conditions for young children.

Figure 2.1 shows how many births were attended by skilled health staff. Again, the situation is more favourable in urban areas than rural ones. The figure shows that in Mozambique, Zambia and India slightly over 30 of 100 births were attended by health care staff in rural areas and between 73 and 83 of 100 births in urban areas. By contrast, in the CIS countries almost all births were attended by skilled staff, in rural areas almost as much as in urban areas. Indonesia shows good figures, too, with 63 attended births in rural areas and 88 in urban areas.

The pressure on girls

In many developing countries, girls have a heavier workload and less free time than boys. Girls face multiple responsibilities that compete for their time, because they complete household chores and caring labour, sometimes including the time-consuming fetching of fuel and water. Girls also face heightened parental resistance to activities outside the home, the threat of violence, and they experience increased discomfort with male-dominated atmospheres. These factors may hinder their participation in public life and paid employment (Levine et al. 2008; Greene et al. 2009). Further, experiencing violence between parents as a child is a risk factor for women experiencing violence from their own partners as adults and for men perpetrating violence against their partners (World Bank 2011b).

Girls and women who specialize in providing unpaid care work face economic risks, because allocation of time to non-market (as opposed to market) work limits the household income and because less paid-work experience or more employment interruption will translate into lower earnings (Heintz 2006). These prospects may hinder girls from developing aspirations apart from building a family, having children and providing unpaid household chores. They may feel that it is pointless to dream or may not believe it makes sense to aspire to a decent job, advanced study or a car, things they have no control over (Greene et al. 2009). The coping strategies adopted at household level in response to negative economic shocks underscore the importance of taking these dynamics into account when considering the linkages involving growth, employment and poverty. For countries without publicly supported systems of social protection, households and communities become a safety net of last resort (cf. Heintz 2006).

Mothers play an important role for girls' entry into adolescence. Studies have shown that increasing the share of household income controlled by women, through either their own earnings or cash transfers, changes spending patterns in ways that benefit children (World Bank 2011b). Improvements in a woman's own education positively impact the education of her daughters. Research on the effects of household- and district-level factors on primary school enrolment in 30 developing countries show a strong positive effect of a mother's education, independent of other factors and circumstances studied. As the researchers conclude, "mothers with more knowledge are in a better position to get their children into school", though they rightly immediately add, "[h]owever, many women in the developing world have not been to school at all" (Huisman and Smits 2009, 191).

The adolescent fertility rate

A telling statistical yardstick for the future of millions of girls and young women is the adolescent fertility rate (AFR), the number of yearly births per 1,000 females in the 15–19 age group. AFR figures indicate the level of teenage pregnancy and motherhood in a country. Before going into the implications of early motherhood, let us have a closer look at the AFRs in the 14 DFL countries. On the surface there is a close relationship between the total fertility rates (TFRs) and the AFRs. The correlation between TFR and AFR is high in both 2000 and 2009 (twice R = 0.87). Based on 2009 data (World Bank 2011a), four countries have relatively high TFRs and high AFRs, and there is a group of countries with quite low values on both indicators and a middle group. However, Brazil and Kazakhstan depart from this pattern, the Latin American country having a low TFR and a relatively high AFR, Kazakhstan a relatively high TFR and a quite low AFR.

In spite of the high correlations, the two quantities have shown different patterns of development over the last decade. The TFRs developed rather unevenly and unequally across countries, with five even having higher TFRs in 2009 than in 2000. Yet on balance the AFRs of all 14 countries fell in the course of the 2000s – an agreeable trend against the backdrop of the disadvantages in life of early motherhood that will be detailed. In the four-country group with the highest AFRs, Malawi and Mozambique showed the most rapid rate decrease between 2000 and 2009, both with 45 per 1,000. Angola and Zambia showed a slower decrease. Whereas the AFRs of Angola and Malawi showed a regular downward trend, those of Mozambique and Zambia started to fall only from 2002 on, in both cases after a rise in the five years before. Nevertheless, the AFR for Mozambique has remained on top.

India, Brazil and Zimbabwe make up a country group with medium-high AFRs, though from very different backgrounds. The early 2000s showed a clear downward trend in the Brazilian AFR. Nationwide campaigns for AIDS prevention, reproductive health policy strategies toward adolescents, sexual education at schools and massive exposure in the media regarding negative consequences of unplanned pregnancy among young people all spoke out in favour of a decline of adolescent fertility (Berquó and Cavenaghi 2005). However, the 2005–9 figures demonstrate no further fall of Brazil's AFR. In India the regular decrease of the nation's AFR in the 2000s continued the 1990s trend. Though the AFR remained much lower in urban than in rural areas, the latter caught up; as a result, the decrease between 1993 and 2006 was slightly larger in urban areas (24%) than in rural areas (20%). Remarkably, in the states neither urbanization levels nor poverty rates are decisive per se for AFR levels; regional habits and attitudes seem more important in India. According to the 2005–6 National Family Health Survey, roughly 8 per cent of all Indian women by then aged 20 to 24 became mothers before 16, when health risks are quite large (see below); 22 per cent of this cohort became mothers before age 18, and 42 per cent before age 20 (Moore et al. 2009).

By 2009, in the other seven DFL countries adolescent fertility rates were below 50; also in South Africa, Botswana (both 49) and Indonesia (44). The current Indonesian rate is particularly remarkable. Though arranged marriages have been largely replaced by "love marriages", socio-cultural and religious pressures to marry and have children remain strong (Situmorang 2003). Low AFRs in the CIS countries have to be projected against a larger background of generally low fertility rates, often hiding deteriorating health and health care conditions, premature adult mortality and related family obligations for young women, leading to a lack of life perspectives for many of them. Kazakhstan partly escapes from this picture, with births concentrated in women aged 25 to 35 (SAK 2009).

Early marriage and early motherhood

Child marriage or early marriage is defined as a "marriage carried out below the age of 18 years, before the girl is physically, physiologically, and psychologically ready to shoulder the responsibilities of marriage and childbearing" (IPPF 2007b, 7). The UN Convention on the

Elimination of All Forms of Discrimination against Women (CEDAW) explicitly outlaws child marriage and stipulates 18 as the minimum marital age for males and females. It has been argued that child marriage violates a number of rights laid down in the Convention for the Rights of the Child – the right to life (article 6), the right to health and the right to freedom from abuse and exploitation (article 24), the right to education (articles 24, 28 and 29) – and for that matter undermines a number of MDGs. Child marriage is a clear obstacle to eradicating poverty, achieving universal primary education (UPE), promoting gender equality and improving maternal and child health. It is a perceived violation of the development rights of girls and young women, before they are physically, emotionally and socially mature. Child marriages also bear multiple social risks. Child brides are particularly vulnerable to domestic violence because of the typically wide age gap between child brides and their spouses, and child marriage is linked with poverty because it affects particularly the poorest and the worst educated in the population (World Vision US 2008; Plan UK 2011, 3; Hervish and Feldman-Jacobs 2011; Santhya and Erulkar 2011).

Figure 2.3 shows that data are available for seven of the 14 DFL countries on the distribution of marriages by age of bride in the period 2000–9. Unfortunately, the figure does not distinguish between marriages under 18 and marriages over that age. The figure shows that in Azerbaijan more than one in five marriages involved women in the 15–19 group, followed by Ukraine, Kazakhstan and Brazil, with around 15 per cent of marriages. In South Africa marriages in this age group are rare, but in other sub-Saharan countries early marriage is quite common. In a 2006 survey in Malawi, half of all women in the 20–49 group reported being married or in union before their 18th birthday. Among women with secondary or higher education, however, the latter share fell below 20 per cent. As the survey report notes, schooling is a key strategy in delaying marriage (NSO/UNICEF 2006, 26). In Zambia various surveys indicate that early marriages are still quite common for girls. According to the 2005 Labour Force Survey, 19 per cent of young women between 15 and 19 were married, against only 2 per cent of young men the same age. Obviously, social pressure to marry early is great in Zambia. In another official Zambian survey (2008), one-third of all respondents said they had been forced to marry. In these cases females mainly reported pregnancy (CSO 2007b, 2009).

Child marriages often accompany early motherhood because contraceptive use is low in these marriages (IPPF 2007b, 7). Figure 2.2 shows the distribution of live births by age of the mother, available for 8 of 14 DFL countries in the late 2000s. It shows that almost one in five women in Brazil and South Africa are 15 to 19 when they give birth to a child. However, countries with large shares of early marriages and early motherhood do not fully overlap, in part because many women are single or living in union when giving birth. Such is notably the case in South Africa.

One in three of all early married girls lives in India. In that country, where in 1976 the legal marriage age was lifted from 15 to 18, marriage law is widely violated, in rural areas in particular. Some change can be noted: between 1993 and 2005–6 the national median age at first marriage increased seven months, from 17.2 to 17.8 years. Yet the latter figure implies that still nearly half of all women marry below the legal age of 18. Education matters here. By 2005–6 the share of women 20 to 24 and married before the legal age was as high as 60 per cent in the states of Jharkhand and Bihar but as low as 12 per cent in Himachal Pradesh and Goa – the states with, respectively, the lowest and highest educational levels. Statistical analysis confirms the inverse relationship between early marriage and education (Moore et al. 2009; IIPS/Macro International 2007).

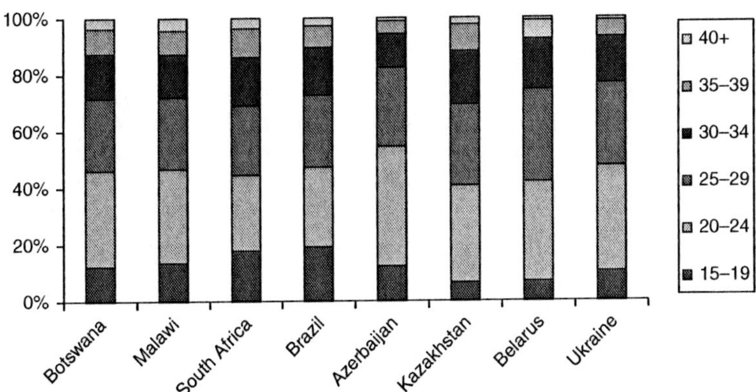

Figure 2.2 Distribution of live births over age of mother

Note: The age group 15–19 includes live births of mothers younger than 15, which is in South Africa 6%, in Brazil 0.8% and in the remaining countries negligible.

Source: UN data: Table 10, Live births by age of mother and sex of child, 2000–9; Botswana, 2006; Malawi, 2008; South Africa, 2009; Brazil, 2009; Azerbaijan, 2009; Kazakhstan, 2008; Belarus, 2008; Ukraine, 2007.

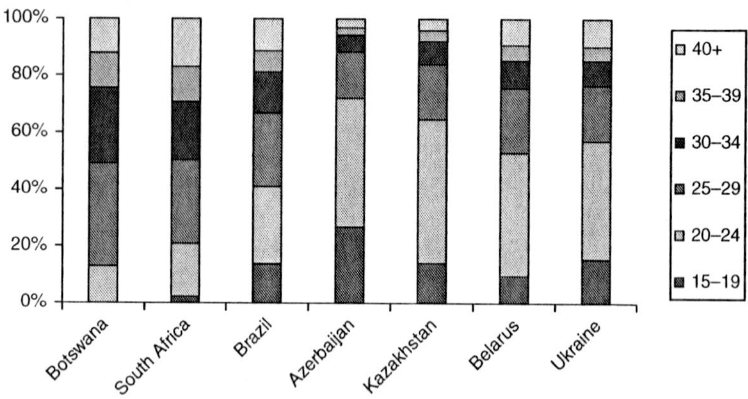

Figure 2.3 Distribution of marriages over age of bride

Source: UN data: Table 23, Marriages by age of groom and by age of bride, 2000–9; Botswana, 2006; South Africa, 2008; Brazil, 2009; Azerbaijan, 2009; Kazakhstan, 2008; Belarus, 2009; Ukraine, 2008.

Health risks of early motherhood

Early motherhood is associated with health and social risks. Pregnancy- and childbirth-related deaths are the main cause of death of 15- to 19-year-old girls worldwide. A devastating chronic disability is obstetric fistula, an injury to a woman's birth canal that leaves her leaking urine and/or faeces. Malawi and Mozambique are among the top-ten countries with such early motherhood risks, and Zambia is at position 17 (Rowbottom 2007). Moreover, babies of young mothers are also at greater risk than those with mothers between 25 and 29, particularly for preterm birth, low birthweight, stillbirth and babies' death, as well as late physical and cognitive development (Temin and Levine 2009; Plan UK 2011, 3).

In particular for India, there is overwhelming evidence of the dramatic health effects of early marriage and motherhood. In health terms millions of adolescent girls in India are disadvantaged. As for food intake, access to health care and growth patterns, they are worse off than their brothers. By the time they reach adolescence, many are grossly underweight and stunted. Pregnancy at an early age further exacerbates their poor health (Jejeebhoy 1998). The outcome of the 2002–4 Household Survey showed that pregnancy complications were highest among adolescent mothers; no surprise there. Delivery and post-delivery complications, too, and maternal mortality risk were highest in adolescent mothers (IIPS 2005). The perinatal mortality rate is also high among adolescent mothers' infants. Combined with their already poor health status, these risks are especially large among the poor and illiterate (IIPS/Macro International 2007). The Indian evidence definitely fits Rowbottom's (2007, 1) conclusion: "The future is compromised for most adolescent girls who become mothers [....] Their children are more likely than those of older mothers to be malnourished and have developmental problems."

Early motherhood is also associated with social risks. "Early marriage and high fertility limit such women's opportunities for education and employment and can severely diminish their chances for advancement in life" (UN Dept 2010c, vii). For South Africa, research indicates that teenage motherhood has a strong negative effect on high school completion. By contrast, higher education in particular may bring lower rates of teenage motherhood (Worku-Yergou Belay 2007). These relationships go both ways, because school attendance may provide at least some protection and school-based programmes might improve health (Lloyd 2007). However, the relationship between reproductive events and education seems to be changing. In sub-Saharan Africa other risks of leaving school during adolescence currently may exceed the risks associated with the traditional demographic reasons of early marriage and childbirth. Lloyd and Mensch (2008) found in a comparative analysis of surveys in francophone (West) Africa that such risks include exam failure, financial constraints and distance. This may be the case in some southern African countries as well, though in Brazil and India the constraints posed by early marriage and/or childbirth may still be important – or of renewed importance, as in Brazil. Again, particularly in India early marriage constrains adolescent women's opportunities to obtain higher education and severely restricts their autonomy. Yet in India, too, promising initiatives are under way to delay early marriage and childbearing, recognized as they are as essential barriers to women's labour participation, autonomy and empowerment. An example is the Haryana programme (see Box 2.4).

Box 2.4 The Haryana programme in India

A conditional cash transfer (CCT) programme in the state of Haryana is attempting to provide incentives for delayed marriage. The project aims to improve the nutritional and health status of adolescent girls between 11 and 18 years of age, to train and equip them to improve home-based and vocational skills, to promote awareness of health hygiene, nutrition, home management and child care and to take all such measures as will facilitate their marriage after they attain the age of 18 years or older. Though India has a large and still growing number of relatively small-scale initiatives and programmes aimed at economically empowering adolescent girls and improving their reproductive health, political intentions at the national level still have to be translated into large-scale programmes. At the same time, continuity of implementation must be ensured at the grass roots level (Santhya et al. 2008; Moore et al. 2009; Vij 2010).

The HIV/AIDS pandemic

As for health, without doubt the threat of the HIV/AIDS pandemic, with its personal consequences for many friends and relatives, is the most radical experience for the current generation of sub-Saharan African girls and young women – and to a lesser extent for their peers in the other seven DFL countries. In 2009 an estimated 33.3 million adults and children were living with HIV, two-thirds of whom (67%) were in sub-Saharan Africa. In 2009 2.6 million people were newly infected with HIV, 69 per cent in sub-Saharan Africa. In 2009 1.8 million AIDS-related deaths were registered, 78 per cent in sub-Saharan Africa. It is clear that that region bears a disproportionate share of the global HIV burden (UNAIDS 2010).

In the past decade the number of people living with HIV increased, but from the mid-1990s the number of newly infected persons and from 2004 the number of deaths decreased. In southern Africa the incidence and impact of HIV among children under 15 has been reduced; there were fewer children newly infected and fewer AIDS-related deaths among them. Worldwide, more than 5 million people are receiving HIV treatment. "As HIV testing expands, systems are strengthened to monitor the health status of people living with HIV, and [if] access to treatment is provided at the appropriate time, AIDS-related mortality is likely to further reduce", UNAIDS (2010, 29) declares. HIV prevention programmes aim at behavioural change, comprehensive and correct knowledge and condom promotion. Country HIV progress reports show condom availability and uptake improving and comprehensive and correct knowledge about HIV increasing slightly, particularly among 15- to 24-year-olds (UNAIDS 2010, 2011).

In 2009 almost 52 per cent of people living with HIV worldwide were women; it was 51 per cent a decade earlier. In 2010–11 more than a quarter (26%) of all new HIV infections were in young women aged 15 to 24. HIV is the leading cause of death of women of reproductive age.

In southern Africa young women are up to five times more likely to become infected with HIV than young men (UN Women 2011a). This growing gender gap is recognized by the Joint UN Programme on HIV/AIDS (UNAIDS 2011, 19): "The growing proportion of women and girls among people living with HIV highlighted the harmful consequences of gender inequality." A year earlier, UNAIDS (2010, 10) phrased the quest for gender equality in a more pronounced way: "Protecting women and girls from HIV means protecting against gender-based violence and promoting economic independence from older men." However, income inequality is also at stake on a world scale. As Bill Clinton put it, "People in rich countries don't die from AIDS anymore, but those in poor countries still do – and that's just not acceptable" (UNAIDS 2011, 35).

Many now recognize that the needs, circumstances and aspirations of adolescent girls and young women have been overlooked in HIV prevention programmes, taking into account the comparatively substantial body of literature on the impact of HIV and AIDS on *adult* women. The UNAIDS 2011 Report states: "Special attention is needed for young girls, as more girls living with HIV due to mother-to-child transmission are surviving and entering adolescence, in part due to increased availability of antiretroviral treatment (ART). These girls have particular sexual and reproductive health needs which need to be considered" (UNAIDS 2011, 36). It has been argued that "greater gender equality and empowerment of women would not only possess intrinsic value, but is also arguably a prerequisite for fighting HIV/AIDS and for successfully addressing its consequences" (Arrehag et al. 2006, 7). Others have argued in the same vein, establishing that the empowerment of women tends to reduce the risk of contagion. Cornia states that reducing discrimination in employment, income and social roles increases women's independence and ability to negotiate sexual contacts on their own terms, adding: "This particularly benefits young girls, who because of existing social norms often get infected at a much younger age than men" (Cornia 2007, 5; cf. IPPF 2007a; Pulerwitz et al. 2010).

HIV/AIDS in the 14 countries

With an estimated 5.6 million people living with HIV in 2009, South Africa's epidemic prevalence remains the largest in the world (UNAIDS 2010). By then the country's HIV/AIDS rate for those in the 15–49 group was estimated at 16.3 per cent, the world's fourth-highest proportion, though in 2004 the estimated rate of 18.8 per cent was even higher (WHO 2011). In KwaZulu-Natal province HIV prevalence in 2006 even reached 39 per cent (Bhana and Pattman 2009, 69). Gender, race and sexuality obviously are key factors underlying HIV risk in South Africa. New HIV infections disproportionately affect poor young females, and in South Africa the young and the poor are predominantly black. In 2008 HIV prevalence in the African population was eight times higher than among coloureds and 40 times higher than among whites and Indians/Asians (derived from HSRC 2009, 79).

However, there are also clear signs of hope. Based on national surveys conducted between 2001 and 2009, South Africa, Zambia and Zimbabwe succeeded in reducing new HIV infections overall by more than 25 per cent; they were three of the estimated 22 sub-Saharan countries where this occurred. HIV prevalence is also decreasing in Botswana, where between 2002 and 2009 the annual number of AIDS-related deaths declined by half. Developments are less clear in Angola, Malawi and Mozambique (UNAIDS 2010). Mostly there seems a transition in higher HIV prevalence towards the poor and remote rural areas and away from urban areas. This has, for instance, been observed in Malawi (Arrehag et al. 2010).

One of the few hopeful signs from Zimbabwe since 2000 has been the downward trend in its observed HIV prevalence rate, the first such decline in southern Africa. The trend reflects a combination of high mortality and declining HIV incidence, related in part to changes in sexual behaviour. Notably in rural Zimbabwe condom use among women the last time they had sex with a non-regular partner has gone up, as did (at least between 1999 and 2005–6) modern contraceptive use by married women aged 15 to 29. Among married women 15 to 19, that use tripled, from 10 per cent in 1999 to 35 per cent in 2005–6 (Republic of Zimbabwe 2010b, 32; UNAIDS/WHO 2009; additional information WHO). At the same time, the exodus of health workers from Zimbabwe in the course of the 2000s, the near collapse of the health system and the deterioration of medical facilities have heavily frustrated the struggle against the pandemic. After 2006 diminishing access to safe water sources and other essential infrastructural provisions came to the top. During 2010 and 2011 the UN Office for the Coordination of Humanitarian Affairs (OCHA) warned that under these conditions Zimbabwe was highly vulnerable to malaria, cholera, measles, typhoid and other epidemic outbreaks. In August 2008 large areas of Zimbabwe were struck by a cholera epidemic (website UN OCHA).

In the CIS countries the prevalence of HIV/AIDS is quite limited, except in Ukraine. With a rate between 1.6 and 1.8 per cent by 2008, adult HIV prevalence there was higher than in any other country in Europe or Central Asia (UNAIDS 2010). In Ukraine injected drug use remains the driving force behind the spread of HIV; female sex workers are a main risk group. Yet since 2000 the epidemic has shifted from high-risk groups to the general population through heterosexual transmission. The highest HIV incidence is among 20- to 24-year-olds. Two-thirds of all new HIV infections are among those aged 20 to 34, and about two in five newly infected are women (World Bank 2009; Dabash et al. 2006).

Brazil stands out for early and strong government intervention on HIV/AIDS. Since 1998 the AIDS death rate has steadily declined, an achievement attributed to the country's treatment policies. Throughout the 1990s a range of NGOs, governmental and grass roots organizations joined to address what was earlier thought a hopeless situation. The government reduced treatment costs by reverse-engineering antiretroviral drugs and negotiated substantial drug price reductions from pharmaceutical multinationals. Though its health care system continues to raise bureaucratic obstacles, the results of Brazil's AIDS programme are impressive (Biehl 2007). As former president Lula da Silva notes (in UNAIDS 2011, 29): "The Brazilian response to AIDS [...] stands out for its early adoption of prevention strategies, focusing primarily on condom use. In 1986, condom use in the first sexual intercourse was only 9 per cent; by 2008, it had reached 60 per cent. Today, our country is the world's largest governmental buyer of condoms."

In India and Indonesia, according to the US Department of State (2011f, 2011g), stigmatization and discrimination against persons with HIV/AIDS were pervasive in recent years. For India the State Department referred to Human Rights Watch (HRW) reporting that many doctors refused to treat HIV-positive children and that some schools expelled or segregated them because they or their parents were HIV-positive. The Indian government seems to have shaken off its earlier rather slack approach to HIV/AIDS. In October 2009 the Ministry of Labour and Employment issued a policy document concerning the pandemic, departing from the viewpoint that HIV/AIDS "is a major threat to the world of work and that it has shown maximum impact on the most productive segment of the labour force". The use of such economic arguments may help to push for more active government policies, also towards health in general (cf. Das et al. 2009).

Effects of HIV/AIDS on growth and progress

HIV and AIDS clearly undermine people's ability to make life choices that they highly value and to live a decent life. The first measurable impacts of its spread are most likely felt in education quality and child mortality rates, with rises in teacher absenteeism and deteriorating services in public hospitals, first for non-HIV-infected patients; what mostly follows are a rapid increase in orphanhood, the educational system's collapse and widespread impoverishment (Cornia 2007). In Mozambique, Zambia and other southern African countries with high HIV/AIDS prevalence, sectors that have proved most vulnerable are health and education (see Box 2.5). The pandemic has aggravated problems of finding skilled health and education staff caused by lack of schooling facilities as well as by the brain drain. Yet in the course of the spread of the disease, other essential services, like the water and sanitation sector, electricity supply and transport, are hit heavily as well, as are smallholder agriculture and parts of manufacturing (UNDP 2007a, 2007b).

Economic growth and social progress have been seriously hampered in all seven African DFL countries. For example, it is estimated that in ten years' time the average income in Zambia fell by 10 per cent because of HIV/AIDS and that the incidence of those living under the US$2 per day poverty line increased by 3 per cent. The estimates also indicate growing income inequality resulting from HIV/AIDS (Salinas and Haacker 2006, 12). In Botswana, with the world's second-highest infection rate (after Swaziland), the spread of HIV/AIDS was the main cause of the fall of the country's HDI between 1990 and 2000 (Government of Botswana 2009, 33). A study of Malawi demonstrates that HIV/AIDS and poverty are mutually reinforcing: HIV/AIDS acts as a vehicle for impoverishment at the individual, household, community and national level, exacerbating poverty by killing people at their most productive ages, leading to premature loss of human capital and income and increasing income and asset inequality (Arrehag et al. 2006, 5).

Box 2.5 HIV/AIDS and tuberculosis in southern Africa

Research shows the baleful combination of HIV/AIDS and tuberculosis (TB), one of the main opportunist infections but largely a curable one. About 77 per cent of Malawian TB patients are also infected with HIV. In 2005 the country's TB cure rate was 75 per cent; the stated aim was to bring it to 80 per cent by 2011 (IMF 2007; UN 2008). In 2009 the Mozambican TB cure rate had increased to 82 per cent (Republic of Mozambique 2010). TB is a major health problem in South Africa, too. In 2005 three in five new TB cases were HIV positive. South Africa shows many examples of drug-resistant TB spreading rapidly in communities of people living with HIV, resulting in very high mortality. Moreover, it is spreading among health care workers, of whom many are women. Nevertheless, successful completion of TB treatment increased from 65.5 per cent in 2004 to over 76 per cent in 2008 (UNAIDS/WHO 2009; SSA 2010).

Prevention of HIV/AIDS in South Africa

The fight against HIV/AIDS in South Africa has a troubled history. Ambitious government plans as of 1994 and 1997 to combat AIDS turned out to be vulnerable to obstruction by provincial health bureaucracies and lack of professional health staff. By the time President Mbeki entered office (1999), official estimates of the number of HIV-positive cases stood at four million. Yet Mbeki and his Minister of Health, resisting a rapid roll-out of antiretroviral therapy (ART), challenged the link between HIV and AIDS, as well as ART's efficacy, and suggested that medical scientists and anti-AIDS activists had racial motives. Finally, under pressure from civil organizations, in July 2002 the Constitutional Court ordered the government to provide antiretrovirals to all HIV-positive pregnant mothers at all public hospitals free of charge "without delay". Under further court pressure the government rolled out what has become the largest ART programme in the world (Butler 2005; Brouard 2011). As a group of South African researchers, medical specialists and care providers concluded, "Particularly in the case of HIV/AIDS, denialism and failures in leadership have led to unnecessary loss of life and a runaway epidemic" (*The Lancet* 2009). The group also pointed at the major inequalities remaining in health status and health service access across the country. They referred to the fact that only 14 per cent of citizens are able to access the private health care sector and yet benefit from up to 60 per cent of national health expenditure; moreover, nearly eight in 10 doctors worked in the private sector – a huge mismatch. Though inequities still are part of everyday life in South Africa, concerning the policies and programmes needed to fight AIDS, a consensus has emerged between government and civil society, including a sense of urgency and funding (Brouard 2011). Trade unions play an active part. Unions in sectors heavily exposed to HIV infections – the COSATU-affiliated unions of mineworkers, communications and transport workers and unions of clothing and textile workers, teachers and retail workers – pushed employers and bargaining councils to engage in HIV/AIDS prevention, treatment and care (NALEDI 2008, 37–44).

South African health authorities and activists have united to fight AIDS. They can feel supported by progress in that fight. The country has one of the world's highest levels of HIV testing and HIV-status awareness in its general population. In 2009–10 a mass campaign to screen people for the disease led 7.6 million people to be counselled and tested for HIV and 4.4 million to be screened for TB and identified 1.4 million HIV-positive people (UNAIDS 2011, 44, 67). What is more, from 2004 on, HIV data collected at antenatal clinics suggested that HIV infection levels were levelling off, first among adults, somewhat later among those 15 to 24. This may well be attributable to the considerable increase in condom use among males and females aged 14 to 22 already observed between 1998 and 2002 (UNAIDS/WHO 2008; Dinkelman et al. 2008). As said above, in the 2000s new HIV infections in South Africa fell by over 25 per cent. The worrisome fact remains that HIV prevalence continues very high for women 25 to 29. A nationwide survey in 2008 found nearly one in three in this age group (32.7%) to be HIV positive – the same proportion as in 2002 (HSRC 2009, 63–4).

Sexual and gender-based violence (SGBV)

Striking in the DFL project was the commonly experienced threat of violence, particularly of sexual and gender-based violence (SGBV), among the young women that participated. Clearly, for many this threat was never far away in their daily lives. Under these conditions, empowering girls and young women means involves a great deal of organizing against SGBV, including creating safe conditions and places.

This commonality of experience definitely applied to those from South Africa. Violence is epidemic there, a blot on the nation's reputation (see Box 2.6). The South African gender-based violence level is extremely high in international perspective. The female homicide rate is six times the global average, and 50 per cent of these women are killed by partners. Over one in four men (28 per cent) admit to have raped (*The Lancet* 2009). According to a 2008 study by the South African Police Service (SAPS) and the Centre for the Study of Violence and Reconciliation, only 4 per cent of reported rape cases ended in conviction. In most cases attackers were the victim's friends or family members, which contributed to a reluctance to press charges. A poor security climate and societal attitudes condoning sexual violence against women contribute to the problem. According to a report released in June 2009 by the trade union Solidarity, 45 per cent of rapes were perpetrated against children; nearly nine in ten child rapes were never reported to the police. The pervasive domestic violence included physical, sexual, emotional and verbal abuse, as well as harassment and stalking by former partners. According to NGOs, about one in four women were in an abusive relationship, but few reported it. The government financed 39 shelters for abused women, but more were needed, particularly in rural areas. The government continues to conduct domestic violence awareness campaigns (US Dept of State 2011k). Crime and violence also hit South African women in various unexpected ways. In a number of surveys, many women operating small businesses in the informal sector list crime atop the constraints on sound business. Thus, high crime rates produce a vicious circle: they contribute both to reduced business activity and to a brain drain and thus contribute to poverty and unemployment (cf. Kingdon and Knight 2007).

Box 2.6 Sexual harassment

"We have challenges in [the] South African Post Office in one of the biggest mail centres. One of the top managers has been suspended for two months due to sexual harassment. One woman stood her ground and made the accusation. This is a sensitive issue and has been difficult for the victim. She is a pastor and is determined to expose the manager. Most of the other young women workers have admitted getting jobs by sleeping with the accused and are very afraid to come forward and testify against the accused. There seems to be a great deal of threat and the young women fear losing their jobs. Even amongst the women union members it is difficult to take the case forward for e.g. the gender officer at the Company is trying to stop the investigation from continuing.... As CWU we are trying to come up with the campaign and sensitize young women around sexual harassment." Mathapelo, member of Communications Workers Union (CWU), South Africa (Decisions for Life project website).

As various reports emphasize, in South Africa young girls' vulnerability to HIV infection in the face of gender inequalities is compounded by the fact that they increasingly have older partners and not rarely are targeted by older men (the notorious "sugar daddies") for sex. In general, they find very little support and guidance in daily life, where emphasis is placed on men's dominance of women and girls, who in contrast are widely expected to be passive and innocent in sexual matters (Bhana and Pattman 2009, 69–70; HSRC 2009, 64–5). In particular for South Africa, the relation between HIV infection and sexual and gender-based violence is underpinned by research outcomes. For example, it has been found that among South African young women experience of intimate partner violence increases the odds of becoming infected with HIV by nearly 12 per cent (UNAIDS 2011, 36). A South African MDG evaluation report, which has taken up the challenge of these and related findings, recommends, among other things, improving access to basic health care, with specific focus on improved health issues impacting women; realising greater access to safer sex practices by making female condoms available; providing guidance and support to help young girls take decisions about their bodies, sexuality and life, especially against predatory older men (SSA 2010, 83). As is practised in quite a few current prevention programmes in neighbouring countries like Mozambique (UNDG 2010d, 105–6), the MDG report emphasizes the importance of community action.

As for the other sub-Saharan countries, much evidence has been gathered on how widespread gender-based violence has become. In Angola's capital Luanda, a 2007 study indicated that nearly four in five women (78 per cent) had experienced some form of violence since the age of 15; over one in four reported abuse in the 12 months preceding the study. On 3 November 2010, two NGOs, Plataforma Mulheres em Acçao and the Open Society Institute, walked to the National Assembly in Luanda to encourage the legislature to pass a law against domestic and family violence. Five of the demonstrators were detained for five hours and later released (US Dept of State 2011a). In spite of the presence of many NGOs, the position of women in Angola remains difficult, and enforcement of human and women's rights weak. Also, in comparison with Mozambique, the building of a civil society and related social structures there still seems in its infancy.

As for Mozambique, a 2010 survey indicated that 21 per cent of female respondents reported an act of physical or sexual violence perpetrated by a man during the past year – an outcome only slightly lower than that for Angola's capital. Sexual harassment was reported to be pervasive in business, government and even schools (US Dept of State 2011j). It is rather shocking to read in the Mozambican MDG evaluation report that "some parents are afraid to send their daughters to school where male teachers dominate, due to the fear of sexual harassment" (Republic of Mozambique 2010, 53).

Even if cohabiting or married women are the primary breadwinners, as is often the case, for example, in Botswana, many among them continue to perceive the headship of households and families as an exclusively male domain. In Botswana these perceptions are a major source of tension, not rarely ending in domestic violence (Mookodi 2004). A detailed qualitative study revealed for that country a close relationship between alcohol abuse and gender-based violence, which in turn makes female victims vulnerable to HIV infection (Phorano et al. 2005).

In the largest DFL countries, urban violence against women has attracted much attention – as have countermeasures. Based on interviews with women in six Brazilian states, an Amnesty International (2008) report provides a shocking account of their experience of urban violence, suffering attacks and violence at the hands of criminal gangs and law enforcement officials alike. Some cities have taken refuge in unorthodox measures to avoid violence against women. For instance, Rio de Janeiro has passed a bill reserving some subway cars and commuter trains for women after "hundreds of female commuters deluged the state legislature's hot line with complaints about fondlers" (De Ruyter et al. 2009, 14). The Lula administration pushed back against Brazil's plague of violence against women. In 2006 the government passed the *Maria da Penha* law; it provided the first clear definition of domestic violence, offered protections for women experiencing domestic violence and tripled the severity of sentences for offenders. Also, each state secretariat for public security operates *Delegacias da Mulher* (DEAMs), police stations dedicated exclusively to addressing crimes against women, totalling over 400 countrywide (website OECD-SIGI/Brazil; US Dept of State 2011d). Yet Amnesty International's case – that the continuing gap between what the legislation promises and what women experience is mainly caused by the authorities' failure to address persistent problems in the criminal justice system – is strong. AI claims that this is especially true for women in the most marginalized communities: "A police force which consistently violates their rights and discriminates against their communities can command little respect or confidence from women seeking to defend their rights" (AI 2008, 35).

In India similar countermeasures have been taken (see Box 2.7). For instance, in the megacity of Mumbai some commuter buses and two compartments on every train are marked "women only". Yet outside rush hours train compartments suffer from a lack of security. In response, the female head of the Rail Ministry announced that in the 2010 budget there would be provision for female security officers on the trains (Plan UK/Plan International 2010, 61). Like Brazil, India has set up all-women police stations to address domestic violence against women (US Dept of State 2009). In Indonesia, too, the police nationwide operate special "crisis rooms" or "women's desks", where female officers receive criminal reports from female and child victims of sexual assault and trafficking and where victims find temporary shelter (US Department of State 2011g).

Box 2.7 Harassment of women in India

"The notion that the world is now a safer place for women to work, earn, and live is a myth. What goes on at the workplace is far away from being quoted or reported anywhere, because one, it is all so subtle, and second, I need the job. And this is all 'they' need to know to be able to harass any woman at her workstation!" (Preeti, 24 years old, employee at a kids' apparel outlet, India (Decisions for Life project website))

Orphanhood

Orphanhood is one of the ugliest effects of the HIV/AIDS pandemic and a huge problem in most sub-Saharan countries, including our seven. Based on debates and documentation from the DFL project, it is identified as a major risk, one that could definitely ruin the life prospects of many girls. Beegle et al. (2010) present a statistical picture, based on national demographic surveys, that looks somewhat reassuring. Available evidence suggests considerable resilience among extended families in absorbing orphaned children. In sub-Saharan countries overall no significant increases are found of child-headed households or children living outside the household environment on the streets. Most common for children's living arrangements with rising adult mortality is an increasing propensity for them not to reside with relatives other than a parent. In most countries but not all, grandparents play a growing role as caregivers. Surviving parents play a substantially more prominent role in the care of paternal orphans than do other members of the extended family network. However, maternal orphans are much less likely to reside with their father than paternal orphans with their mother (Beegle et al. 2010, 1729, 1743).

As for caregivers in AIDS-stricken families, the available evidence leaves a more disquieting picture. Children heavily burdened with the role of caregiver are tasked far beyond a child's "normal" responsibilities. They may experience high personal costs – loss of friends, isolation, as well as a major emotional burden – though young caregivers also voiced benefits of having the responsibility of caring for a loved one (Robson et al. 2006). Moreover, outcomes of the 30-country research already mentioned indicate that overall the absence of one of the parents decreases a child's chances of enrolment in primary education (Huisman and Smits 2009, 190). An overview of orphanhood in the African countries at stake is given below.

Taking the share of orphans in the population under age 18 as the point of departure, the orphanhood problem is largest in Zimbabwe, followed by Mozambique, South Africa and Zambia (2009 estimates from UNICEF 2012). In Zimbabwe the share in 2009 was 24 per cent, whereas in the other three countries it was about 19 per cent. Of the country's 1.4 million orphans, about a million lost one or both parents to AIDS. In 2005 a record 22 per cent were double orphans (Beegle et al. 2010, 1733). Zimbabwe seems an exception to the rule in that the incidence of child-headed households is low; an official estimate mentions 100,000 children living in such households (Government of Zimbabwe 2009). In Mozambique 670,000 children orphaned by AIDS add to the huge number of orphans from the civil war, bringing the total number to about 2.1 million orphans aged 17 or under. In the 2000s there was nearly one double orphan due to AIDS for each non-orphan in the Mozambican schools, an outcome regarded as alarming by the country's 2010 MDG report. This ratio was about the same for boys and girls (Republic of Mozambique 2010, 91–3). A hopeful sign may be that Mozambique's total orphan rate in recent years has stabilized (Beegle et al. 2010, 1743).

In South Africa 1.9 million of the estimated 3.4 million orphans lost one or both parents to AIDS. At least one in three orphans are believed to live in chronic poverty. Only about half of them proved to be covered by official child support grants. Moreover, Leibbrandt et al. (2010, 56) found a disparity between paternal and maternal orphans: three in four children whose father died received such grants, but less than two in five of those whose mother died did. Where both had died, the percentage was slightly above that of maternal orphans. Overall, South African orphans were less likely to receive a child support grant than children with both parents. In Zambia about 850,000 of the 1.2 million orphaned children counted in 2005 lost one parent or both to AIDS (UNDP 2007b); though the AIDS incidence levelled off, the number of Zambian orphans continued to increase, to 1.3 million in 2009 (UNICEF 2012).

In the other three African countries the orphanhood situation is only slightly less poor. The figure of 150,000 children in Angola losing one or both parents to AIDS may seem relatively modest, but as in

Mozambique this number is in addition to the immense problems caused by the civil war. About 1.5 million children 17 or under were orphaned due to all causes – 15 per cent of all children of that age (UNICEF country statistics). In Malawi the 2006 Welfare Monitoring Survey found 1,110,000 orphans, one in seven persons under 20. One in five orphans had lost both parents; about half were orphaned due to AIDS (NSO 2006). Governments, supported by UN-sponsored programmes, try to keep orphaned children in school. In the late 2000s primary school attendance rates of orphans in Malawi remained at par with those of non-orphans (cf. Government of Malawi 2010, 39). Botswana's problem is of the same magnitude, with orphans numbering about 16 per cent of the population under 18, of whom AIDS was responsible for around two in three (UNICEF country statistics). In 2009 in the seven African countries, there were over 9.8 million orphans, of whom over 5.3 million owed their status to AIDS.

Mobility out of poverty?

Even if someone is poor, perceiving opportunities to move out of poverty and climb up in society is quite important for his or her perspective in life. A positive perception can give individuals a boost – can, for example, stimulate a girl's desire to continue her education. By contrast, the perception of a considerable risk of falling (back) into poverty may work out negatively by discouraging initiatives towards education or a (better) job. That risk may be especially important for girls and young women, because in many developing countries they run the risk of becoming a member of a female-headed household – or indeed its head. As will be seen, the odds of staying in poverty are above average for these households. Empirical studies of upward and downward social mobility near the poverty line and of the economic, social and psychological mechanisms behind such movements are few, though the World Bank's Moving Out of Poverty studies (Narayan and Petesch 2007) offer valuable insights. Among much else, these studies revealed data from many countries and produced case studies covering India (Krishna 2007) and Brazil (Perlman 2007). Rather than go into their outcomes, which are still difficult to generalize from, this section confines itself to a broad overview of four DFL countries.

In South Africa mobility out of poverty appears considerable. However, mobility *into* poverty was equally so; obviously in the 1990s both movements were of the same magnitude. By 2000 about two-thirds of those below the lower-bound poverty line could be called chronically poor, as they had not moved out of poverty in the five years before. The largest groups among them were the rural poor (in 2000 about a million households), female-headed households, the elderly, former farm workers, migrants, street homeless and AIDS orphans (Aliber 2003). The situation of the female-headed household seems to have improved somewhat in the 2000s, most likely due to increased state social grants (Leibbrandt et al. 2010). Yet for 2005–6 it was reported that 45 per cent of the country's female-headed households, compared with one in four male-headed households, still lived below the lower-bound poverty line. The incidence of poverty was by far highest in rural areas, mostly the overcrowded former homelands, with poverty rates more than double those of urban areas (Armstrong et al. 2008). Taking up informal work has not been a way to alleviate poverty either. In 2003, 42 per cent of the informal self-employed earned less than the US$2 a day poverty line figure, more than double the share of poor among all employed (Kingdon and Knight 2007; Casale et al. 2004) – a ratio that hardly seems to have changed in the course of the 2000s (cf. SSA 2010).

In Mozambique, between 1996–7 and 2008–9 poverty fell somewhat, in particular among female-headed households, but it remained very high. In 2008–9, 58 per cent of female-headed and 54 per cent of male-headed households lived below the poverty line (Republic of Mozambique 2010). Mobility out of poverty remained low. Between 2002 and 2005 18 per cent of rural people rose above the poverty line but 15 per cent fell below it. In rural areas large numbers remained untouched by progress: 56 per cent of the rural extremely poor in 2002 still belonged to the same category in 2005 (Hanlon 2007).

Because of India's size, getting more than a snapshot of the dynamics of mobility in and out of poverty is impossible. Research covering 106 villages in three states has shown that in 25 years, 9 to 14 per cent of the originally poor households, depending on the state, succeeded in escaping poverty, while 6 to 12 per cent fell into poverty, resulting in a net poverty reduction of 1.9 to 3.2 per cent (Krishna 2007). State and regional development antipoverty programmes may bring about higher net gains, but notably the relatively backward states encounter major problems. First, they experience the awkward combination of rapid population growth and low economic growth. Second, they seem unable to initiate effective and strong antipoverty programmes – partly for organizational reasons, partly because of financial constraints. In the last two decades the central government has pursued the credo of liberalization, which has led to scaling down public investment in

agriculture, rural development and infrastructure. Finally, financial liberalization led most banks to avoid backward states, small farmers and small-scale industries. As a result, from the 1980s on, inequalities in per capita income and in growth rates across states have both increased (Kundu and Sarangi 2009). Physical indicators for the last decade also point to continuing widespread poverty as well as the persistent urban versus rural divide. The (abundant) evidence can be limited to one issue. In 2007–8, according to official MDG reporting, 51 per cent of Indian households had no toilet facility – 66 per cent of rural households against 19 per cent of urban households (CSO/Government of India 2009, 19).

In the 1990s Indonesia showed a relatively high rate of mobility out of poverty (measured by the proportion below the low national poverty line). Remarkably enough, the crisis that hit the country in 1997–8 did not affect that rate negatively. Comparing 1993, 1997 and 2000 data, the persistence of poverty turned out to be rather low over generations. A child growing up in a chronically poor household was 35 percentage points more likely to remain poor as an adult than a child who grew up in a non-poor household (Pakpahan et al. 2009). Scattered information on developments after the turn of the century may cast doubt if such rather high mobility out of poverty has continued. Physical indicators, including access to improved sanitation facilities and safe water sources, suggest that in the 2000s, for many Indonesians urban living conditions deteriorated while conditions in rural areas were stable or improving. Additional income and consumption figures suggest that in the past decade the poorest 30 per cent of city dwellers were stuck in poverty (ADB 2009; Mishra 2009; WHO 2011).

3
Education and Skills of Young Women

Introduction: the MDG2 + 3 goals

Millennium Development Goal 2 aims to achieve universal primary education (UPE); more specifically, it aims to ensure that, by 2015, children everywhere, boys and girls alike, are able to complete a full course of primary schooling. The UN Development Group Task Force on the MDGs writes: "Since 2000, considerable progress has been made toward achieving UPE. Some of the world's poorest countries have dramatically increased enrolment, narrowed gender gaps and extended opportunities for disadvantaged groups [. ...] The deficit in Sub-Saharan Africa remains large with over 30 million children still denied a primary education"; but it adds: "Progress, however, has not been universal [...] many children from marginalized social and economic groups do not have access to primary schooling. Inequalities, disparities and combined forms of exclusion persist and are often hidden" (UNDG 2010b, 9–10). This chapter details the achievements in young women's education and skills in the 14 DFL countries and the factors that contribute to improvement.

MDG3 aims to promote gender equality, empower women and eliminate gender disparity in primary and secondary education no later than 2015. As already noted, gender parity does not always imply progress for girls and women, though for education, particularly for primary education, gender parity is important. A wide range of factors affects girls' enrolment and attainments in primary, secondary, tertiary and vocational training. To take just one, women's education has a strongly negative correlation with fertility, though causality can go both ways (Worku-Yergou Belay 2007; Buvinic et al. 2009). Urbanization also correlates with lower fertility rates, a phenomenon in part due to higher opportunity costs for education and employment for those living in cities (cf. UNICEF 2012). This chapter compares women's and men's educational achievements.

The importance of education

Education is closely related to labour force participation and higher earnings: "Girls with more schooling participate in greater numbers in the labour force when they grow up, and they are able to earn more for their families and society" (Levine et al. 2008, 18–19). The universal "law" that earnings correlate with education is basically confirmed for females in the DFL countries. This phenomenon is called "the economic returns to investment in schooling." Using data from the *WageIndicator* 2010–11 survey, our findings reveal that highly educated young women aged 30 or younger in the survey have higher earnings – measured as the median value of the hourly wages – than mid-level educated women and these in turn have higher earnings than the least educated women in this age group (Tijdens and Van Klaveren 2012). The survey includes data for 10 DFL countries: Mozambique, South Africa, Zambia, Azerbaijan, Belarus, Kazakhstan, Ukraine, Brazil, India and Indonesia. As for the two exceptions, in Brazil the least educated young women have slightly higher earnings than their mid-level educated sisters but less than the highly educated, and in Ukraine the least educated have slightly higher earnings than either the mid-level or the highly educated.

Education is important not only for the women and their families; it is vital for the country's economic growth, too. For governments, providing good-quality, accessible education serves economic growth, but it also safeguards equality of opportunity, which thrives where universal access to public services, like education, is provided (CGD 2008). In many countries, strong pressure from households, trade unions, women's organizations and other NGOs works to narrow educational gaps, not least because doing so might serve to reduce poverty.

Literacy

In 2008 there were just under 800 million illiterate adults, around 17 per cent of the world's adult population. This datum is in immense contradiction with the importance of literacy. To cite the website of the American organization ProLiteracy: "[...] the ability to read and write is the basis for all other education; literacy is necessary for an individual to understand information that is out of context, whether

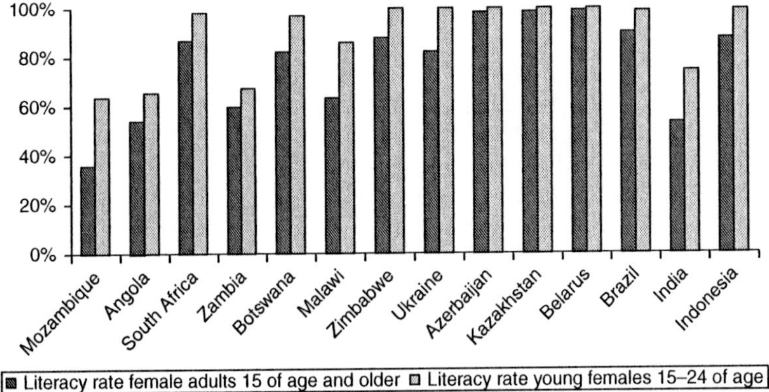

Figure 3.1 Female adults 15 and older (2009) and young females 15 to 24 (2005–9), % literate

Source: UIS 2011.

written or verbal. Literacy is essential if we are to eradicate poverty at home and abroad, improve infant mortality rates, address gender inequality, and create sustainable development." Literacy as a concept has proved both complex and dynamic; it continues to be interpreted and defined in a multiplicity of ways. Yet the most common understanding of literacy is as a set of tangible skills – particularly the cognitive skills of reading and writing – that are independent of the context in which they are acquired and the background of the person acquiring them (UNESCO 2006). In many countries, however, a "lighter" definition is used in surveys: respondents are asked whether they and the members of their household are literate as opposed to needing to demonstrate the skill.

Progress towards UNESCO's goal of halving adult illiteracy rates by 2015 has been disappointing. Of the nearly 800 million who are illiterate, two-thirds are women. Sub-Saharan Africa and South and West Asia account for 73 per cent of the global adult literacy deficit. Literacy rates in these regions are increasing too slowly to counteract the effects of population growth, resulting in an increase of the absolute numbers of illiterate people (UNESCO 2011). From cross-country research in Africa, it has been learned that literacy rates cannot be explained by variation in national per capita income. As will be shown below, even in the poorest countries there is significant variation in achieved literacy, suggesting that learning can occur even in resource-challenged environments (Lloyd and Hewett 2009). However, the fact remains that for many countries international educational goals are unlikely to be reached by 2015.

Figure 3.1 shows the literacy rates of females 15 and older for 2009, as well as the literacy rates of females 15 to 24 years old, with data for the latest available year in the period 2005–9. The 14 countries vary largely with respect to female literacy rates. In South Africa, Botswana and Zimbabwe, in all the CIS countries, in Brazil and in Indonesia, literacy of young females is almost 100 per cent, whereas it is slightly over 60 per cent in Mozambique, Angola, Zambia and India and above 80 per cent in Malawi. The figure reveals an encouraging trend when comparing the literacy rates of young females to the total female population 15 and older. Countries with relatively low literacy rates for females at large univocally show major progress, with the rate for the young females 8 (Zambia) to 28 percentage points (Mozambique) higher. Differences between the rates for the large countries – India (21 percentage points), Indonesia (12) and South Africa and Brazil (both 11) – indicate their tremendous education efforts in recent years. Though this improvement in literacy may not immediately pay out in the labour market, it has brought millions of girls and young women to a better starting position in life – or put otherwise, it has very basically empowered them.

Inequalities in education

Following calculation of the inequality-adjusted HDI (IHDI) with losses for inequalities in education, as discussed in Chapter 1, in 2011 the largest inequalities were found for India (40%), followed by Malawi (35%) and, at some distance, Brazil (26%). The other African countries were in the 18 to 24 per cent loss range, as was Indonesia (20%). With 5 to 8 per cent losses, the smallest educational inequalities were in the CIS countries (UNDP 2012). These results fit in with other international publications, all concluding that educational problems are concentrated in several sub-Saharan countries and parts of South Asia, including India and Pakistan. The *World Development Report 2012* relates the sizable education gaps persisting for girls from poor households in these countries to a combination of poverty and other factors of exclusion – ethnicity, caste, remoteness, race, disability and sexual orientation. On top of these factors, girls from rural or ethnic subgroups are often worst off. The report stresses that in many countries gender disparities remain large only for those who are poor, with reference again to India (World Bank 2011b, 12–13). Other publications have also emphasized the relationship between household poverty and social exclusion, on the one hand, and low girls' enrolment in education on the other, noting, for example, that in sub-Saharan Africa only 17 per cent of girls enrol in secondary school (cf. Levine et al. 2008). It is in a number of African countries and in India that within-country inequalities in various fields are largest and, combined, often exert a devastating influence on living conditions. Low participation in education and the substandard living and health conditions of the poor hamper the cognitive development of girls in particular, as was discussed with respect to India.

In recent years a number of organizations have made pleas for conditional cash transfer (CCT) programmes as a means to fund mainly primary education and attract (some may say force) the poor to participate in education (e.g., UNGEI 2011). Brazil's Bolsa Família programme is an early example of such an approach (see Box 3.1). Others warn against a one-sided emphasis on funding. For example, Lloyd (2009) refers to the observation that in at least four sub-Saharan countries both male and female teachers hold female pupils in low esteem. Be that as it may, it is assumed that many girls respond better to female teachers.

Box 3.1 Brazil's Bolsa Família programme

In Brazil in 2004, five income-transfer programmes were combined as Bolsa Família, a means-tested programme targeted at the poor and extremely poor, based on self-declared income. Families are required to adhere to a number of conditions in order to receive the benefit. Children under seven must be taken to health clinics at regular intervals to be monitored and to receive vaccinations. All children between 6 and 15 are required to be enrolled in schools; they have to attend at least 85 per cent of classes. The benefit level of the Bolsa Família programme is relatively low (50 per cent of the pension level) because it is regarded as an income supplement rather than replacement (Ferreira et al. 2010; Holmes et al. 2011).

Primary education: enrolment

Between 2007 and 2010, that 89 per cent of the world's girls in the official secondary school-age group enrolled in secondary school against 91 per cent of boys indicates a further closing of the world-wide gender gap in primary school enrolment; in other words, a higher gender parity index (GPI), here 0.98. For the sub-Saharan region the comparable figures are, respectively, 74 and 78 per cent (GPI of 0.95), again indicating an overall increase and a smaller gender gap. Yet the sub-Saharan figures for both genders are the world's second lowest. It should be added that enrolment rates in many developing countries give too rosy a picture of attendance and of survival rates to the last primary grade. Globally, the last rate is calculated for 2006– 76 per cent through administrative data and, based on survey data, 91 per cent between 2005 and 2010; the sub-Saharan totals are, respectively, 15 and 5 percentage points lower (UNICEF 2012). In many countries the gaps between enrolment and survival, indicating dropout numbers, are considerable, but statistical gaps and anomalies abound. Some sources suggest that on a world scale girls' dropout rates are falling more rapidly than boys'; other sources are less sure (UNDESA 2010; World Bank 2011b; WDR 2012). The UN's MDG2 evaluation is as follows: "While the existing data are insufficient to provide an accurate and complete picture, it appears that in spite of the significant success in initially enrolling children into primary school, nearly one in three of those who do enrol in sub-Saharan Africa and South and West Asia drop out before completion of the cycle" (UNDG 2010a, 10).

Table 3.1, presenting enrolment rates in primary education in the 14 countries, shows high rates for three of the four CIS countries (one is missing) and for South Africa and Brazil, whereas rates are low in the other African countries.

Table 3.1 Net enrolment rate in primary education and its GPI and the survival rate to last grade and its GPI, 2005–10 (latest available year)

	Net enrolment (%)	GPI	Survival to last grade (%)	GPI
Mozambique	90	0.94	34	0.91
Angola	75*	0.97*	?	?
South Africa	90	1.02	?	?
Zambia	94	1.03	52	0.95
Botswana	88	1.02	?	?
Malawi	94	1.05	42	0.99
Zimbabwe	92*	1.02*	?	?
Ukraine	89	1	98	1
Azerbaijan	85	0.98	97	0.97
Kazakhstan	98*	0.99*	99	1.01
Belarus	96	1.02	?	?
Brazil	94	0.98	?	?
India	81*	0.95*	94	1
Indonesia	98*	1*	83	1.07

Note: GPI = gender parity index.

Source: UIS 2011; (*) UNICEF 2012.

In 2009 in 12 of 14 DFL countries, the net enrolment rate in primary education was above 85 per cent, whereas it was 81 per cent in India and 75 per cent in Angola, as Table 3.1 shows. Indicated by the GPI, in six of the 14 the net enrolment rates are slightly higher among girls (GPI > 1.00), in two countries they are equal, and in the remaining six countries enrolment rates are slightly higher for boys. In five of seven African countries boys have a slight disadvantage. However, when looking at the survival rates (indicating how many children continued to the last grade), the picture changes. In India and in three CIS countries (one CIS country's information is missing), at least 94 per cent of children enrolled in primary education continue to the last grade. In Indonesia the figure is 83 per cent, but in Zambia only 52 per cent, and in Mozambique the survival rate falls even deeper, to 34 per cent, while no information is available for the remaining African countries and for Brazil (UNESCO 2011; UIS 2011).

Primary education: country overview

In South Africa recent figures indicate a net enrolment rate in primary education of 94 per cent, two points lower than that registered for 2000. In contrast, higher enrolment of girls persists, giving a GPI fixed around 1.02. Thus, the conclusions in South Africa's MDG report seem partly justified, partly not: "Primary education in South Africa is characterized by very high rates of enrolment and retention. These rates show strong gender equity, and where small differences do exist, they are in the girl child's favour. Universal primary education is already effectively a reality." Still, the report warns: "Whilst the girl child has an improved participation rate in school, an undesirable number of girls continue to drop out of school due to pregnancy. Therefore there is a need to address the primary causes of teenage pregnancy and entrenched poverty" (SSA 2010, 49).

Malawi is an interesting case from a policy perspective. In 2005 the government made primary education free for girls and scrapped primary school fees to encourage enrolment. In the five African countries involved in this global school fee abolition initiative (SFAI), it led to an overall increase in total primary school enrolment in the following year ranging from 12 to 51 per cent. In Malawi, however, the impact on school quality was clearly negative, indicating that free primary education is no quick fix; it requires planning, adequate financing, resources and stakeholder involvement at local and school levels. Hidden costs, as for exercise books and textbooks, played a negative role here (Mugoni

2005; UNDG 2010a, 2010c). In a way, the Ukrainian case contains a similar warning. While education in Ukraine is free, universal, and compulsory until age 15, the public education system suffers from chronic underfunding, and children from poor families continued to drop out of school before turning 15 (US Dept of State 2011l).

In Zimbabwe in the course of the 2000s, the educational system felt heavy constraints: mortality and morbidity of staff, pupils and parents from HIV and AIDS; youth gang violence; emigration of qualified teachers; and poverty bringing an inability to pay school fees. Though enrolment rates in primary education officially fell by fewer than 10 percentage points between 2000 and 2009, the Department of Education admitted in 2009–10 that teachers' vacancy rates were extremely high across all educational levels and that quality losses were huge. Moreover, international donors indicated from 2007 on that they witnessed low enrolment rates, particularly among girls. If a family was unable to pay tuition costs, it was most often girls who left school or never began. In 2006, in collaboration with UNICEF and other partners, the government launched a National Girls' Education Strategic Plan to increase the likelihood of achieving the UPE goal and ensuring that girls stayed in school. The plan's effects are still rather unclear (Republic of Zimbabwe 2010a, 2010b; US Dept of State 2011n).

In listing causes for Brazil's pervasive inequality, Skidmore (2004) ranks prominently the systematic neglect of universal public education (UPE), with free tuition at federal universities versus underfunding of the public system of primary and secondary schools. Public primary education remains in bad condition; children are in school only four hours a day, and the dropout rates of girls in particular are high by international standards. Most of the middle and upper classes send their children to private schools. Indeed, the OECD (2008) criticized Brazil because of its low level of expenditure in education, in particular because its expenditure was heavily skewed towards tertiary education students. According to the OECD, though Brazil is likely to reach the formal UPE goal by 2015, qualitative problems will by no means be solved by then.

At first sight India seems on track to achieve the MDG UPE goal by 2015, especially considering that the country has come from far. Only about 55 per cent of those born between 1950 and 1970 attended primary school or higher. According to the MICS 2000 survey, 27 million school-age children in India, one in four, did not attend school; in this group girls were a majority – 57 per cent. At the time India's exclusion rate was 15 per cent, meaning that 15 per cent of children would likely never attend school (UNICEF 2005). For 2006–7, the country's *gross* enrolment rate in primary education was 81 per cent, with gender parity improving to 95 per cent – major progress in view of the GPI rate of 76 per cent in 1991 (CSO/Government of India 2009). Yet two reservations are relevant. First, domestic sources suggest less reason for optimism. The 2005–6 National Family Health Survey outcomes present a much lower primary *net* enrolment rate; namely, 83 per cent – 85 per cent for boys, 81 for girls (again, 95% girls-to-boys parity). The dropout rates are still comparatively high, though there are few gender differences. As UNESCO (2010, 60) states, "For India, the big challenge is keeping children in school once they enrol." (See Box 3.2.) Second, at primary school level especially, the gaps between children from different income groups continue to be large. Whereas in 2005–6, 96 per cent of children from the population's wealthiest 20 per cent attended primary school, fewer than seven in ten children from the poorest 20 per cent of families did so (IIPS/Macro International 2007). As a result, large numbers of girls and young women still lag behind in educational level. In 2005–6 more than one in three (37 per cent) Indian females aged 15 to 19 had fewer than six years of education: 45 per cent in the rural areas against 19 per cent in urban settings (IIPS/Macro International 2007; Moore et al. 2009).

Box 3.2 School programmes in India

In India, the Sarva Shiksha Abhiyan (SSA) programme aims to enrol all 6 to 14 year-olds by 2015, retain them in school and provide them with quality education at least till grade 8 – a tougher requirement than meeting the MDG UPE goal by 2015 as such. On the World Bank India website, impressive accounts can be found of activities in subprogrammes under the SSA. The account of Seema Bishnoi, teacher and warden of a residential primary school in one of the poorest parts of Rajasthan, tells of the huge difficulties to be overcome in catering for 11- to 16-year-old daughters of poor illiterate parents who either dropped out of school or have never been to school at all. Yet it also tells of the opportunities that learning offers these girls – teaching hygiene, playing with the computer, learning to bike – all bringing positive behavioural changes (UNGEI website; Ravallion 2009, 22).

The figures suggest that Indonesia is on track to achieve the UPE goal by 2015. Yet here, too, some reservations are needed. As with Brazil, reports from international bodies point to the poor quality of the country's primary education and stress such shortcomings as lack of adequate infrastructure and a large share of teachers without minimum teaching requirements (Bank Dunia/World Bank 2007). In spite of enrolment rates close to one, dropout rates remain considerable. The country's statistical bureau has pointed to unequal income distribution as decisive. For example, in 2007 dropout rates for junior high school were, respectively, 3 and 11 per cent among children of the non-poor and children of poor households (BPS 2009). High dropout rates in the transition to secondary school are a particular worry, especially for girls, who clearly have a lower probability of continuing (see Box 3.3). Indonesian researchers relate this outcome to such factors as low household income, inability to pay for secondary education, religious background and distance to school. However, they identify employment opportunities as a fourth factor; such opportunities in the nearby community affect school enrolment in the transition period negatively – a disquieting outcome (Suryadarma et al. 2006a).

Box 3.3 Taking girls off school?

There has been much debate on the effects of the 1997–8 economic crisis in Indonesia on girls' education. The crisis had major effects on purchasing power of most Indonesians, with the share of those under the poverty line tripling the 1996 figures. Though the rebound was sharp, a majority of those below the poverty line in 2002 would not have been there but for the crisis (Ravallion and Lokshin 2007). In 1997–8 there were substantial cuts in the share of household budgets allocated to schooling, concentrated among the poorest. It is less clear whether these cuts hit girls' education more than boys'. The results of Thomas and Frankenberg (2007, 551) "suggest that poor households in both urban and rural areas are investing less in the schooling of their young children (ten to fourteen years old), and urban households are allocating resources to protect the schooling of adolescent males", though they add that "[t]he jury is still out on whether there was any long-term impact of the disruption on learning and performance in the labour market" (552). Based on an in-depth study, Levine and Ames (2003) go one step further. They conclude that regarding school enrolment from 1997 to 1999, girls fared better than boys, but they admit that daughters only caught up with sons' enrolment in regions relatively less affected by the crisis. The worldwide crisis of 2008–9 has likely led to the same pattern of effects. In the poorest families mostly girls may have been taken off school, notably in regions most heavily hit by the crisis. Elsewhere, education obviously has been regarded too important to be neglected; often bottom-up initiatives have been taken to keep girls in school (cf. Hossain and Eyben 2009).

Secondary education: enrolment

From 2007 to 2010, 55 per cent of the world's girls in the official secondary school-age group enrolled in secondary school against

Table 3.2 Net female enrolment rate in secondary education and its GPI and net female attrition rate and its GPI, 2005–10 (latest available year)

	Net enrolment (%)	GPI	Net attrition (%)	GPI
Mozambique	15	0.91	20	0.95
Angola	?	?	17	0.81
South Africa	84	1.05	?	?
Zambia	26	0.82	36	0.95
Botswana	64	1.15	44	1.22
Malawi	24	0.95	20	1.05
Zimbabwe	?	?	45	1
Ukraine	85	1.01	85	1
Azerbaijan	94	1.03	82	0.99
Kazakhstan	89	0.99	95	1
Belarus	?	?	97	1.02
Brazil	85	1.1	80	1.08
India	?	?	49	0.83
Indonesia	68	0.98	59	1.04

Note: GPI = gender parity index.

Source: Net enrolment rate and related GPI: UIS 2011, except: South Africa, SSA 2010; Zambia, UNDP 2008; net attrition rate and related GPI, UNICEF 2012.

65 per cent of boys (UNICEF 2012), a significantly lower proportion than enrolled in primary school. Gender parity also fell considerably, to 0.85. The sub-Saharan region's comparable figures are quite low: 24 and 30 per cent, respectively, implying a lower GPI (0.80) than primary education (0.95) as well. Again, the sub-Saharan figures are, for both genders, the world's second lowest.

Table 3.2, which presents the enrolment rates in secondary education in the 14 countries, shows high rates for three of the four CIS countries (Belarus is missing) and for South Africa and Brazil, whereas they are low in the other African countries.

Generally, secondary education pays off. There is much evidence that returns on investment in secondary schooling are nearly everywhere pronounced – even more pronounced for girls in countries where their average education is low and lags behind that of boys. A review of 42 countries shows that an extra year of secondary schooling for girls can increase their future wages by 10 to 20 per cent; the corresponding amount for boys is about 5 to 15 per cent (Psacharopoulos et al. 2004, cited in Morrison and Sabarwal 2008, 2). Everywhere, for individuals, every step up in educational level contributes to a corresponding poverty reduction. Junior secondary school graduates in Indonesia, for example, are 27 per cent less likely to be poor than primary school graduates (Alatas 2011, 70).

Secondary education: country overview

Data on secondary education enrolment by country and gender is limited, particularly so for the southern African countries. From the available figures for 2005 to 2010 (the latest available year) Mozambique has by far the lowest net enrolment rate in girls' secondary education (15%), followed by Malawi (24%) and Zambia (26%). With respectively 84 and 64 per cent, South Africa and Botswana show higher enrolment for girls (figures for Angola and Zimbabwe are lacking). South Africa and Botswana also have more girls enrolled than boys, but the other three countries have negative gender parity rates. In the poorest countries the statistics may paint an overly optimistic picture. In Mozambique, for example, research shows that for large parts of the population serious constraints on access to secondary education for girls persist. The obligation to pay matriculation fees is a substantial barrier. Distance is another, not least because families are less willing to send girls to live alone or with relatives or friends in areas with secondary schools than they are to send boys. Third, traditional paternalism plays a major role, especially in rural areas: girls are expected to be "married off" to other families or to spend most of their time on household activities (Van den Bergh-Collier 2007, 10; World Bank 2008, 87).

In Zambia and Malawi a similar complex of constraints on girls' secondary education attendance prevails. Though in Malawi the ratio of girls to boys in secondary schools rapidly increased in the 2000s, the government's MDG evaluation notes: "Some of the factors that force girls out of school could be: early marriages and pregnancies, family and cultural responsibilities" (Government of Malawi 2010, 26). In 2006 a survey of Malawi's National Statistical Office revealed large enrolment differences along spatial and socio-economic divides. For example, the urban enrolment rate in secondary schools was triple the rural rate. Yet girls nearly consistently had a higher enrolment rate than boys after controlling for the urban/rural divide and for employment status and level of education of the head of the pupil's household (NSO 2006).

Constraints on the education of girls and young women vary considerably across the CIS countries, though the available figures on secondary education for three countries (Belarus data is missing) are quite close: net enrolment rates between 85 and 94 per cent, and gender parity near or slightly above one. The strongest constraints are reported from Azerbaijan. Women NGOs of that country complain that women are expected to function primarily within a family; single women are widely perceived as a failure once they have passed the marriageable age of 21 to 23 years. The prevailing code of "family honour" limits women's mobility in Azerbaijan; it places them in a vulnerable position if they have sex before marriage or decide to live independently. Families often limit daughters' access to higher education through not allowing them to enter universities in farther-off cities (Center Women and Modern World et al. 2009).

The rise of Brazil's net enrolment rate for girls in secondary education – up to 85 per cent in 2008 and with a GPI of 1.10 higher than boys' enrolment – may mask considerable problems with educational quality. As with primary education, the quality of Brazil's secondary schools has been much criticised. The OECD (2008) notes that, with on average 32 students, class size in secondary education is quite large. Though Brazil's formal enrolment rates are high, equalling the CIS countries', actual school attendance is much lower, and the rates of grade repetition are high, too. Moreover, in the mid-2000s female writers criticized Brazil's educational system for not having special programmes for young women who became pregnant. Controlled for other factors, a childless girl was eight times likelier to be enrolled at school than a young mother with at least one child. Berquó and Cavenaghi (2005, 13), after presenting this and other evidence, developed a plausible relation with the poor quality of public education, which, "associated with limited job opportunities, might induce a great number of young women to start families as the most attractive choice of their lives." The findings of Cardoso and Verner (2006) also show that early parenthood has a strong impact driving teenagers out of school. They stress that poverty also lowers school attendance and that reducing school's costs could improve the school attendance record. In Brazil schoolgirl pregnancy likely explains a higher share of secondary school dropouts than the 5 to 10 per cent range it explains in other countries (cf. Temin and Levine 2009, 35).

Indonesia succeeded in two decades in having the net enrolment of girls in secondary schools increase by 20 percentage points and nearly fully bridge the gap with boys, bringing enrolment for 2007 to 59 per cent, with the GPI rising from 0.83 in 1991 to 0.98 sixteen years later (ADB 2009; UIS 2011). Actually, however, the government hardly facilitates education for the poor at all; thus, gaps in educational achievement between rich and poor households steadily increased during the past decade. In 2010 only 53 per cent of 16- to 18-year-olds from the poorest 20 per cent of households completed junior secondary school, compared with 87 per cent from the richest 20 per cent (Alatas 2011, 70–1). Pupils from poor families prove to be highly vulnerable to dropping out during the transition to secondary school, a fact already noted and one that obviously did not really change in the late 2000s. By Alatas' account (2010, 72), programmes promoting greater access to education for the poor largely fail to reach poor households, and for many Indonesian households secondary education's costs are still prohibitively high. The low quality of secondary education, lower also than in comparable countries, may also affect parental enrolment decisions negatively.

Comparable Indian education figures are missing for secondary schooling, too. For 2006–7 the country's *gross* enrolment rate in secondary education was 57 per cent – considerable progress, as this rate was 41 per cent in 1991. But gender parity improved from just 0.60 to 0.82 (CSO/Government of India 2009; ADB 2009). In spite of progress, in neither outcome does India compare favourably with many Asian countries. Its results do not match the rule that Asian women study longer than Asian men, and its parity ratio was one of the lowest of 41 Asian economies. UNESCO (2010) concluded that in 2005 over three in 10 Indian females (30.7%) aged 17 to 22 were in "education poverty" – that is, they had under four years of education – a figure nearly double that of males of the same age (15.6%). Gender differences match up with large differences across income categories and spatial divides and compound differences in primary education enrolment and completion. The composition of the 40 million youngsters enrolled in India's secondary education is skewed towards the urban areas (in 2005–6, 64%, against 49% in rural areas) and extremely skewed towards children from the middle and upper classes: 83 per cent of children from the population's wealthiest 20 per cent attend secondary school against only 29 per cent of children from the poorest 20 per cent. Also, secondary school enrolment varies widely across states: in 2005–6 from 92 per cent in Kerala to only 22 per cent in Bihar and a poor 4 per cent in Jharkhand (IIPS/Macro International 2007).

Vocational training

Enrolling in technical and vocational education and training (TVET) can be important for improving the labour market position of girls and young women. TVET prepares for the acquisition of specific knowledge and skills for the world of work, usually in a specific occupation, trade or job requiring expertise in a particular group of techniques or technology. In practice, TVET programmes are quite heterogeneous and encompass a wide range of fields of study – from teacher training programmes to commercial studies to technical fields in industry and engineering (UNDESA 2010, 61). The facts and figures presented below should be projected against a global trend to defer specialization in secondary education and push vocational content to post-secondary education. Specialized, occupation-specific TVET programmes in the formal school system are being reduced worldwide (UIS 2011, 51). In low-income countries such a reorientation can result in improvements if narrow technical approaches are replaced by broader programmes more attuned to addressing young women's needs – starting from the assumption that in these countries "the constraints on young women's employment are much more complex than simply lack of relevant vocational skills" (Katz 2008, 6).

What figures there are suggest that in sub-Saharan countries TVET is still in an early stage of development, though perspectives may be promising, also for its graduates. UNESCO statistics indicate that in 2009 in this region about 3 per cent of all students enrolled in lower secondary education were in TVET programmes, as well as about 16 per cent of those enrolled in upper secondary education. Four in ten of the latter TVET enrollees were females. The figure was slightly higher in South Africa (43%), though that country, with one in ten in TVET programmes among upper secondary education students, fell below the regional average. Yet South Africa is a clear example that TVET graduates are in short supply and often have a strong labour market position. In the mid-2000s in both the public and private sector, having a vocational qualification contributed more towards wages than having just a diploma, with or without a matric certificate (finished high school). Interestingly, in South Africa a vocational qualification was more important for higher wages for females than for their male counterparts (Bosch 2006; Bhorat et al. 2009). In Zambia finishing a vocational education programme also seems a clear-cut labour market prerequisite. According to a 2004 survey, technical educational, vocational and entrepreneurship training (TEVET) was provided to nearly 33,000 Zambian students. Strikingly, women outnumbered men in many categories, including business, law and information technology. The survey revealed that most TEVET graduates had found a job after six months (AfDB/OECD 2008, 626–8).

In the large DFL countries TVET still seems in its infancy, with a large majority of employers not up to make use of the skills of its graduates. The infancy stage definitely applies to India's TVET system. Indian researchers found that in 2005 the categories of formal and informal vocationally trained made up less than 12 per cent of the 15–29 group in the labour force: 14 per cent of the young males, 9 per cent of the young females. For the formally trained the overall share was 3.7 per cent: 4 per cent for males, 3 per cent for females. India's figures compare poorly with other countries' (NCEUS 2009a, 2009b). The gender disparities reported in Indian TVET are large, with girls accounting for just 7 per cent of enrolment at the secondary level and their courses concentrated in such traditional areas as nursing and sewing. Moreover, public awareness of the potential of TVET is very limited, and the labour market benefits of a TVET diploma are not immediately apparent (Rajput 2009; NCEUS 2009b).

Until a decade ago the TVET situation in Brazil was only a fraction less bad; even in 2009 UNESCO statistics counted only 13 per cent TVET enrollees among upper secondary education students, though they also indicate 57 per cent females at this level (UIS 2011). By then, in rather outdated conditions, students mainly learned classical manufacturing trades. However, Brazil embarked upon a programme of expanding and modernising its institutes of education, science and technology. Since 2003 their number has nearly tripled, and their scope has broadened, though expansion proponents also acknowledge that there are still considerable qualitative shortcomings (Downie 2011).

Vocational training seems more solidly grounded in Indonesia, but a closer look shows that this mainly concerns the institutional set-up. Trade unions and employers' organizations are more structurally involved in TVET implementation and planning than in most other DFL countries. UNESCO statistics show Indonesia has a relatively high share, 38 per cent, of TVET enrollees among upper secondary education students and 41 per cent females among TVET students (UIS 2011). Alatas (2011, 73–4), highly critical of Indonesia's public training centres, characterizes them as unprepared to meet demands and often in bad condition. She pleas for a broad training curriculum, including not only training in technical skills but also soft "life" skills. As already stated, such an approach can be particularly advantageous for young women.

The CIS countries' situation differs from both other country groups'. In the days of the former Soviet Union, technical vocational education was highly valued and emphasized there. Among regions of the world, central and eastern Europe still have the highest TVET enrolment as a percentage of upper secondary education students, though this percentage is falling: 50 per cent in 1999, 47 per cent in 2009 (UIS 2011). With 45 and 43 per cent, respectively, in 2009, Belarus and Azerbaijan fit in with this picture; moreover, both show substantial female shares in TVET: nearly half in Belarus, 58 per cent in Azerbaijan (UIS 2011; ETF 2010 [Belarus]). In Azerbaijan, given the resistance against enrolling in tertiary education, for many girls TVET at upper secondary level seems the highest attainable. In Belarus most VET profiles are seen as too narrow and outdated, oriented as they are towards narrow specialist jobs in manufacturing. The development of new, broader VET standards is currently under way (ETF 2010). With 26 per cent TVET enrolment in Ukraine and 25 per cent in Kazakhstan, participation in these countries is much lower; the same holds for the female shares, with only about one in three girls and young women enrolled in TVET. These and other figures suggest that TVET in these two countries has lost relevance for females; it still largely departs from output standards from the Soviet era and neglects growth in service sector occupations.

Tertiary education

The global trend is that male dominance in tertiary education has been reversed in the last two decades. In or around 2007, for 166 countries with available data, women's share in tertiary education was 50 per cent or more in 102 countries (UNDESA 2010, 62). For the eight DFL countries for which the latest available data cover a year between 2005 and 2010, the picture is mixed. Four countries confirm the worldwide trend, with gross enrolment rates of female students in tertiary education clearly higher than those of males. On top are Kazakhstan and Belarus, with gender parity indices of over 1.40, followed by Ukraine (1.27) and South Africa (1.26). In Indonesia the gross enrolment rate of females is nearly at par with men's (GPI 0.96), while in India (0.70), Azerbaijan (0.68) and Malawi (0.51) the young women lag (UIS 2011; SSA 2010 [South Africa]). If the focus is on the three countries for which data specify participation on the highest level of tertiary education (ISCED level 6) by gender, female students continue in the majority in Ukraine (GPI 1.44) and Belarus (1.27). In Indonesia their share at the highest level falls to about one in three, however.

Figures for the CIS countries justify a closer look at tertiary education there. In Belarus university-level education has growingly been "feminized", with young women enrolling in much larger numbers than their male peers. Even traditionally, more females than males were in Belarus's higher education, but the gender parity rate kept rising, from 1.11 (1991) via 1.32 (2000) to 1.44 (2008). At a gross rate of 91 per cent in 2008, female enrolment in tertiary education is very high in Belarus, equalled only by Ukraine among DFL countries. However, traditional gender division is still visible in Belarus, with female shares about 70 per cent in teacher training, economics, law and medicine, while men comprise about the same share of those studying science, technology, architecture and construction (Government of Belarus 2005). Tertiary education in Kazakhstan shows similar development, albeit at a lower enrolment rate; in 2008 the gross rate for females was 45 per cent. Here, too, though the women-to-men parity gap continues closing, to 1.45 in 2008, it does not always translate into female employment (see Figure 3.2). In rural areas especially, unemployment among better-educated women is considerable. Sharp labour market segmentation and mobility problems related to the huge distances in the country seem the main explanations (cf. World Bank 2004). Due mainly to already mentioned family constraints on young women's tertiary education, data for Azerbaijan tell a completely different story. Besides lagging behind the male rate, female enrolment in Azerbaijani tertiary education (19% in 2008) is far below that in other CIS countries.

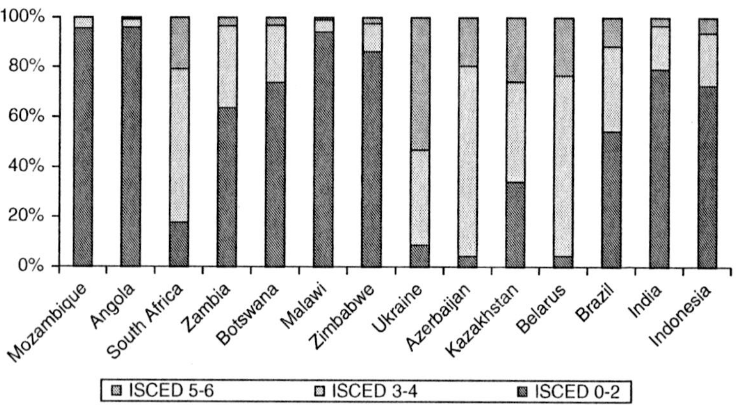

Figure 3.2 Female employed population by highest level of education completed; distribution over three educational categories: low (ISCED 0–2), middle (ISCED 3–4), high (ISCED 5–6)

Source: ILO Laborsta database; national statistics; Mozambique, 2003; Angola, 2001–2; South Africa, 2009; Zambia, 2005; Botswana, 2005–6; Malawi, 2006; Zimbabwe, 2009; Ukraine, 2008; Azerbaijan, 2008; Kazakhstan, 2008; Belarus, 2009; Brazil, 2007; India, 2004; Indonesia, 2008.

Growth in India's higher education system is impressive. The 11th five-year plan (2007–12) outlines major expansion, including funding for 30 new central universities, five new Indian institutes of science, education and research, eight new Indian institutes of technology (IITs), seven new Indian institutes of management and 20 new Indian institutes of information technology. Qualitative progress is impressive, too. Yet besides praising progress, a World Bank policy review stressed related societal contradictions. To cite just one example of many: "Delhi's new metro is a 21st century marvel while rural roads in many states are in poor repair and often impassable" (World Bank 2006b). In tertiary education India and Malawi have the largest gender gap among DFL countries, with India showing up slightly behind Malawi. In 2006–7 India's women-to-men enrolment ratio in tertiary education was only 0.69. It cannot be denied that in 1991, when the ratio was 0.54, the situation was even worse for girls and young women, but progress has been comparatively limited (CSO/Government of India 2009; ADB 2009). Enrolment differences by gender are reflected in large gender gaps in skill levels. In 2004–5 the share of graduates and above (ISCED levels 5–6) among men more than doubled that among women: 7.9 against 3.7 per cent, or 47 per cent women-to-men parity. Projections for 2017 suggest that graduate and above shares will increase to about 10 per cent for men and 5 per cent for women by then, implying about 50 per cent parity (NCEUS 2009a).

Regionally, sub-Saharan Africa lags, with 40 per cent females, or GPI of 0.66, in tertiary education (UNDESA 2010, 64). Distance learning may offer the region's girls and young women major opportunities for tertiary education – though the immediate cause can be nasty. In 2001 and 2005 serious gender-related violence and sexual exploitation at the University of Zimbabwe were reported (Republic of Zimbabwe 2010b). Such problems likely add to the explanation of the success of the Zimbabwe Open University (ZOU), the country's only distance learning university. Since its conception in 1999 ZOU has averaged about 20,000 students, nearly half of all Zimbabwe's total; it clearly meets a demand. An interesting wider initiative is eLearning Africa, which includes an annual conference, a web portal and a news service, disseminating information about learning opportunities in conjunction with computers, the Internet, mobile devices, radio and audiovisual media in Africa. The platform aims to enhance knowledge, expertise and skills while also serving as a catalyst for the African community of practice in this field. The ultimate aim is to facilitate and accelerate the UPE goal (website eLearning Africa).

Female skill levels

In social research, skills refer to a complex and multidimensional concept. Yet in most countries skill levels are predominantly measured by educational attainment; measures of other skill dimensions are lacking. For the DFL countries there are data for the educational attainment of women and men in the labour force. The country's figures exhibit huge mutual differences. Based on national statistics (mostly accessible through ILO Laborsta), the shares of the female labour force with at least secondary education (ISCED 3 and higher) vary from 4.5 per cent in Mozambique and Angola to over 90 per cent in Azerbaijan, Belarus and Ukraine. These shares are higher for women than men in four of 13 countries for which there are data: the latter three CIS countries and Brazil. Moreover, in Botswana and Azerbaijan women's shares approach men's, and in 2008 the Indonesian female share of secondary or higher educated was less than 3 percentage points below the male share. The gender skills gap, as reflected in the labour force, is particularly large in India, where only 21 per cent of women in the labour force (versus 45% of men) are at least secondary educated. In this respect Mozambique, Angola, Zambia and Malawi show large gaps, too. Yet despite all problems and against all odds, in the 2000s development of female participation in education was impressive, lifting the skill levels of women in many countries while sometimes even outperforming men.

Female progress is most evident at the tertiary education level, as revealed by comparing tertiary-educated men and women (ISCED 5 and 6) in the labour force. In South Africa and Indonesia – in addition to the already mentioned Brazil, Azerbaijan, Belarus and Ukraine – the female labour force shares at the tertiary education level have recently surpassed those of the males: in all but Indonesia by 3 to 5 percentage points, in Indonesia by 1 percentage point. Brazil is a particularly interesting case. Though female labour participation in that country is lower than male, the Brazilian Labour Force Survey 2007 counted over five million women in the labour force educated at tertiary level against fewer than four million men. For most countries, computing the educational attainment of the population at large leads to outcomes different from those referred to above, especially if limited to the population 25 and up. For our 14 countries, computations of the UNESCO Institute for Statistics indicate higher female than male shares only in Azerbaijan and Brazil (UIS 2011, Table 18). Such statistics do not include the massive educational advance of the current generation of adolescent girls and young women. In concentrating entirely on these figures, their progress in other countries, such as South Africa and Indonesia, may be missed. For example, in Indonesia in 2008 13 per cent of the 25- to 29-year-old women in the labour force were educated at ISCED levels 5–6, twice the share of the tertiary educated in the Indonesian female labour force at large (ILO Laborsta database).

However, some caveats remain. Within the female population of particularly the larger countries, divides according to space, employment status and race persist. In two of the three DFL countries with a large population, the spatial divides in education are large. This is first and foremost the case in India. In 2005–6, 37 per cent of Indian females aged 15 to 19 had fewer than six years of education: 45 per cent in rural areas against 19 per cent in urban. Variation across states was also huge. In Bihar (the third-largest state, with over 100 million inhabitants) young females with under six years of education made up 61 per cent, in Jharkhand 56 per cent and in Chhattisgarh and Uttar Pradesh (the largest state, about 200 million inhabitants) both 45 per cent. By contrast, in Kerala only 2 per cent of all adolescent females had fewer than six years of education, in Himachal Pradesh 7 per cent, in Goa 8 per cent, in Tamil Nadu 12 per cent and in Maharashtra (the second-largest state, over 110 million) 17 per cent (Moore et al. 2009). Divides in Indonesia are only slightly less deep, both along the urban-rural line and across regions, as measured by enrolment rates in primary and junior secondary schools (Suryadarma et al. 2006b; BPS 2009). By contrast, Brazil's education seems on track to escape from this pattern. In the 2000s nearly all Latin American countries succeeded in leaving the sharpest urban-rural divides behind, in both primary and secondary education; in Brazil too this divide became less pronounced (Lopez 2008).

A second caveat is that national statistics, depending on the (varying) treatment of unemployment, may hide much lower educational levels among female unemployed or economically non-active. For South Africa we were able to analyse 2009 Labour Force Survey data in this respect (courtesy Statistics South Africa). The unemployed showed overrepresentation of those with secondary education, both non-completed and (albeit to a lesser extent) completed, and underrepresentation of the tertiary educated, for women slightly more than for men. Whereas in 2009, 21 per cent of employed females had tertiary education, only 6 per cent of unemployed women did. Obviously, in the South African labour market completion of tertiary education enlarges job opportunities and substantially diminishes unemployment risks. Already in the early 2000s, completion of secondary schooling (having a matric qualification) no longer enhanced the probability of finding work, notably for black youngsters from 16 to 25. Ever more South African employers questioned the level of standard grade matric qualifications and their usefulness as screening devices (Dias 2005). Obviously many still do so.

A third caveat applies to the racial divide, which still proves to be highly relevant in the South African labour market. At 14 per cent in 2005, the share of tertiary-educated African (black) women in employment was less than half that of such educated employed women in South Africa's other three population groups (SSA 2005). Analyses of South Africa's income inequality suggest the persistence of discriminatory pay and hiring practices. The decrease of average wages in the rainbow nation since 1995 worked out quite negatively for large parts of the target group. First, those between 18 and 30 were disproportionally hit, men and women alike, though the decline was larger for women. Second, the (extra) income derivable from (better) education remained virtually absent for young Africans. Returns to education fell dramatically for them, while young whites saw pronounced increases. It has been suggested that the jump in education was not large enough for young Africans to benefit (Casale 2004; Hoogeveen and Özler 2005). There are quite a few indications that these mechanisms are still prominent.

For Brazil, based on census data on São Paolo's urban labour market, Lovell (2006) conducted a highly interesting study of distribution of completed years of education by gender and race. From 1960 to 2000, school completion rates increased overall. Both white and Afro-Brazilian (black) women achieved consistently higher levels of education than men. Yet racial inequality persisted for both sexes. Lovell concluded that in 2000 racial inequality in São Paolo was higher among women than men, largely due to Afro-Brazilian women's underrepresentation at the highest levels of the education system. Another study extends conclusions on racial discrimination to the Brazilian labour market at large, particularly respecting wage discrimination of blacks. Yet this study did not analyse the gender component (cf. Arcand and D'Hombres 2004).

4 Employment of Young Women

Introduction

MDG3 aims at promoting gender equality and empowerment of women, among other ways by increasing the share of women in non-agricultural paid employment. Paid, non-subsistence employment outside agriculture is essential for young women's perspectives. This full chapter is dedicated to employment issues touching young women, discussing employment perspectives and women's labour force participation. The focus then shifts to formal and informal employment, an important distinction in the 14 countries. Why do some countries notice a decrease in informal employment, while others do not? Next to be covered are unemployment and underemployment, the transition from school to work and child labour. Migration, addressed in Chapter 2, comes to the fore again because most migration flows are driven by employment opportunities and wage differentials. A chapter about employment cannot be written without detailing the female employment structure by industries and occupations, discussing the distribution of women workers and the female share in these industries and occupations. The Decisions for Life (DFL) project targeted eight occupations in the services sector that offer young women perspectives on work. The chapter ends with a description of these occupations.

Labour force participation

As the Commission on Growth and Development (2008) notes, women's participation in the labour force has developed differently since 1980. Female labour participation rates (LPRs) – also called activity rates or employment-to-population ratios (EPOPs) – have risen in industrialised countries, as well as in Indonesia and other developing countries, but decreased in India, China and Russia. The commission concludes that the reasons behind these trends are yet poorly understood and that more work is needed to understand the available data, including whether they capture informal work by women. Moreover, even data collection is weak. According to the commission, estimates of women in the labour force are not comparable internationally, "reflecting the fact that for women, demographic, social, legal, and cultural trends and norms determine whether their activities are regarded as economic. In many countries large numbers of women work on farms or in other family enterprises without pay, while others work in or near their homes, mixing work and family activities during the day. Countries differ in the criteria used to determine whether such workers are to be counted as part of the labour force" (CGD 2008, 123). Be that as it may, we here in modesty report on LPRs for our cohorts, females aged 15 to 29.

As Figure 4.1 shows, LPRs for all three five-year cohorts between 15 and 30 vary widely across the 14 countries. They are highest in Mozambique (for all three groups), followed by Angola and Malawi. LPRs are also relatively high in Kazakhstan and Brazil. The activity rates for the sub-Saharan countries show a great deal of variety, with low rates of young females in particular in South Africa, Botswana and Zambia. Besides different statistical treatment across countries, this variation is due to differences in school attendance and levels of inactivity. Overall, India has the lowest LPRs for our target group. With less than 40 per cent, the Indian LPR for those 25 to 29 is especially low; in the other 13 countries the activity rate for this cohort is over 50 per cent.

The development of LPRs per five-year cohorts in our countries in the 2000s displays varying patterns, except for the LPRs for the 15–19 female cohort, which developed rather homogeneously. In all eight countries whose data covers this decade (2003–8 for South Africa and 1999–2005 for Ukraine), that cohort's LPRs decreased. The decrease – more than 6 percentage points – was most substantial in Azerbaijan, Kazakhstan and Belarus; in India and Indonesia the fall was 2.5 to 4 percentage points, while in South Africa, Ukraine and Brazil it was marginal. At the same time, the LPRs for the 20–24 female cohort showed an increase in two countries: Brazil (4 percentage points) and South Africa (2 points). The other five countries revealed a decrease. The labour participation of females 25 to 29 went up in most countries, with the exception of Ukraine and Indonesia; rather remarkable is the 5 point LPR decrease for this cohort in Indonesia between 2000 and 2008. The increase of labour participation for those 25 to 29 was substantial in Kazakhstan

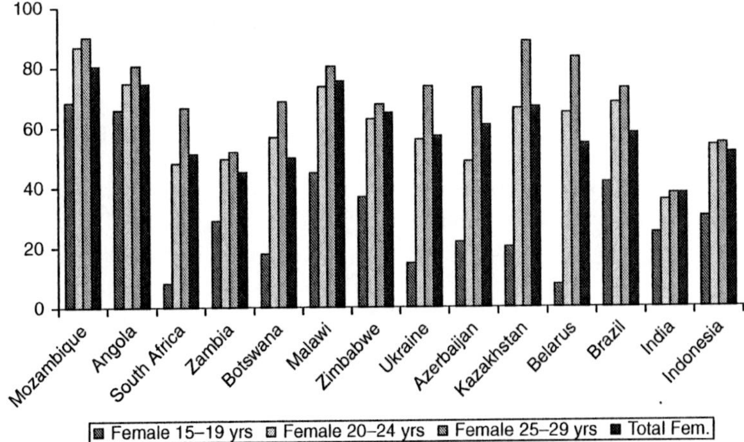

Figure 4.1 Female labour force participation rates by age (% of population in the labour force)

Note: In Ukraine figures apply to formal labour market; in all other countries figures apply to total labour market.

Note: Zambia females 12–19 years.

Sources: Mozambique, est. EAPEP 2008; Angola, est. EAPEP 2008; South Africa, LFS 2008; Zambia, Census 2000; Botswana, LFS 2006; Malawi, est. EAPEP 2008; Zimbabwe, LFS 1999; Ukraine, LFS 2008 formal labour market; Azerbaijan, LFS 2008; Kazakhstan, LFS 2008; Belarus, est. EAPEP 2008; Brazil, LFS 2007; India, Census 2001; Indonesia, LFS 2008.

(11 points) and Brazil (7 points). India's rather marginal increase was remarkable in view of the long-term decrease in Indian female LPRs noted by the Commission on Growth and Development.

Absorption and allocation

As the *World Development Report 2012*, focusing on gender equality and development, states: "For an economy to be functioning at its potential, women's skills and talents should be engaged in activities that make the best use of those abilities. But, as the stories of many women illustrate, this is not always the case. When women's labour is underused or misallocated – because they face discrimination in markets or societal institutions that prevents them from completing their education, entering certain occupations, and earning the same incomes as men – economic losses are the result" (World Bank 2011, 3). In the course of this book, we come across factors explicitly working or discriminating against girls and young women. Other factors, more implicit or hidden, involve the orientation of a country's educational system, among other things. Such factors may frustrate young men's positions in the labour market, too, though mostly they seem to work out more negatively for young females.

When reviewing the 14 countries against this background, particularly in CIS countries underutilization shows up, revealing a major qualitative mismatch between skills offered by the education system and employers' labour demand. For instance, one in five Ukrainian employers, a fraction higher than any other eastern European country's, regard the skills of available workers as a major obstacle to the firm's operation and growth. An important role may be played by the fact that output standards in Ukraine's higher education are still largely based on the planned economy of the Soviet era (World Bank 2009b, 2010; Nijssen and Grijpstra 2006). Part of the mismatch is the immense underutilization of the skills of Ukrainian women that various statistics suggest. The outdated higher education system may be a factor here, but so too is strong labour market segmentation, excluding many women from better-remunerated jobs (cf. Pignatti 2010).

Statistics suggest underutilization in other CIS countries, too, in particular caused by problems reallocating education and labour from manufacturing and agriculture to the service sector. State planning definitely did not help. Throughout the 2000s Belarusian official labour agencies continued to advertised a future for traditional "male" jobs in manufacturing while industrial jobs were already in decay (Government of Belarus 2005; World Bank 2009d). In Azerbaijan in 2008 nearly half of all women employed were classified in elementary occupations against fewer than one in six men employed, whereas their skill levels hardly differed. Yet a statistical bias may well play a role here. In the Azerbaijani wholesale and retail industry, for example, six of seven women workers were classified as having an elementary occupation against only one of four men (authors' calculations based on ILO Laborsta database). This rather unlikely outcome may point at a reflexive tendency to label women's work "unskilled" or "elementary" – a tendency that, though on the way out, can be noticed worldwide.

Box 4.1 Brazil's labour shortages

In rapidly expanding economies and industries, labour allocation problems may take a completely different shape: shortages of skilled labour may be prominent here. Such shortages may even have the potential to derail a country's growth scenario. Brazil is a case in point. Currently its shortages of qualified labour are a hot item in discussions among economists and politicians, Brazilians and foreigners alike. Against the backdrop of the size of these shortages and the nation's aspirations, it is evident that the traditional solution – immigration – is no option; it is widely acknowledged that a government-driven effort to improve the quality of education is needed (cf. Anderson et al. 2012). As it is, the current situation definitely opens good labour market perspectives for high-skilled young women.

Formal and informal employment

The 2003 International Conference of Labour Statisticians defines informal employment as own-account workers and employers in their own informal sector enterprises, family workers, members of informal producers' cooperatives and employees holding informal jobs. More specific rules apply in each country. For example, in Brazil workers with a labour card (Carteira de Trabalho) or contributing to a social security fund are considered in formal wage employment (but see Box 4.1). In India informality is defined as the absence of employers' and workers' organizations ("the unorganized sector"). In South Africa the formal sector consists of registered businesses; the informal sector does not (Saget 2006). In all 14 countries informal work is important for female employment, though the share of informal work varies widely, from 96 per cent of India's female labour force to 17 per cent of Ukraine's. Shares in Mozambique, Angola, Malawi and Zambia are around nine of ten working women, in Indonesia seven, in Azerbaijan and Brazil six, in Botswana four and in Kazakhstan three. For Belarus no data are available.

These figures indicate that large numbers of working women might be beyond the reach of such labour market institutions as collective bargaining, minimum wage setting and labour inspection (see Chapter 7 for a detailed discussion). The figures also indicate that though large numbers of women lack employment protection associated with labour contracts and social security, they do not pay taxes. However, ILO *Global Employment Trends* for 2011 and 2012 indicate that the total employment shares of those in vulnerable and poorly paid jobs have steadily declined over the past ten years. Informal labour is predominantly an agricultural phenomenon. In Kazakhstan, with three in ten workers – men and women – in informal jobs, six in ten informal workers held a job in the agricultural sector in 2009. Almost half of the remaining informal workers were self-employed, and the other half were working mostly in formal enterprises and to a lesser extent in informal enterprises (ILO 2012). Particularly when agricultural employment in part consists of subsistence agriculture, informal work is likely.

The impact of the economic crisis on the informal employment rate is not yet fully clear. South Africa, with its comparatively up-to-date and detailed labour statistics, provides some evidence. In that country employment fell continuously, from 13.7 million in 2008's second quarter to 13.2 million in the second quarter of 2011, with the first recovery in that year's third quarter. Initially employment losses were relatively larger in the informal than the formal sector and hit male employees harder. From 2009's third quarter on, the situation was reversed; more layoffs took place in the formal economy. Also, in the latter period females were hit harder than men, with the net result that four in five jobs lost in 2008–11 were female (authors' calculations based on SSA 2009a and 2011). The ILO (2010c) suggests that adjustment in the informal economy was more rapid, and employers in the formal economy were resorting to layoffs only after a delay.

That women are overrepresented in informal employment is not by necessity negative, because it includes self-employment and owning a business offering opportunities for women. In the 2000s many Ukrainian women started a "women's business" – small businesses in garment production or services such as hair and beauty salons. Women with a university degree used it in education (private tutoring) and commercial services (consultancies). In the skilled labour force many women chose voluntary informal self-employment, with higher average earnings than salaried women in comparable occupations (Lehmann and Pignatti 2007; Pignatti 2010). In the other CIS countries necessity seems to have dominated from the outset, fewer job opportunities in the formal sector being at the root of the switch to self-employment. That was clearly so in Azerbaijan, where the strong growth of female employment between 2003 and 2008 nearly fully was translated into more female own-account workers and contributing family workers (ILO Laborsta Database). Here, "[...] women have increasingly looked to the informal sector to supplement family income, although such work is usually unprotected and involves long hours for little pay" (ADB 2005, xii).

Policies matter for informal workers in the labour force. The relationship between economic growth, social policies and informality's increase or decrease is in part driven by national policies – specifically, how perspectives of formalization for individual workers relate to expansion of the social security net. In the 2000s new government subsidies, lower business taxes and improved access to credit in Brazil made being formal beneficial for firms. Moreover, non-compliance with labour and social security regulations seems on the way back due to tightening of labour inspections, resulting in a tripling of the number of workers registered with a labour card (Berg 2009). Under some conditions informalization goes almost unnoticed. In South Africa the number of formal sector workers employed in the standard employment relationship under more or less stable conditions, including clear and written contracts and transparent wages, seems to erode rapidly. A 2003 estimate was that about 6.1 million workers, or 47 per cent of the South African labour force at large, belonged to such a "core" (Von Holdt and Webster 2008). Along the same lines, we estimate the number of core workers for 2009 as slightly over 5.0 million, or only 38 per cent of the labour force (based on SSA 2005; SSA 2009a, and Labour Force Survey 2009 data put at the disposal of AIAS by Statistics South Africa). This outcome implies that over six in ten workers, quite a vulnerable majority, have virtually no access to the country's "labour market arena" (cf. Ordor 2011). Along with high inactivity rates, it also implies that large groups, even majorities, of youngsters are not familiar with (formal) labour and decent work.

Box 4.2 What is a decent job in Indonesia?

"Decent work means a work that can give you prosperity and enable to improve yourself. For example, if your job is boring like data entering, but you get highly paid for that, that's for me still considered decent. But another example is when your salary is low but your job is interesting where you are put to travel and meet people like journalists – that is also decent. At least you get one of the benefits, either prosperity or self-improvement. My current job is not decent for me, because my salary is low and it's boring". (Retno, 25 years old, marketing employee at KFC, Jakarta, Indonesia (Decisions for Life website)).

"I hope that the World Day for Decent Work can really make a realistic program for the improvement of the Indonesian working conditions. I am concerned about the wage of Indonesian workers. There are some that still earn a wage lower than the provincial minimum wage, or the wage being late paid by the company, or even worse not getting paid". (Isabella, 25 years old, head of LIA English Course, Branch Medan, Indonesia (Decisions for Life website)).

"May Day or any other labour day will not give any impact to the workers conditions if there is no good program with it. What's important for me is that as an outsourced worker, I really want the outsourcing system to be disallowed in Indonesia. And decent work means for me decent wage." (Khofiya, 25 years old, teller of Jabar Bank, Indonesia (Decisions for Life website)).

"In my point of view, decent work relates to three things which are working hours, decent wage and a reasonable overtime payment." (Andi, 25 years old, Indonesia (Decisions for Life website)).

"We can call a work decent when there's a balance between our job responsibility and the income. Working environment is also a factor that is considered to have decent work, where there is gender equality in the company and no sexual harassment." (Nila, 25 years old, marketing coordinator, Indonesia (Decisions for Life website)).

Unemployment and underemployment

In Chapter 1 we referred to the ILO projections on new labour market entrants and youth unemployment. The ILO researchers were the first to nuance their outcomes, indicating that many discouraged young people may leave the labour market as officially surveyed if they see no job prospects. This discouragement effect leads to many girls and young women disappearing from the (un)employment statistics; millions of girls worldwide live through major problems in the transition from school to work (Morrison and Sabarwal 2008; Katz 2008; ILO 2011a). Labour market experts have recognized the inadequacy of the conventional unemployment data; their reservations are widely echoed in the development literature. Yet such shading has hardly reached the general public, notably not that in high-income countries. The statistical bureaus of various DFL countries, trying to find solutions to measuring unemployment, have mostly taken refuge in concepts of underemployment, forced inactivity and idleness (cf. Dewan and Peek 2007). If self-reported, this counting may lead to doubling the official youth unemployment rates, as has been the case in Indonesia (cf. Van Klaveren et al. 2010b). Another option is that employment below a certain (marginal) income has been counted as underemployment, as has been tried for Indian agriculture (Bosworth and Collins 2007; see also Box 4.2).

Chapter 1 discussed widespread unemployment of young South Africans (see Box 4.3). In most DFL countries their peers are in similar conditions; female unemployment is usually one and a half to twice the male unemployment. For example in 2007, 28 per cent of Brazilian girls 15 to 19 were officially unemployed (boys 17%), 18 per cent of young women 20 to 24 (men 10%) and over 13 per cent of those 25 to 29 (men 6%; IBGE 2008). As for Indonesians, in 2009 over 12.6 million of them 15 to 24 were in neither education nor employment, with exactly four of ten unemployed or underemployed – the latter defined as the share of the population working less than 35 hours per week and prepared to take on more work or to be fully employed. Nearly two in three of these un- and underemployed were young women (BPS 2010). For some time the nation's high youth unemployment rate has been a major concern and has driven the current authorities' preoccupation with job creation (Chowdhury et al. 2009). Indonesia was also one of the first nations to volunteer to be a lead country in the UN's Youth Employment Network (YEN), created within the Millennium Declaration's framework. Jointly the CIS countries are an exception, with unemployment rates of young females only slightly higher than males'. For example, in 2008 in Ukraine, 18.5 per cent of girls 15 to 19 were employed against 15 per cent of boys; rates for those 20 to 24 and 25 to 29 – 13 and 7 per cent, respectively – were about equal (based on ILO Laborsta database).

Box 4.3 Unemployed in South Africa

"Everybody has dreams and goals they wish to one day achieve, but at times things don't go as planned. I too had dreams of my own that I wanted to see come true when I finished school[....] I wanted to study Political Science[....] In 2008, I completed matric. Like every child it was one of the most nerve-wracking experiences, but at the same time an exciting experience ever. [...] I was very happy to see that I passed my matric with two distinctions [....] Unfortunately I did badly on mathematics. Therefore I couldn't get a place at University[....] Instead of sitting and doing nothing, I got myself a job at PnA as a cashier and floor assistant. The contract was for three months and it expired. What is strange though is that I was the only person terminated as I was regarded a bad influence when I told my colleagues about joining a trade union as I was now in contact with the young women from Decisions for Life, who taught me about choices I had to make as a young women. As much as I think one day I will find a job or a scholarship to study politics and or trade unionism, my hopes are bleak as unemployment is high in South Africa." (Hlezipi, Boksburg, South Africa (Decisions for Life website)).

Child labour

In a number of countries and in various industries and occupations, young women workers may feel the threat of child labour: extremely low wage rates for child workers may crowd out (slightly) older workers. It may seem unlikely that our target group of relatively higher skilled women would feel such pressure "from below", but signals from participants in the DFL project led to the decision to devote a section to child labour.

Child labour affects a large number of young adolescents: worldwide it is estimated that 150 million children 5 to 14 are engaged in it. The prevalence of child labour has fallen in recent years, and the incidence of hazardous child labour is declining sharply. Nevertheless, the individual consequences remain quite serious. Labouring children usually cannot complete their education, as is evidenced by the relation of school enrolment to child labour. They will face problems escaping poverty. Child labour is gender-segregated by occupation, as is adults' work. For example, though overall boys make up a majority, most children involved in domestic labour are girls (UNICEF 2011). Many children do domestic chores in others' households, mostly for extremely low pay or, in the worst cases, for none at all. The ILO estimates the number of those 5 to 17 in domestic work worldwide at 15.5 million for 2008, of which 11.3 million are girls (73%). In this category 4.9 million girls were only 5 to 14 (Simonovsky and Luebker 2011, 9).

The incidence of child labour is highest in sub-Saharan Africa; Zimbabwe is one of the world's worst examples. Human Rights Watch (HRW) and other NGOs reported in 2009 that adults and children were subject to forced labour while digging for diamonds in the Marange diamond fields. When in 2010 the Zimbabwean economy showed signs of recovery, the Chinese-owned Shurungwi gold, chrome and nickel mines sought children under 18 to work long hours under appalling conditions (IRINnews 2010) – though the country's labour law states that "no person under 18 shall perform any work likely to jeopardize that person's health, safety, or morals." Moreover, children were trafficked internally to be farm workers or domestic servants (US Dept of State 2011n). In South Africa a 1999 survey found that, when leaving out fetching fuel and water, about 400,000 children 5 to 17, 3 per cent of this age group, worked 12 or more hours per week (cited in UN 2005, 19). In the 2000s compliance with the labour law seems to have decreased the numbers of child labourers – albeit, as a South African children's rights lecturer and researcher argues, at the cost of deepening poverty in rural areas (IRINnews 2009).

Child labour also exists in other DFL countries, notably Brazil, India and Indonesia. In Brazil it is a major problem, concentrated in private households and agriculture. Many an adult female domestic worker takes her girl children to the workplace, where they assist her. Data for 2007 showed that 4.8 million of the 44.7 million between 5 and 17, nearly 11 per cent, were at work. Over three in five worked in agriculture (IBGE 2008). For India there is evidence that in 2008–9 women in low-paid work felt an income drop, leading to increasing indebtedness, greater use of child labour and children's removal from school (SEWA 2009). The government's 2004 national survey estimated the number of working children 5 to 14 at 16.4 million, but NGOs have reported numbers closer to 60 million (US Dept of State 2011f). Using various statistics, we calculated that in India in 2006, about 21 million children of primary school age were out of school. One may assume that a large majority of them work in the informal sector, often in private homes but also in many industries, and are not rarely exposed to hazardous working conditions (website CRY). In Indonesia, according to the country's statistical bureau BPS (2010) in 2009 2.4 million boys and 1.6 million girls 10 to 17 were in child labour. BPS added that 28 per cent of the boys and over 34 per cent of the girls at stake were in hazardous labour and worked in total over 40 hours per week. The ITUC (2009c) concluded, based on ILO studies, that more than 700,000 children, mainly girls, work as domestic workers in Indonesia. Typically recruited between the ages of 12 and 15, often on false promises of decent wages and working conditions, they may work 14 to 18 hours a day, seven days a week, and earn far less than the prevailing minimum wage.

Migration

Migration is associated with adult men looking for work, but about 105 million women account for almost half the world's population of international migrants (UNDESA 2010, 13–14). Worldwide, cities are growing, pointing to migration flows from rural to urban areas. For many reasons girls and young women leave their villages and migrate to cities in search of the promise of a better life. In South Africa, Johannesburg is often called *Eboli*, or City of Gold (Plan UK/Plan International 2010, 36; cf. also UNICEF 2012). A main driver of migration is the search for work, not offered in rural areas. The desire for further education also drives migration to cities. Other motives may play a role: the attraction of an exciting city life or, for girls, running away from forced marriages or a family life in poverty. The dreams and aspirations of migrating girls and young women for an improved life might come true. Statistics show that girls in cities are more likely than their rural peers to go to school, more likely to find employment in the city than in a village, and less likely to be married early (Plan UK/Plan International 2010, 39).

In 2010 international migrants or the foreign-born population was expected to pass 213 million people. Worldwide, India ranks 10th, with 5.4 million migrants in the country, Ukraine 11th (5.3 million), Kazakhstan 15th (3.1 million) and South Africa 27th (1.9 million). Both having about 55 per cent female migrants, Kazakhstan and Ukraine reveal the highest female shares in the DFL countries (UNDESA 2010). As single-person migration of women is especially associated with vulnerabilities, the UN Development Programme (UNDP) in the Asia-Pacific region has plead for wider international agreements to ensure women's safe migration. Hereby the risks of migrant work should be directly addressed, including human trafficking, vulnerability to violence, HIV/AIDS and loss of earnings (UNDP 2010b). Especially in this region, the worldwide crisis forced many female migrants to return home. In December 2008 the Indonesian Minister of Manpower and Transmigration indicated that 250,000 overseas migrant workers had been laid off and had returned home before their contracts expired. Many were female workers from Malaysia's electronics sector (ILO 2009a).

Recent migration streams have been massive in sub-Sahara Africa. Regional emigrants in 2010 were estimated to be 21.8 million; that is, they constitute individuals born in a sub-Saharan country but living outside their country of birth. Immigrants in sub-Saharan Africa are estimated at 17.7 million, of which nearly half (47%) are women. Zimbabwe, Mozambique and South Africa are in the top-10 emigration sub-Saharan countries; South Africa is also in the top-10 immigration countries. Migration to developed countries generates remittances to developing countries. In 2010 sub-Saharan countries received US$21 billion, almost 5 per cent of remittances worldwide (World Bank 2011c). In the course of the 2000s, large parts of Zimbabwe's population had to take refuge in remittances from migrants to diversify their livelihood survival strategies. A 2005 survey established that half of the households in the two largest cities, Harare and Bulawayo, were dependent on migrant remittances for everyday consumption (Bracking and Sachikonye 2006). If the unrecorded informal remittances to Zimbabweans, estimated at 150 per cent of the official ones, are also taken into account, the total magnitude of these money flows rises to over 17 per cent of the country's GDP, larger than the contribution of agriculture to the GDP (Republic of Zimbabwe 2010b).

Brain drain, or skilled workforce emigration, is a major problem in sub-Saharan Africa. In Mozambique an estimated 45 per cent of the tertiary-educated have migrated. Emigration of skilled medical and nursing staff is an even more prickly problem. A 2010 estimate was that 21,500 (18%) of physicians trained in sub-Saharan Africa and over

53,000 (11%) of nurses trained in the region have emigrated, in considerable part to the USA and the UK (UNDESA 2010). Zimbabwe's ongoing political and economic crisis has contributed to a move of health workers to other sectors –notably the private health sector – and to emigration of skilled health workers. Between 1998 and 2000 alone the country lost about 18,000 nurses and 100 doctors (Republic of Zimbabwe 2010b). In 2000 over half of all physicians born in Zimbabwe appeared in nine major receiving countries (including South Africa, to which most have migrated), as did nearly one in four of Zimbabwe-born professional nurses, mostly in the UK (Clemens and Pettersson 2008). These emigration flows even intensified after the turn of the century. Those who stayed report increased workloads and longer working hours, as well as medical attention coming too late or being inadequate (Chikanda 2005; Connell et al. 2007). An exodus of nurses and physicians also aggravated the already poor status of Malawi's health sector in terms of human resources. In 2004 as many as 28 per cent of physicians trained in Malawi had emigrated; by then it was the highest proportion in seven southern African countries. Here, too, staff shortages and growing numbers of AIDS patients have created a heavy workload for the remaining health workers (Arrehag et al. 2006, 144–5).

The distribution of women workers over industries

The sections above discussed streams on the labour market. Now the labour market structures come to the fore. This section details the distribution of the female labour force over industries, as well as women's shares in industries and occupations. Industry structures vary widely across countries; though the female shares of employment by industry mostly show less variation, the combined result is wide variation in the industrial distribution of the female labour force. A main divide is that between countries in which agriculture is still the main source of (female) employment and countries that are developing into service economies. Clearly four of seven sub-Saharan countries are in the first category: Mozambique and Malawi, where nearly nine of ten women in the labour force are in agriculture; Zambia, where the share is nearly eight of ten; and Angola. It is assumed that over seven in ten Angolan working females work in agriculture (cf. Kyle 2007). Agriculture is also the largest employer in India, with 55 per cent of all females employed, as well as in Indonesia and Azerbaijan, with 40 per cent.

Yet the latter two countries already have a substantial service sector. As Table 4.1 indicates, in eight of 13 countries where data are available,

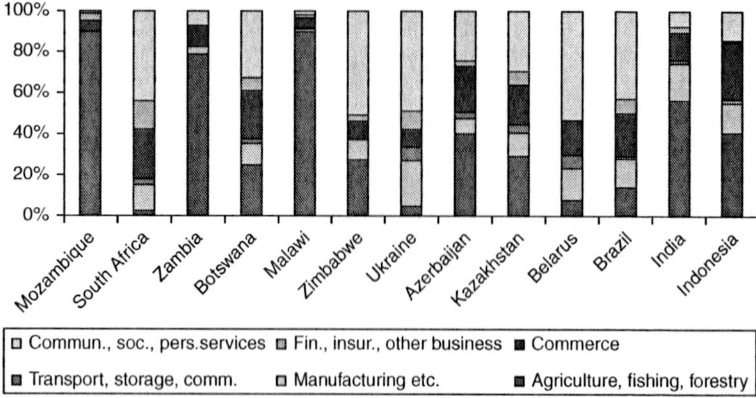

Figure 4.2 Distribution of the female labour force over industries

Note: No data are available for Angola.

Sources: ILO Laborsta database, national statistics: Mozambique, 2002–3, total labour force; South Africa, 2011, total labour force; Zambia, 2005, total labour force; Botswana, 2008, formal labour force; Malawi, 2005, formal labour force; Zimbabwe, 2002, formal labour force; Ukraine, 2008, formal labour force; Azerbaijan, 2008, total labour force; Kazakhstan, 2008, total labour force; Belarus, 2009, total labour force; Brazil, 2007, total labour force; India, 2009–10, total labour force; Indonesia, 2008, total labour force.

the share of services at large in total female employment is over 50 per cent. The eight include three large countries, South Africa (84%), Brazil and Ukraine (both 73%), plus Botswana (65%), Zimbabwe (63%), Belarus (77%), Kazakhstan (60%) and Azerbaijan (53%). Indonesia (45%) makes up its own middle category; at 26 per cent India shows a low share of females in services at large. Shares of services in female employment in agricultural sub-Saharan economies are even lower: Malawi, 9 per cent; Mozambique, 10 per cent; Zambia 18 per cent.

In nearly all countries, transport, storage and communication make up the service industry that contributes least to the female labour force, the range being from 0.1 per cent in Mozambique to nearly 7 per cent in Ukraine. In all countries commerce, under which label wholesale and retail, as well as restaurants, hotels and catering, are grouped, is a prominent employer for females. It is the largest service employment category for females in five countries: first and foremost Indonesia, with total female employment nearly 28 per cent; then India (13%), Zambia (10%) and Mozambique and Malawi (both 5%). In all other countries commerce is the second largest "servicer" in terms of female employment: South Africa (24%), Azerbaijan (23%), Brazil (21%),

Kazakhstan and Botswana (both 20%), Belarus (17%), Ukraine (9%) and Zimbabwe (8%). The relatively low commerce share in Ukraine may be attributable to a blurred distinction with our next category, finance, insurance, real estate and other business services, which in Ukraine also accounts for 9 per cent of female employment.

Except for South Africa (over 13%) and Ukraine, the finance etc. category is substantially less important for women's employment, contributing from 7 per cent in Brazil to 3 per cent in India and just 1 per cent in Indonesia. In contrast, community, social and personal services, including public administration, defence, education, health, social work, other community services, and private households, are of major importance to women's employment, particularly where agriculture is less important. The higher the share of the female labour force in agriculture, the lower the share in community, social and personal services (R = –.92). In nine of 13 countries community, social and personal services make up the largest single service category, in Belarus and Zimbabwe even accounting for over half of all females employed. In Brazil, South Africa and Ukraine this amounts to more than four in ten women; in Kazakhstan and Botswana, around three in ten; in Azerbaijan, two in ten; in Indonesia, one in ten. In the agriculture-dominated countries, India, Zambia, Malawi and Mozambique, the share falls below 8 per cent.

A look at detailed figures on subsectors of community, social and personal services (not shown in Table 4.1) shows that in the CIS countries education stands out as a major source of female employment, contributing 12 (Azerbaijan) to 21 per cent (Ukraine) of the total female workforce. In Brazil, South Africa and Botswana the share is about 10 per cent; in the other countries it is substantially lower. Ukraine shows up with a substantial 17 per cent share in health and social work, whereas in the other CIS countries, South Africa and Brazil, this subsector employs 6 to 7 per cent of females. Comparable figures are much lower in the other countries, with fewer than 2 per cent of women working in health and social work in India and Indonesia. In most countries public administration and defence contribute to female employment only to a limited extent. Botswana is the exception, with a 10 per cent share, followed by Ukraine with 7 per cent; the other countries show shares below 5 per cent. The public administration of India contributes just over 2 per cent, and that of Indonesia slightly more than 1 per cent.

As already indicated, a specific, vulnerable category hidden in the figures for community, social and personal services is that of domestic workers. According to the official statistics they make up considerable parts of the female workforces of Brazil (16% of all employed females) and South Africa (15%). For Botswana (7%), Indonesia (4.5%) and India (4%) the statistics indicate a much lower incidence of domestics, though in the latter two countries NGOs assume a multiple of the official numbers of domestics employed would be more accurate (cf. Tijdens and Van Klaveren 2011b).

In our countries manufacturing, the third employment category after agriculture and services, is less important for females than many debates on globalization's effects on women workers might suggest. Even with mining, utilities and construction included, only one country in 13 employs over one in five females in manufacturing at large: Ukraine, with 22 per cent. In the other four large countries, one in six to seven females employed can be traced to manufacturing: 18 per cent in India, 15 per cent in Indonesia, 14 per cent in Brazil, 13 per cent in South Africa. Among the smaller countries only Belarus (16%) shows a similar share of females working in manufacturing at large.

The female share in industries

Another relevant angle is the female employment share within industries. Figure 4.3 presents an overview of the percentages of women in five industries and in total employment. For six countries an industry division is available only for the formal sector. Here, women's shares in employment vary: from 23 per cent in Malawi and 24 per cent in Zimbabwe to 44 per cent in Brazil and even 53 per cent in Ukraine. In the countries with detailed industry figures related to total employment, women's shares go from 28 per cent in India and 38 per cent in Indonesia, via 43 per cent in South Africa and 49–50 per cent in Azerbaijan, Kazakhstan and Belarus, up to 55 per cent in Mozambique.

The figure also depicts the share of women in five major industries. In seven countries women are overrepresented in agriculture, implying a larger share than they have in employment at large there. In particular in Malawi and Mozambique agriculture is female dominated, whereas only in Brazil is formal labour in agriculture quite male dominated. In contrast, manufacturing in most countries is male dominated. Only in three countries are women overrepresented in manufacturing compared with their share of total employment; namely, Botswana, India and Indonesia. When manufacturing is treated in greater detail below, reasons for these differences are gone into.

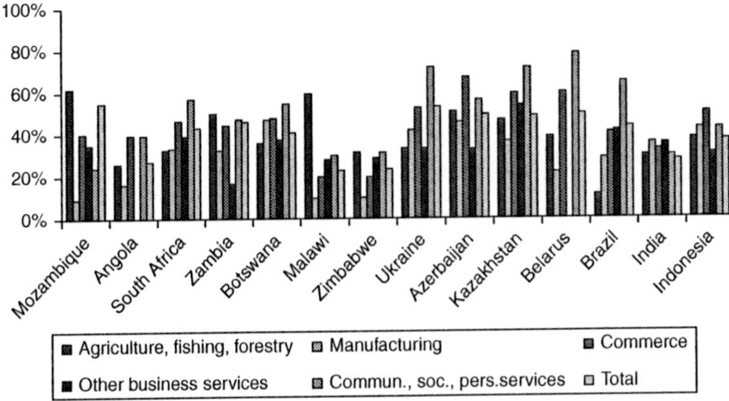

Figure 4.3 Women in five industries and in total employment (%)

Note: For Angola data on other business services are missing.

Sources: ILO Laborsta database, national statistics: Mozambique, 2002–3, total labour force; Angola, 2007, formal labour force; South Africa, 2011, total labour force; Zambia, 2005, total labour force; Botswana, 2008, formal labour force; Malawi, 2005, formal labour force; Zimbabwe, 2002, formal labour force; Ukraine, 2008, formal labour force; Azerbaijan, 2008, total labour force; Kazakhstan, 2008, total labour force; Belarus, 2009, total labour force; Brazil, 2007, formal labour force; India, 2009–10, total labour force; Indonesia, 2008, total labour force.

Commerce shows sizable shares of women employed, albeit not in Malawi and Zimbabwe (20%). In all four CIS countries women make up majorities of commerce employees, up to two of each three employed in Azerbaijan. Indonesian commerce also employs a majority of women (51%), in contrast to India (33%), Brazil (41%) and South Africa (47%). Overall, in commerce women are overrepresented in eight countries: Angola, South Africa, Botswana, Azerbaijan, Kazakhstan, Belarus, India and Indonesia. In finance, insurance, real estate and other business services the picture is largely the other way around, with men overrepresented in ten of 14 countries. Only in Kazakhstan is the share of women above 50 per cent in the finance sector, but in a majority of countries women make up around a third of this industry's workforce.

The figure's fifth major industry is community, social and personal services. In seven of 14 countries – South Africa, Botswana, Brazil and the CIS countries – this industry is clearly female dominated: females make up between 55 and 79 per cent. In another six countries female shares are lower but still higher than the national averages; only in Mozambique is the female share (25%) lower than that average. Although for some countries detailed figures are lacking, it is evident that these relatively high shares are predominantly due to four highly feminized subsectors: education, health and social work, other community sectors, private households. Across countries female shares in the fifth subsector, public administration and defence, are considerably lower.

The distribution of women workers over occupations

Now to change the subject from industries to occupations. Unfortunately, compared with industry figures, occupational statistical data are available in fewer countries. Only for nine of 14 countries do figures indicate the distribution of the female labour force over occupations and women's shares in occupations. Let us first concentrate on distribution of women workers over occupational groups. Labour force surveys commonly measure occupations using ILO's International Classification of Occupations (ISCO). ISCO is a hierarchical classification, with nine major groups at the highest level of aggregation. Not all countries have classified the occupations encountered in their labour force surveys into these nine groups, however; some have used seven or even only six groups. A few countries call a group "skilled agricultural workers" and classify unskilled agricultural workers as "elementary occupations", whereas other countries use "agricultural workers" without further reference to the skill level. In some countries a tenth group is added: domestic workers. That group is not included here, but readers are referred to the authors' publication on this highly vulnerable category of majority female workers (Tijdens and Van Klaveren 2011b). Nevertheless, the data available allow for a lively sketch of the female employment structure by occupation.

As **Table 4.1** shows, distribution of employment by occupation varies surprisingly little across countries, with one exception. In Zambia almost 80 per cent of the female labour force is employed in the occupational group "agricultural workers". Consequently, Zambia's remaining groups are of little importance. Indonesia follows, with 35 per cent of women working in agricultural jobs; then Botswana, with 22 per cent. In the remaining countries the percentages of female agricultural workers vary from under 1 per cent in South Africa to 16 per cent in Kazakhstan.

Relatively few women work in the group "legislators, senior officials, managers". Its contribution to female employment ranges from 0.1 per cent in Azerbaijan to 7 per cent in South Africa. The occupational group with the highest skill level, "professionals", is slightly more

Table 4.1 Distribution of women workers over occupational groups

	South Africa	Zambia	Botswana	Malawi	Ukraine	Azerbaijan	Kazakhstan	Belarus	Brazil	Indonesia
Legislators, senior officials, managers	6.2	2.5	3.5	1.2	6.0	0.1	5.1		4.2	1.0
Professionals	6.1	1.5	4.7	17.2	17.1	16.6	17.8		9.2	5.4
Technicians, associated professionals	14.4		8.6		15.4	4.2	12.2		8.5	1.5
Clerks	16.5	8.2	10.9	11.6	6.1	4.9	3.2		11.5	4.1
Service and sales workers	14.7	4.3	23.0	24.0	19.9	3.9	18.7		20.3	25.3
Skilled agricultural workers	0.3	79.0	22.1	9.3	0.9	12.8	16.3		13.8	34.9
Craft and related trades	3.4		6.6		3.8	6.8	4.4		3.5	10.4
Plant & machine operators, assemblers	2.9	4.5	1.2	8.2	5.6	2.0	2.0		5.8	2.1
Elementary occupations	20.8		19.4	28.5	25.2	48.7	20.3		23.2	15.3
Domestic workers	14.7									
Total	100	100	100	100	100	100	100		100	100

Source: ILO Laborsta database, national statistics: South Africa, 2011, total labour force; Zambia, 2005, total labour force; Botswana, 2005–6, formal labour force; Malawi, 2005, formal labour force; Ukraine, 2008, formal labour force; Azerbaijan, 2008, total labour force; Kazakhstan, 2008, total labour force; Belarus, 2000, total labour force; Brazil, 2007, total labour force; Indonesia, 2008, total labour force.

important for women's employment, with shares ranging from 1 per cent in Zambia to around 17 per cent in Malawi, Ukraine, Azerbaijan, and Kazakhstan. The importance of the group "technicians and associate professionals" varies from 1.5 per cent in Indonesia to 17 per cent in South Africa. The group includes accountants, teachers and social workers, among others. Taking the three groups ranked highest together, their share in the female labour force is largest in Ukraine (39%), followed by Kazakhstan (35%) and South Africa (33%); it is lowest in Indonesia (8%) and Zambia (4%).

In importance, clerking as an occupation ranges from 3 per cent in Kazakhstan and 4 per cent in Indonesia to over 19 per cent in South Africa. In six of nine countries the "service and sales workers" group is of larger importance to the female labour force; its shares in female employment range from 4 per cent in Zambia to 25 per cent in Indonesia. Joint shares of these two groups particularly important to the DFL project are in the range between 22 per cent (Kazakhstan) and 36.5 per cent (South Africa), Zambia (12.5%) and Azerbaijan (8%) being exceptions. In Brazil (32%) and Indonesia (29%) about three in ten working women can be found in these two occupational groups.

Two occupational groups are of relatively little importance for female employment. The groups "craft and related trades" and "plant and machine operators, assemblers" contribute in all countries less than 11 per cent of the female labour force. By contrast, the unskilled group of elementary occupations is important in all countries. In summary, in Zambia and Indonesia agricultural workers form the main occupational group. In Botswana the service and sales workers are the largest group; in South Africa, Malawi, Ukraine, Azerbaijan, Kazakhstan and Brazil the elementary occupations are the largest. This overall picture implies that unskilled and semi-skilled occupations are most important for women's employment in all nine countries.

The female share in occupations

For the female share of each occupational group, Table 4.2 presents an overview of women's percentages in the ten occupations and total employment. For three countries figures are available only for the formal sector. Here, women's employment shares vary from 41 per cent in Botswana and 23 per cent in Malawi to 48 per cent in Ukraine. Where figures cover the total labour force, women's shares of the total go from 38 per cent (Indonesia), via 43 per cent (South Africa), to 48–50 per cent (the four CIS countries).

Table 4.2 Women workers in 11 occupational groups (%)

	South Africa	Zambia	Botswana	Malawi	Ukraine	Azerbaijan	Kazakhstan	Belarus	Brazil	Indonesia
Legislators, senior officials, managers	30.9	41.3	30.5	32.0	38.6	6.3	38.3	45.0	36.1	22.1
Professionals	48.9	29.2	45.6	22.0	63.5	54.4	67.9	67.0	58.6	53.0
Technicians, associated professionals	55.3		62.7		64.5	52.5	65.4		46.7	28.5
Clerks	69.3	50.3	69.7	41.0	84.6	41.0	72.9	88.0	58.6	41.7
Service and sales workers	44.3	41.7	64.8	19.0	68.3	34.3	66.6		57.5	52.9
Skilled agricultural workers	32.8				39.1	31.8	48.7		32.7	38.0
Craft and related trades	11.2		33.5		13.8	36.6	22.9	28.0	20.7	33.8
Plant & machine operators, assemblers	15.1	23.1	10.4	11.0	21.4	18.3	10.8	16.0	20.4	12.3
Elementary occupations	41.8		48.5	27.0	52.2	71.7	47.8		55.3	32.8
Domestic workers	96.0									77.7
Agricultural workers		50.2	42.2	18.0						
Total	43.6	46.4	41.1	23.0	48.3	49.5	48.9	50.0	42.2	37.7

Source: ILO Laborsta database, national statistics: South Africa, 2011, total labour force; Zambia, 2005, total labour force; Botswana, 2005–6, formal labour force; Malawi, 2005, formal labour force; Ukraine, 2008, formal labour force; Azerbaijan, 2008, total labour force; Kazakhstan, 2008, total labour force; Belarus, 2000, total labour force; Brazil, 2007, total labour force; Indonesia, 2008, total labour force.

In most DFL countries, four of nine occupational groups turn out to be female dominated. In one group they form substantial minorities (sometimes majorities), and in four groups smaller minorities. Women do remarkably well in two of the three highest level occupational groups. In five of nine countries the group "professionals" shows female majorities, with Ukraine and Kazakhstan showing more than 60 per cent females in the group. In five of seven countries (no data for Malawi and Zambia) the group for technicians and associate professionals is female dominated; Botswana, Ukraine and Kazakhstan show even more than 60 per cent women. At semi-skilled level, the group for (administrative) clerks is most feminized of all: in all nine countries it contains over 40 per cent women, in six countries there is a female majority and four countries (South Africa, Botswana, Ukraine and Kazakhstan) show over 60 per cent women, with Ukraine (85% women) on top. The other semi-skilled group in the service sector at large, "service and sales workers", follows closely. Here there are female majorities in five countries, and three countries (not South Africa, but again Botswana, Ukraine and Kazakhstan) have over 60 per cent females. Taken together, in 11 of 18 cells of the groups "clerks" and "service and sales workers", women form majorities.

In most of our countries women also have a strong presence in the elementary occupations. In three of eight countries (no data for Zambia) these occupations show female majorities, with Azerbaijan on top (72%) followed by Brazil (55%) and Ukraine (52%). In Botswana, Kazakhstan and South Africa alike, over four in ten workers in elementary occupations are female.

In four groups women form minorities, with overall only one country exception left. With shares of 30 to 42 per cent, they still form substantial minorities in the high-level group "legislators, senior officials, managers"; exceptions are Indonesia (22%) and Azerbaijan, where only 6 per cent women are counted. Except in Zambia, where they are 50 per cent, women form considerable minorities among (skilled) agricultural workers. Women have less presence in the craft and related trades, with shares ranging from 11 (South Africa) to 37 per cent (Azerbaijan). Finally, in "plant and machine operators, assemblers", the share of women in all nine countries drops below 25 per cent.

The eight targeted occupations

To refresh the reader's memory, we relist the eight large service sector occupational groups which the DFL project targeted: bookkeepers, call centre operators, receptionists in hotels, housekeepers in hotels, IT programmers, salespersons/cashiers in retail, secretaries, and travel agency intermediaries. The authors undertook to provide insight into the socio-demographic characteristics of the target group: household composition, presence of partner and children, age and education, as well as earnings per occupation and per country and working hours (Tijdens and Van Klaveren 2011a). The data stem from the *WageIndicator* survey, covering the period between January 2008 and April 2011; the selection looks at women 15 to 30 in the eight occupations in seven countries: Belarus, Brazil, India, Indonesia, Kazakhstan, South Africa and Ukraine. The occupation showing up most frequently in the database is salesperson/cashier in retail, followed by secretary. Only a few housekeepers in hotels, followed by hotel receptionists (sometimes called front-office workers), completed the survey. It should be noted that the data of the young women in the eight occupations are not representative and that differences do not necessarily reflect differences across countries in the share of these occupations in the female labour force.

Overall, nine in ten women surveyed were employees, whereas fewer than one in ten were unemployed. Yet in Ukraine only seven in ten were employees, and more than two in ten unemployed. Receptionists in particular had a high percentage of unemployed (almost two in ten), whereas unemployment was lowest among IT programmers, with fewer than one in twenty reporting so. As for household composition, the women surveyed lived in households with two to four members, the largest households being in Indonesia and the smallest in Ukraine and Belarus. Almost half of the women lived with a partner. More than two in ten women lived with children. In South Africa this share was one in three; it was less than two in ten in Brazil, India and Ukraine. More than three in ten housekeepers lived with children, yet only one in ten receptionists did. The average age was 25.3 years, though in India and South Africa the women surveyed were slightly older than in the other countries. The women in this study were on average well educated. Those in Ukraine had the highest educational levels, followed by those in Indonesia and India. In Brazil and South Africa half of the women had a middle-level education. The housekeepers had the lowest education, and the IT programmers the highest.

The IT programmers clearly had the highest median earnings, followed by the bookkeepers and the travel agency intermediaries. At the bottom of the wage distribution were the housekeepers in hotels, followed by the hotel receptionists, the secretaries and the salespersons/cashiers.

India had the longest average working week, followed by Brazil; the shortest working week was noted in Ukraine, followed by Kazakhstan. The incidence of shift work or irregular hours was highest in Belarus and Ukraine, closely followed by India. Evening work was particularly reported in India, then in Kazakhstan. Saturday and Sunday work was found to most frequently occur in Brazil. The front-office workers in hotels most often reported shift work or irregular hours, whereas secretaries and bookkeepers hardly ever did. The hotel housekeepers worked Saturdays most often, followed by the hotel receptionists and the retail salespersons/cashiers. The receptionists in hotels reported to work Sundays most often, followed by the housekeepers.

5
Wages and Working Conditions of Young Women

Introduction

This chapter treats another important labour market feature relevant to young women: wages and working conditions. Wage rankings are looked at by industry, followed by a discussion of the gender pay gap. The focus then shifts to job quality, particularly to working hours, workplace sexual harassment and violence, and combining work and family life. Especially for employed young women, compliance with labour legislation and collective bargaining outcomes are essential, but at the same time in nearly all countries they constitute an Achilles' heel: a problem addressed at the chapter's end.

Wages: industry rankings

For nine DFL countries, a ranking of official earnings of male and female workers by industry is available (see Table 5.1). Rank 1 indicates that the industry at stake has the highest average earnings, whereas rank 14 or 15 points at the lowest earnings. The table shows that the finance and insurance industry has the highest average earnings in four of nine countries and the second highest in another two. In contrast, agriculture and fisheries are ranked 14th and 15th, indicating that these industries have the lowest average wages across the nine countries. On average, mining follows finance and insurance, with the second-highest wages, with public administration and defence in third place and the utilities sector in fourth. Remarkable are the low overall positions of education (ninth rank) and especially health and social work (13th).

For six countries (Azerbaijan, Botswana, Indonesia, Kazakhstan, Ukraine and Zambia) the ranking of female earnings across the same

Table 5.1 Ranking of earnings of men and women in total, by industry

	Azerbaijan 2008	Botswana 2005–6	Brazil 2007	Indonesia 2008	Kazakhstan 2008	Zambia 2005	Malawi 2006	South Africa 2009	Ukraine 2008	Total rank
Agriculture	14	13	8	15	14	10	10		14	12
Fishing	15			14	15					14.7
Mining	1	2	5	7	3	3		5	2	3.5
Manufacturing	9	11	2	10	6	7	6	6	7	7.1
Utilities	7	1		3	10	2	9	1	5	5
Construction	4	8	7	9	4	6	11	7	8	7.1
Wholesale, retail	11	10	6	12	9	8	8	7	9	8.9
Hotels, restaurants	8	12		13	7	9	7		12	9.6
Transport, storage, communication	5	6	4	8	5	5	2	2	4	4.6
Finance, insurance	2	3		2	1	1	1	4	1	1.9
Real estate, renting, other business	3	4		5	2		12		6	5.3
Public admin., defence	6		1	1	11		5		3	3.8
Education	10	5		4	13		3		11	7.7
Health, social work	13	7		6	12				13	10.2
Other community and personal services	12	9	3	11	8	4	4	3	10	8.2
Private households				16						x
Min.	1	1	1	1	1	1	1	1	1	
Max.	15	13	8	16	15	10	12	7	14	

Source: ILO Laborsta database.

15 industries (not shown in Table 5.1, data again derived from ILO Laborsta) can be separately analysed. In these countries the size of the wage differences across industries (highest to lowest) correlates to a large extent (0.53) with incidence of informal labour. Most likely formal labour feels the competition of informality in a number of industries, resulting in wage pressure. The rank order is somewhat different from the overall wage order. Again, in all six countries the lowest average female earnings are found in agriculture and fishing, ranks 14 and 15, and finance and insurance earnings are overall highest – though in Azerbaijan women in mining are on top and in Botswana women in utilities, earning even more than those in finance and insurance. Yet for females overall, the real estate and renting industry ranks second, followed by mining (3rd place) and public administration and defence (4th).

Again, average earnings in education (10th) and health (13th) are relatively low. That is also the case with earnings in manufacturing: in the total ranked seventh but among females 12th. In four of six countries manufacturing pays females on average less than both wholesale and retail (overall 10th) and the hotel and restaurant sector (8th). Compared with European countries, where agriculture; wholesale and retail; and hotels, restaurants and catering time and again show up as the "usual suspects" for low wages (cf. Van Klaveren and Tijdens 2008), earnings rankings in the DFL countries seem less clear-cut, notably concerning the wholesale and retail and hotels industries, with their large shares of women in employment.

Wages: the gender pay gap

The distance between male and female wages is indicated by the gender pay gap (GPG), calculated by dividing the gap between male and female wages by the value of the male wages. Table 5.2 collects data from seven DFL countries on this gap, by industry: the six countries just discussed plus Brazil. The table shows a large GPG in Zambia (46%) and Azerbaijan (43%), a relatively small one in Botswana (19%) and Brazil (22%). In Zambia the extremely large pay gaps in mining, manufacturing and utilities contribute to the large total. In Botswana the small GPG is due to the very small GPGs in agriculture, utilities, construction, transport, storage and communication, and real estate, renting and other business. In some countries a few industries even show a negative GPG, indicating that women have on average higher earnings than men; for example, in Brazil the GPG is –6 per cent in manufacturing and –2 per cent in transport, storage and communication. Such negative

Table 5.2 The gender pay gap, by industry

	Zambia	Botswana	Ukraine	Azerbaijan	Kazakhstan	Brazil	Indonesia
Agriculture	47	4	12	22	28	71	23
Fishing				17	27		−20
Mining	53	−13	49	20	30	39	31
Manufacturing	55	52	29	25	34	−6	22
Utilities	53	2	23	21	24		23
Construction	−65	13	14	46	26	?	−29
Wholesale, retail	44	36	20	7	23	54	10
Hotels, restaurants	4	33	16	9	43		19
Transport, storage, communication	17	12	26	41	16	−2	−17
Finance, insurance	6	31	31	35	35		−3
Real estate, renting, other business		13	8	58	14		−19
Public admin., defence			16	22	22	9	1
Education		36	15	28	10		1
Health, social work		36	12	33	11		14
Other community and personal services	18	31	28	47	37	39	−7
Private households						23	41
Total	46	19	25	43	31	22	14

Source: Tijdens and Van Klaveren 2012; Zambia, hourly earnings, 2005; Botswana, monthly earnings, 2005–6; Ukraine, monthly earnings, 2008; Azerbaijan, monthly earnings, 2008; Kazakhstan, monthly earnings, 2008; Brazil, hourly earnings, 2007; Indonesia, hourly earnings, 2008.

GPGs is attributable to women's performing skilled office or lab jobs, whereas men predominantly perform unskilled manufacturing, drivers' or storage jobs.

The table reveals that in the seven countries the GPG ranking is not the same across industries. For example, in Azerbaijan the GPG is smallest in the wholesale and retail sector. In no other country is the GPG in this sector smallest across the industries. In Kazakhstan the GPG is smallest in education, and in Brazil for manufacturing. In both Indonesia and Ukraine mining has the largest gap. Although no straightforward industry-related picture emerges from the table, one can compute an overall ranking of the GPG across industries not controlled for national labour force size. In the seven countries jointly, the smallest overall GPG is in real estate and renting, closely followed by public administration and defence, with wholesale and retail in third place. Overall the GPG is highest in manufacturing; being relatively large in Botswana, Indonesia, Kazakhstan, Ukraine and Zambia. The second- to fifth-highest GPGs are in other community services, finance and insurance, mining, and utilities. In most countries these industries employ relatively low shares of women. Although further research is needed here, it seems that if jobs within an industry are highly gender segregated, the GPG is also large. Yet as shown in a few instances, gender segregation can favour female workers (see Box 5.1).

Box 5.1 The salary checker in Mozajarplata, Belarus

"Before my maternity leave I worked as a secretary in a large company. When I gave birth to a child, my employer made me a choice – either I go to work two months after the birth of my son, or I get dismissed. I knew that the employer attempted to violate my rights. So I sent the question to Mozajarplata by lawyer and quickly got detailed advice. So I managed to keep the job[....] However now I realise that I do not want to linger in a secretary position. I try to understand what is a dream job for me. And immediately appreciate all options from a financial point of view – Salary Checker became my "tool at hand". My formula of a dream job is challenging duties and decent salary. And I'm sure that soon I'll find such a job." (Elena, 26 years old, Belarus (Decisions for Life project website)).

Job quality

In high-income countries many debates among researchers and policymakers, including trade unionists, focus on job quality or decent work. Over the years researchers from the EU, North America and Australia have invested time and energy to explore and define the meaning of "quality of work". Common sense has grown around the idea that shop floor workers should have structural opportunities to improve jobs and limit health risks at work. Also, wages are often regarded as an aspect of job quality. Opinions really start to diverge when it comes to indicators for measuring and judging job quality, but even here ever more common ground can be found. If wages are left out, these main elements or dimensions of job quality can be derived from the "northern" debates: use of skills; possibilities for learning and career development; reasonable working hours; health and safety at work; gender equality, non-discrimination; adequate work-life balance, possibilities to combine work and family life; social dialogue and worker involvement; and work-related stress within limits (cf. Van Klaveren and Tijdens 2008).

The debates in the Decisions for Life project touching upon job quality showed clearly that participants chose their priorities by taking into account daily experience and colouring their choices with comments on day-to-day practice, as a number of boxes in this book testify. Three priority areas, not necessarily in order, were regulating or limiting working hours; fighting workplace sexual harassment and violence; combining work and family life, jointly with the overarching wish that employers better comply with legal regulation and collective bargaining results (see Box 5.2). The next sections build on these debates and devote attention to working hours, workplace sexual harassment and violence, combining work and family life, and the compliance issue.

Box 5.2 Open letter to the Prime Minister about working in the IT industry

"PIT.Ua – Union of Information, Communication and Business Technologies Professionals – pays your attention to the fact that IT industry is one of the most perspective industries all over the world and in Ukraine in particular.... PIT.Ua, within the framework of the international social project Decisions for Life conducted a campaign of questioning working women of IT-industry with the aim of discovering their basic needs and requirements. We are bringing to your attention the most important needs:

Flexible working hours – possibility to work unperformed hours in suitable time

Convenient work place – modern information technologies allow women to work from home

Renewal and/or raising the level of proficiency during maternity leave

Courses for raising the level of qualification, paid by the organisation or the state

Decent work terms – a comfortable workplace: arm chair, cosy table, sofa for rest for expectant mothers." (Ukrainian Union of Information, Communication and Business Technologies Professionals, Ukraine (Decisions for Life project website)).

Working hours

Statistics and stories alike point to the long hours that young women predominantly must work in the DFL countries and their negative consequences on social and family life. For example, Arlene, a 30-year-old South African call-centre worker participating in the DFL project, says: "Working at company A put a lot of strain on my personal life. I worked very long hours and hardly saw my kids and family. My relationship with my boyfriend suffered because of the long hours. We have since separated." Louise Plaatjes, a SASBO union organizer active in the South African DFL campaign, stresses the long hours for call-centre workers in the finance sector. She says they are often exploited by labour brokers.

As Figure 5.1 shows, working hours per week are long for female workers in the five countries where detailed industry data exist. In Zambia hours are extremely long in restaurants and hotels (58.5 per week), followed by finance and insurance and wholesale and

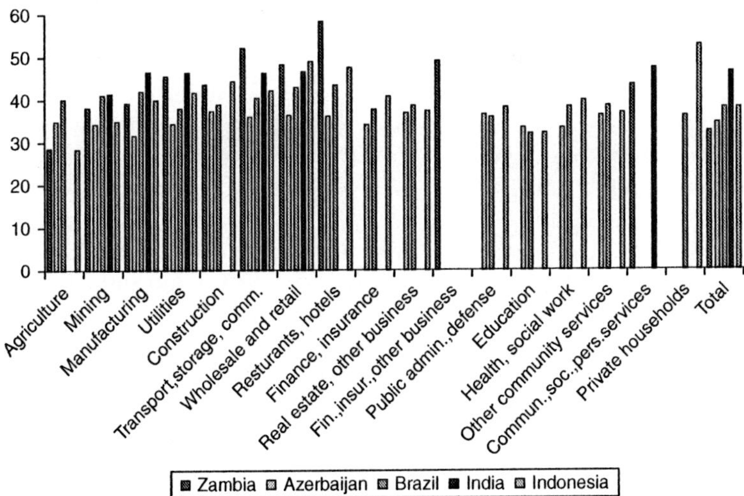

Figure 5.1 Female work actually performed per week, by industry

Source: ILO Laborsta 4A.

Table 5.3 General legal limit for working hours, per day and per week

	General limit working hours per day	...hours per week
Mozambique	8	48
Angola	8	44
South Africa	9 in case of 5 d/w or 8 in case of >5 d/w	45
Zambia	n/a	n/a
Botswana	n/a	48
Malawi	n/a	n/a
Zimbabwe	no limit	no limit
Ukraine	n/a	n/a
Azerbaijan	n/a	40
Kazakhstan	8	40
Belarus	n/a	n/a
Brazil	8	44
India	9	48
Indonesia	7–8	40

Note: n/a = not available.

Source: Derived from ILOLEX database, http://www.ilo.org/ilolex/english/index.htm; last accessed 10 March 2012.

retail (both 49). In Azerbaijan weekly working hours are relatively short: 35 hours on average, ranging from 32 to 38 in various industries. Working hours range from 32 in education to 43 in finance and insurance and wholesale and retail in Brazil. At 39 hours on average, Brazilian women have no extremely long weeks. In India female average working hours are extremely long (nearly 47), and they are long in each industry, varying from 42 to 48. In Indonesia the picture is diverse. In finance and insurance the average working week for females is 41 hours, slightly above the national average of just over 40, but working hours are very long in wholesale and retail (49) and hotels and restaurants.

In most countries working hours are subject to regulation. Table 5.3 shows the general legal limits for working hours per day and per week. Exceptions may apply, for example for specific occupations or industries. Comparing reported and regulated hours, in Indonesia the average reported hours for females are above the legal limit in eight industries, while in only seven are they below the limit.

Workplace sexual harassment and violence

Violence against women occurs in every country of the world to a greater or lesser extent, with numerous serious consequences for the women themselves and for society generally. Gender-based violence is perhaps the most widespread and, unfortunately, socially tolerated of human rights violations; it reflects and reinforces inequalities between men and women. As the ITUC has noted, from a trade union perspective violence against women is not only a violation of human rights but also a type of violence with a direct and detrimental impact on a woman's access to paid work. Violence pervades a country's culture, and workplace violence pervades the world of work (ITUC 2009a).

As seen in Chapter 3, all DFL countries report sexual harassment and violence as a major problem. South Africa, for example, has reported that with the growing inroads of flexibility clauses and labour brokers into employment relationships, "opportunities for exploitation and harassment have grown tenfold and a number of women workers recount how male supervisors demand and receive sexual favours in order to secure some women places in the daily or weekly shifts" (Ndungu 2009, 3). South Africa and other countries widely report the practice of male employers or leading staff pressing for sexual favours when offering jobs to girls or young women or in exchange for better working conditions, schedules or financial improvement. Malawi has also reported such practices (cf. Kateta 2009). At the mid-term DFL meeting in March 2010 in Maputo, Patricia Nyman, national gender coordinator of SACCAWU, the South African service sector union, politicized the incidence and impact of workplace harassment and called it an "organisational conspiracy against young working women. [...] Sexual harassment on the job is a key problem. If you want to keep your contract you have to abide by the manager's invitation to go out with him, if you refuse, he does not prolong your contract".

In India sexual harassment of women in the workplace includes physical and verbal abuse from male supervisors, restricted use of toilets and denial of lunch breaks (US Dept of State 2011f). Sexual harassment in the workplace is also reported as widespread in Indonesia. Constraints on mobilizing women workers against harassment seem even larger there than in other developing countries. Researchers in Indonesia have observed that female workers are highly reluctant to voice abuses by management and fellow workers (Rachmawati and De Ruyter 2007). Similar findings come from Azerbaijan, where large-scale surveys of international NGOs found that about 30 per cent of women had experienced sexual harassment from an employer or a co-worker. Another survey revealed the broad belief in Azerbaijan that women should quit their job if they experience sexual harassment at work (Center Women and Modern World et al. 2009).

Combining work and family life: a legal framework for young women

To combine work and family life, high-income countries usually apply a range of legal arrangements and clauses in collective agreements. We inventoried the extent that these regulations were present in our 14 countries. Table 5.4 shows results for paid holidays and paid sick leave (see also Box 5.3). Of the African countries Zambia provides the

Table 5.4 Duration of paid annual leave and arrangements for paid sick leave

	Duration annual leave	Paid sick leave
Mozambique	no info	in collective agreements only
Angola	no info	no info
South Africa	21 calendar days	up to 30 days in 36 months
Zambia	2 days per month	no info
Botswana	15 working days	up to 14 working days
Malawi	18 working days if working 6 days a week or 15 working days if working 5 days a week	up to 4 weeks sick leave
Zimbabwe	during every public holiday if it occurs on a day on which one would otherwise have been required to work	up to 90 days sick leave on full pay per year
Ukraine	24 calendar days	no info
Azerbaijan	21 calendar days	no info
Kazakhstan	24 calendar days	no info
Belarus	24 calendar days	no info
Brazil	30 calendar days	no info
India	12 calendar days of annual leave for every 240 days worked (there is no general law stipulating a minimum paid leave for all workers)	Only workers covered by the employees' state insurance act 1948 can claim a sickness benefit. There is neither minimum income guaranteed nor special employment protection during sick leave.
Indonesia	12 calendar days	The entrepreneur shall be obliged to pay the worker's wages if the worker does not perform work because the worker is taken so ill that he or she cannot perform the work

Source: Van Klaveren et al. 2009a–g, 2010a–g.

longest paid annual leave (two days a month), followed by South Africa (21 calendar days a year), Malawi (18 days) and Botswana (15 days). In the CIS countries provisions vary from 21 to 24 calendar days. In Brazil leave is 30 calendar days, whereas in India and Indonesia it is 12. In the majority of the 14 countries regulations concerning paid sick leave are absent or only found in collective agreements. In the remaining countries these facilities vary from up to 14 working days per year in Botswana to 90 days in Zimbabwe.

The results of the inventory for statutory paid maternity leave are depicted in Table 5.5, showing that all countries have such regulations in place. Leave ranges from 56 days in Malawi to four months (approximately 122 days) in South Africa and 126 days in the CIS countries. In most countries maternity leave before and after giving birth is regulated, though in some one period or both are not regulated, giving the pregnant woman herself the choice – one that might lead to the risky behaviour of working until close to the date she is to give birth. In South Africa, after the first democratic elections, the rewriting of labour laws brought four key pieces of legislation, among them the Basic Conditions of Employment Act (BCEA; 1997). According to the union movement, not everything in the BCEA represented progress, including regulation of maternity benefits. While setting a minimum

Table 5.5 Maternity leave

	Maternity leave before giving birth	**Maternity leave after giving birth**	**Maternity leave in total**
Mozambique	20 days	40 days	60 days
Angola	28 days	56 days	3 months
South Africa	not defined	42 days	4 months
Zambia	not defined	not defined	84 days
Botswana	not defined	42 days	84 days
Malawi	not defined	not defined	56 days
Zimbabwe	21 days	not defined	98 days
Ukraine	70 days	56 days	126 days
Azerbaijan	70 days	56 days	126 days
Kazakhstan	70 days	56 days	126 days
Belarus	70 days	56 days	126 days
Brazil	not defined	not defined	120 days
India	42 days	42 days	84 days
Indonesia	1.5 months	1.5 months	3 months

Source: Derived from ILOLEX database, http://www.ilo.org/ilolex/english/index.htm; last accessed 10 March 2012.

of four months' maternity leave in total, the law superseded the Unemployment Insurance Fund, which had allowed women six months paid benefits. Already around the turn of the century the SACCAWU union in a parental rights campaign succeeded in securing rights higher than the BCEA minimum at company level, such as increased maternity leave periods, paternity leave and childcare at work (Ordor 2011, 25–8).

In Mozambique improvements for women were linked with a new family law (2005); it secured a broad range of legal rights previously denied Mozambican women and more precisely defined them with regard to property, child custody and other issues. It also raised the minimum age for marriage, from 14 for both sexes to 18 for those with parental consent, 21 for those without it. What is more, steps were taken to guarantee compliance – substantially more than in other sub-Saharan countries. However, information on the newly defined rights has been slow to spread. Five years after it took effect, a survey conducted by the NGO MULEIDE found that nearly two in three women remained uninformed about the family law (US Dept of State 2011j). A 2009 survey in Mozambique confirmed the existence of weaknesses in social and job security; 45 per cent of female respondents said they benefited from maternity leave (Lee 2012).

Box 5.3 "My family and children appreciate what I'm doing"

As a country we had a challenge of crime and poverty, which was the result of the system of apartheid. In 1993 things were so hectic in Transkei because the people wanted to be free[....] At this time I was at school and I was doing standard eight, we would just smell the tear gas from nowhere and we would know that there is protest somewhere. My friends and I used to joke and say "this is how freedom smells like". After voting in 1994 the celebrations were everywhere and we knew then that things would be different for us[....] For children like me, born in the 70s, it was difficult for us because we could see how our parents, sisters and brothers fought for this freedom. I'm grateful to all those who had to die in order for us to enjoy the fruits of freedom[....] It is not nice to be a young woman in South Africa with the HIV/AIDS pandemic, rape, sexual harassment and poverty. We are so lucky in [Retail Store X] even though it changed now. It's good to join a company which can acknowledge the culture, acknowledge that people are sick and care for them putting the HIV/AIDS workplace policy. [Retail Store X] had funds which were kept by the chairman but unfortunately he left and his son took over. Now we don't know what is happening to the fund as most people cannot access it[....] I wanted to be a nurse when I grew up, even though I didn't fulfil that dream but I still have hope that one day I will fulfil my dream[. ...] My daily routine is very busy and linked to this is my challenging role as shop steward, being an employee and being a mother. My day starts at 05h30, I prepare clothes, uniform and lunchbox for my children, serve them breakfast because they are both collected by a taxi at 06h30. After this I clean the house and prepare myself for work because I start to work at 08h45 but I have to be at work at 08h30. I use the train to get to work. I love the train because it's cheap and I get a chance to sing in the church coach. If I'm lucky I get a chair but in most cases I don't but I don't really mind in the mornings but the evenings are a challenge because it is long after a demanding day." (Thabisa, 34 years old, South Africa (Decisions for Life website)).

Compliance, a major problem

Legal arrangements and bargaining clauses should safeguard women's and labour rights as indicated above, like maternity leaves, for the workers at stake. It may be needless to say to labour relations watchers, but many debates in the DFL project focused on the weaknesses and loopholes that left room for non-compliance with the legal framework. The participating women illuminated many examples of weaknesses and loopholes they were familiar with. Often, trade unions in their eyes prove to be too weak (or not daring enough, quite a few young women added) to enforce compliance. The role of the Labour Inspectorates, the main enforcement agency for work issues in all 14 countries, varied across countries and across industries and regions, too. As the short overview below also shows (see Box 5.4), in some cases the inspectorates developed into allies for the workers and their unions, but in others they are still far from that.

Box 5.4 Labour Rights for Women (2012–16)

In 2012, the project Labour Rights for Women was funded from Netherlands Development Aid. This project succeeds the Decisions for Life project and is again a cooperative venture of ITUC, the Wage Indicator Foundation and the University of Amsterdam with national trade unions in 16 developing countries. Labour Rights for Women departs from the understanding that women's labour rights are to a large extent insufficiently protected in the national legislation of the targeted countries. In addition, effective enforcement of the existing national labour laws is a serious problem. Both are largely due to women's lack of capacity to defend their workplace rights and demand improved legal protection, as well as to the insufficient attention to women's issues in the public debate pressing governments to better protect women at work. The project aims to leverage the necessary changes in society by combining awareness raising of the general public with empowering women to defend their own rights, while strengthening women's leadership in collective bargaining and social dialogue.

In South Africa unions have complained for years about the limited capacity of the Department of Labour (DOL) to control compliance with labour regulation. In 2007 trade union researcher Simon K. Ndungu testified that DOL's staff of labour inspectors had been nearly halved in the preceding decade. Bhorat et al. (2010) studied enforcement of minimum wages in South Africa in detail, measuring non-compliance not only by the fraction of workers below the minimum wage but also by the violation's degree or depth – how much below the minimum wage an individual earns. The yardsticks correlated significantly. The researchers found that South African employers' non-compliance as such was, at 36 to 45 per cent, high. Surprisingly, the labour inspectorate's density was partly insignificant in predicting violations of minimum wage regulation, especially so where the degree of violation was very high or very low. Between the extremes a higher density of labour inspectors resulted in a reduced depth of violation. At firm level the rate of unemployment was found to exert the largest negative influence on depth of violation. A positive outcome, by contrast, was that unionized workers had a significantly lower depth of violation than non-union workers. In particular, having a written contract lowered the likelihood that the minimum wage was violated. As was expected, violation rates were considerably higher in the informal sector than in (semi-)formal firms.

In most other southern African countries the Labour Inspectorate situation is even worse. For example, Malawi has an Occupational Safety Health and Welfare Act (1997) that entails companies and the civil service to inform, instruct and supervise employees for their better health. Yet till 2010 Malawi's official inspection capacity was minimal, and enforcement of health and safety standards poor (US Dept of State 2011i). If the most tangible and "hardest" part of job quality is barely subject to government control and enforcement, should one expect violations of well-being at work and work-life balance, regarded as "softer" and lower in the workers' needs' hierarchy, to be enforced? In these countries if enforcement efforts exist at all, they are limited to the formal sector. This also applies to India, where legal provisions regulating conditions of work are mainly enforced in the organized, or formal, sector (ITUC 2011c; US Dept of State 2011f).

In Brazil, tightened labour inspection is actively used to reduce informality in the labour market. Here two significant trends have been observed (Berg 2012). First, in the mid-1990s a new bonus system tied inspectors' salaries to individual performance related to formalizing workers, to collection of employers' contribution to the national unemployment and pension fund, and to the number of workers covered by inspection. Second, teams of labour inspectors were developed to tackle specific, mostly industry-related, problems such as child labour and work accidents. These teams were not bound to the bonus system. Hundreds of thousands of workers have been registered as a result of inspection. Analysing the functioning of the Brazilian labour inspectorate, Pires (2011) argues that improving bureaucratic performance should focus on setting processes in motion for the constant revision of goals and their measures and redefining mechanisms and procedures every time they become hostile to the achievement of desired goals.

In some DFL countries the authorities have curtailed the scope of controls on compliance, mostly to please foreign investors. As a rule, underlying agreements come into the open only accidentally. A notorious example is Azerbaijan; its government can legally conclude bilateral agreements with multinational firms that set aside labour laws. Neither unions nor even labour inspectorates have access to these agreements. It should come as no surprise that labour rights are repeatedly violated by multinationals operating in Azerbaijan (ITUC 2011c). Labour legislation compliance does not necessarily improve under so-called socialist conditions. For instance, in Belarus the law grants women the right to three years of maternity leave with assurance of job availability upon return. However, it has been reported that Belarusian employers often circumvent employment protections by using short-term contracts, then refusing to renew a woman's contract when she becomes pregnant. The state Labour Inspectorate obviously lacks the authority to enforce employer compliance and often ignores violations (US Dept of State 2011c).

6
An Industry Outlook

Introduction

This chapter provides an industry outlook on female employment in the DFL countries. There are various reasons for producing this unusual overview. In the first place, mechanisms allocating labour basically follow industry divisions; with some exceptions, allocation along occupational lines comes second. Translated into daily life terms, most young women looking for a job orient themselves on a specific industry. Job information on the *WageIndicator* websites is also structured this way, with its primary orientation on industries and subsequently on occupations. Secondly, employment prospects differ widely across industries. With globalization and the development of new technologies, these differences will most likely widen further in the near future; foreign investment, international outsourcing and tourism will be the main drivers of change. A third reason for producing an industry overview is that in most countries trade unions are organized along industry lines. As cooperation with trade unions was the lifeline of the DFL project, it was important to serve those involved in the project with industry information.

Employment structures and prospects are specified for the main economic sectors: agriculture, manufacturing, and services. The section on agriculture starts by explaining why this sector gets ample space. After a short section on services at large, most space is devoted to analysing employment prospects in commercial services' three core subsectors of interest – wholesale and retail trades, tourism and call centres – for the DFL project's target group. Finally, a brief look at prospects in two "adjacent" industries, health and public administration and defence, that may also be relevant to the target group. Note that teachers' employment perspectives can to an extent be derived from Chapter 3.

Industries: agriculture

The leading question in treating employment in agriculture came up early in the Decision for Life project and runs as follows: can young women living in urban areas and trying to make a career there rely on a "fallback scenario" in which they reasonably can go back to their families, who live by agriculture, without heavily overburdening those families? An answer to that question is derived from a number of country profiles.

In South Africa from 1995 to 2000, both men and women experienced a massive real income decline, perhaps 40 per cent. As men systematically left the labour market, women systematically entered it. Black women particularly were forced to work in low-income-generating informal labour, partly agriculture based (cf. Leibbrandt et al. 2005; Casale et al. 2004). In spite of expanded social security benefits, lack of basic services causes the burden of poverty to fall heavily on the rural African population. As just one example, in 2005–6, of those concentrated in rural areas, three in four of the poorest 20 per cent had inadequate sanitation, over one in three no electricity (Armstrong et al. 2008). Hours of unpaid labour performed by women (e.g., devoted to collecting firewood and water) increase dramatically where access to public services is limited, lacking or disappearing. Besides health risks (spinal damage), these activities' heavy time demands harm children's (notably girls') schooling and social development and adults' labour market activity (UNDP 2011, 58). Moreover, unlike in other sub-Saharan countries large commercial enterprises dominate farming in South Africa. [Thus] it is questionable whether land redistribution, pushed particularly by young ANC militants will produce substantial employment for young people, girls and boys alike.

For Malawi and Zambia the situation of women in agriculture is well documented, and so the next story is relevant for assessing women's position and perspectives in this sector in Mozambique and Angola, too. In Malawian agriculture poverty, gender inequality and food insecurity are inextricably linked, in particular for women. Most smallholder Malawian households are unable to achieve food and income security in an average year; famine often lurks just around the corner. It is estimated that in most years seven in ten households run out of their self-produced food by December, three to four months prior to the harvest. Over half of full-time farmers in Malawi are women. Women grow crops for home consumption to a much larger extent than men, who are more likely to cultivate cash crops. Chores like wood and water collection are more extensively done by women, such that their total hours are higher (Wodon and Beegle 2006; Winters et al. 2008). Against all odds, NGO projects have succeeded in the food security area, notably through training women in agricultural techniques and use of microcredit programs (Republic of Malawi/EC 2007, 15). In Zambia, too, a large majority of women active in farming are in subsistence farming. However, related to market activities, agriculture is the most female-intensive sector; 60 to 70 per cent of the total working time invested in it is female. Yet it is also the least *skill*-intensive sector in the Zambian economy (Fontana 2004, 57).

As in other aspects, in agriculture Zimbabwe is a special case. Its agriculture has suffered heavily from the policies of Mugabe and his cronies. By the early 2000s, with the huge rise in unemployment and consequent male migration from rural areas, rural female-headed households grew ever more common; such households are nearly always the most disadvantaged. Weak support services, lack of credit, and acute shortages of essential inputs also hurt agricultural production (Government of Zimbabwe 2009). Moreover, food relief programmes as a response have been hijacked, with local officials of the ruling party discriminating against members of the opposition and civil society organizations, such as Women of Zimbabwe Arise (WOZA; AI 2007). Even if these despicable practices now belong to the past, due to the effects of climate change food security may well remain a serious problem for some time to come. The official MDG report adds that the decline of agriculture has also had dramatic effects on the country's manufacturing sector and parts of its service sector (Rep of Zimbabwe 2010b, 7).

Basically, the main lines in the country analyses above are supported by analyses in several international publications. All point to continuous chronic undernourishment and food insecurity in large parts of African agriculture; to its vulnerability to climatic extremes and natural disasters and, consequently, to the vulnerability of much rural employment; and to the bad shape of infrastructure and the overall gendered character of poverty and insecurity in rural sub-Saharan Africa – in short, to the fact that girls and women suffer on average more than boys and men (ECA/AU/AfDB/UNDP 2010; World Bank 2011d; UNDESA 2010; ILO 2011b).

In the three largest DFL countries agriculture fares little better than in southern Africa. In Brazil the majority of the four million farms are very small, and many operate at subsistence level. For many families agriculture is no longer a source of even minimal income, and many struggle to supplement it through salaried labour, handicrafts or other small-scale enterprises. About 27 per cent of rural households are female headed – either because the husband has migrated to the city in search of work or because she is a single mother – in a process that can be termed the feminization of rural poverty (UNDP 2007c; Rural Poverty portal/Brazil).

In Indonesia, land fragmentation, poor bureaucracy and infrastructure and other problems may continue to dog its agricultural sector. As the ILO (2009c, 36) stated, "Government expenditures on energy subsidies in Indonesia are approximately six times larger than public investment in agriculture, indicating scope for reallocation of investment that could promote agricultural productivity and beneficial structural change." In India women play a major role in agriculture and are more than equally involved. In the early 2000s, on average about 60 per cent of all agricultural operations were handled exclusively by women. An estimated one in five rural households are de facto female headed. Currently many farmers seem to prefer women workers to men, but a large proportion of women workers in agriculture receive lower wages than men; female hourly wage rates vary from 50 to 60 per cent of male rates. In India, too, farmers receive little government support (Planning Commission 2007).

In summary, for the African DFL countries and Brazil, Indonesia and India, it is categorically unlikely that many young women living in urban areas and trying to make a career can rely on a fallback scenario in which they can return to their families living from agriculture without burdening them heavily. Nor is it likely that things in the CIS countries would really be different. In this respect the continuous employment decrease in agriculture since 1990 in all four countries may give a clue (ILO Laborsta; for Belarus, Pastore and Verashchagina 2007; website Belstat).

Industries: manufacturing

Chapter 4 showed that manufacturing since the present century's start has developed into a limited source of employment for women, the 14 countries less Ukraine contributing fewer than one in five female jobs. A short qualitative overview capturing South Africa, India, Brazil and Indonesia gives a clue to explaining why manufacturing jobs have become a less promising source of employment for women.

In South Africa throughout the 2000s, the main manufacturing areas continued to be metals and engineering, over three in four workers being male. Moreover, there in particular the share of casual, temporary and subcontracted labour rapidly increased, and the growing vulnerability of those in manufacturing jobs obviously made the industry at large less and less attractive for women, in particular for the higher skilled. From 2000 to 2009 the overall female employment share in manufacturing decreased from 37 to 33 per cent (ALRN 2004; SSA 2009a, 2009b). India's labour-intensive industries, including textiles and garment manufacturing, meet strong international competition. Expansion was already hampered by heavy protection, lack of skilled labour and management capabilities and India's crumbling infrastructure. Under such pressure the long-term fall of the real wage rate connects with the continuation of the trend towards informalization and subcontracting to ever lower levels of the value chain. Employment, in so far as it could be maintained in the 2000s, consisted to a large extent of increased hiring of casual and contract workers and of growing exploitation of girls under 18 years of age (Gupta et al. 2008; NCEUS 2009a; website SOMO).

In Brazil in the past decade, mining and manufacturing did not systematically create higher-productivity jobs than the service sector did, though their wage levels remained rather high (Vargas da Cruz et al. 2008). In 2007 over one in four women (across countries a large share) working in Brazilian manufacturing could be found in textiles, garment and leather. Besides catering to a large home market, textiles and adjacent industries have considerable export potential. Electrical and electronics manufacturing contributes quite limitedly – a fraction less than 3 per cent – to female employment in manufacturing (data, ILO Laborsta). Clearly, since the 1980s Brazil's wage levels have been too high to attract substantial foreign investment in labour-intensive industries.

Of all DFL countries Indonesia seems to have –or perhaps have had – the most potential in labour-intensive industries employing many women. In the past decade relocation from urban to rural areas and shifts to production lower in the subcontracting chains of textile, garment, footwear and furniture production were dominant trends, implying for many workers lower wages and higher insecurity. The about two million women still working in these industries make up majorities of those in such vulnerable, casualized and home-based work. Overall, employment in these industries is declining; since 2005 Indonesia's global market share of textile and garment products has fallen, with the country losing out, notably, to China and Vietnam, which have less labour-protection regulation. Their cheap imports add to the pressure on the domestic industry (Lake 2008; De Ruyter and Warnecke 2008; De Ruyter et al. 2009). Early efforts to attract foreign direct investment in electronics to Indonesia met with little success. And already in the 1990s such investment shifted towards more capital-intensive industries, which employ relatively small numbers of mostly men (cf. Lipsey and Sjöholm 2004).

For all our countries, whether export-oriented, labour-intensive manufacturing can be integrated into a sustainable development model that creates decent jobs for (young) women is a serious question. The most sustainable source of industrial employment is likely the manufacturing of local agricultural products. Investigating the conditions under which such agri-based manufacturing can be feminized may be quite worthwhile.

Industries: services

Services at large

It has already been noted that in eight of 13 countries, the share of female employment in services at large is over 50 per cent; this includes the three large countries South Africa (84%), Brazil and Ukraine (both 73%). Due to the large shares of women in community, social and personal services, their female employment shares in commercial services are much lower: respectively, 40 (South Africa), 30 (Brazil) and 26 per cent (Ukraine). In Botswana 32 per cent of women employed are in commercial services; in Indonesia and Kazakhstan, 30 per cent. While in the other CIS countries shares vary between 25 and 28 per cent, they are much lower in India (18%) and in southern Africa (except South Africa and Botswana); in Mozambique, Malawi, Zambia and Zimbabwe they vary from 9 to 13 per cent. At first sight this variation across countries seems to correspond largely with skilled women's shares (ISCED 3–6) in total female employment; they vary from 96 per cent in Azerbaijan and Belarus and 92 per cent in Ukraine, via 46 per cent in Brazil and 21 per cent in India, to only 6 per cent in Malawi and 5 per cent in Mozambique. Indeed, across 13 countries the correlation is high (R = .47) between the share of skilled women and that of women employed in commercial services. Also, from a qualitative perspective the services industry is important; it shows major potential to provide skilled jobs. Again Brazil leads the way. Calculation based on the ILO Laborsta database indicates that in Brazil 90 per cent of women in the three highest-ranked occupational groups worked in services, broadly defined (for details, see Van Klaveren et al. 2009g, Table 10).

It was noted that commerce (wholesale and retail, together with restaurants, hotels and catering), as the largest or second-largest employment category in services at large, is everywhere important for female employment. Detailed figures that allow differentiation between the two subsectors reveal that in the seven countries for which data are available, wholesale and retail is by far the larger employer of the two, with employment about fourfold that of the restaurant etc. subsector in Brazil, Indonesia and Botswana, sevenfold in Ukraine, and over ten times that in Azerbaijan, Kazakhstan and Zambia. Employment in commerce, a recent development, seems to vary considerably across countries. The trade press suggests expansion in most countries, notably Azerbaijan, Kazakhstan and Brazil. However, South Africa's official statistics indicate the opposite. In that country the commerce industry between 1970 and 2007 was the largest employment growth source for men and women alike, but growth ended abruptly between April–June 2007 and April–June 2011, with an overall 13 per cent drop in employment and 20 per cent in female employment (SSA 2011). This drop may well illustrate the vulnerability of commerce when consumer spending comes under pressure in countries touched by the economic crisis.

Wholesale and retail

What are the employment perspectives for young females in the wholesale and, more particularly, the retail trade? In the sub-Saharan countries two contrasting industry and labour trends seem at hand. First, large food chains are making inroads in the informal market; in South Africa they cater to township dwellers. The rise of supermarkets and shopping malls may imply a shift to formal labour and improvements in job quality, but their less labour-intensive character may on balance reduce retail employment. Jointly with the effects of the global crisis and lower consumer spending, that may well explain the employment fall in South Africa. Moreover, in particular for that country the shift to formal and improved work can be questioned. In the 1990s and early 2000s, retail trade employers' casualization and externationalization of labour accelerated. Fluctuations in demand were addressed by having casual workers work irregular hours. In 2003, in an example of a successful workers' mobilization, the SACCAWU union led a company-wide strike against these practices at the Shoprite supermarket chain (Von Holdt and Webster 2008, 342–3). Yet DFL project meeting reports document that these practices continue with expanded intensity to the present, with Shoprite workers recurrently reacting with strikes. In the smaller African countries supermarkets and the like, now and for the next five years, will provide only limited employment to women; their expansion is likely to destroy informal employment in both retail and agriculture. In Zambia and Malawi there is overwhelming evidence that local small-scale food producers have major problems meeting the quality, hygiene and packaging standards set by the supermarkets (website Regoverning markets).

Early in the global financial crisis Indonesia's retail trade showed a development similar to South Africa's. The strong employment growth of 2000–8 ended as retail suffered from falling purchasing power. The rural poor in particular were buying less food (cf. Hussain et al. 2009). Yet from mid-2009 on, fuelled by an extensive official stimulus package, the Indonesian retail, restaurant and hotel subsectors showed a strong recovery. They added more than 650,000 (formal) about a 40 per cent increase – jobs according to simulations – due to the government stimulus (ILO 2011c, 59). Yet at the same time expansion of "modern markets" by mainly multinational food chains culminated in fierce competition, both mutually and with traditional outlets. This expansion has had a significant impact on employment in traditional markets. Moreover, both wage rates and working conditions seem to have deteriorated elsewhere in retailing; in particular, women's working hours have been lengthened (Suryadarma et al 2007; Pandin 2009).

Tourism

In most of the 14 countries the perspectives of young women in the restaurants, hotels and catering subsector, particularly in three of eight targeted occupations (receptionists and housekeepers in hotels and travel agency intermediaries), may depend to a great extent on the development of tourism – sometimes called the leisure sector. In South Africa, Brazil and Ukraine major sports events have pushed or will push international tourism. With eight million international arrivals in 2010, South Africa was one of the fastest-growing tourism destinations in the world. Its hosting the FIFA football World Cup has meant a considerable boost: international tourist arrivals rose 15 per cent and tourism revenues 4 per cent. The World Travel and Tourism Council (WTTC; website) expects long-term growth of tourism to South Africa to average 8.5 per cent yearly over the coming ten years.

This prediction may imply the yearly creation of 80,000 to 100,000 new jobs. Brazil's hosting the 2014 FIFA World Cup 2014 and 2016 Olympic Games is also expected to boost tourism, as similar events did elsewhere. Women may well find considerable employment opportunities at various levels, from room attendants to managerial positions. In Ukraine some push may be expected from the EUFA Euro 2012 football championship, organized jointly with Poland, though the WTTC's long-term projection for Ukraine indicates falling visitor and employment figures (WTTC 2012).

Major events attracting mass tourism are absent from the other DFL countries. For them international tourism may be stimulated if they succeed in catering to the trend towards sustainable, nature-based tourism, emphasizing tourists' respect for the local culture and the environment. A recent survey found that nature-based tourism is one of several conservation mechanisms that can reduce poverty (UNDP 2011, 76). Authorities and travel and accommodation providers in Zambia and elsewhere have taken up the challenge (see Box 6.1). Lack of skills and training may slow the expansion of tourism as in Indonesia, where since the mid-2000s the tourism sector's demand for skilled labour has outstripped supply. The ILO stresses the need for skills development in the archipelago's tourist centres. Training should focus on developing managerial ability, entrepreneurship, information technology, English language capabilities, general business skills and professionalism. However, a majority of respondents to a 2009 opinion leader survey for Indonesia concluded that training is not enough: low wages and unfavourable working conditions may well undermine the formal tourism sector (ILO 2009b).

Box 6.1 Tourism in Livingstone, Zambia

"My name is Agatha. I live here in Livingstone, am single and happily expecting a baby soon! I am a designer and wedding planner and currently working in a bridal shop although my dream is to eventually run my own business[....] A few years ago I had fallen in love with and dated a Japanese tourist/expatriate who was working here for some time, we really loved each other and we planned to relocate to Japan together eventually. However, when people got wind of my relationship, I received very strong criticism especially from my parents who would never hear of it and threatened to disown me if I pursued the relationship. My friends and relatives also condemned me saying all I wanted from this man was money when in fact we were truly in love[....] Livingstone being a tourist destination has a lot of tourists and expatriate people working here and people generally take anyone befriending such people as being gold diggers. I was very hurt over this situation as my relationship had to end in order for me to have peace. I now realise I had the right to make my own decision in this matter." (Agatha, attending a Decisions for Life meeting, Livingstone, Zambia (DFL project website)).

Call centres

Besides tourism, in South Africa the government's 2005 strategic reorientation program (ASGI-SA) identified the call centre industry as demanding special priority attention. Since then, expansion of this subsector seems to have lived up to the authorities' expectations. Earlier estimates hold that about three-fourths of the centres' workforce is female, implying that call centre jobs as a whole make up about one in four women's jobs in business services. From the outset employers in this new industry tried to keep unions and collective bargaining out (Benner et al. 2007), and in the input of South African women to the DFL project, such negative employer attitudes repeatedly came to the fore.

The country with the most impressive call centre story is India (see Box 6.2). It is part of a wider story in which expansion of the IT (information technology) annex of the BPO (business process outsourcing) industry has been the cornerstone of the growth of the country's services sector at large since about 1980. In 2005 Thomas Friedman, in *The World Is Flat*, gave stunning examples of sophisticated business activities outsourced (or to be so) from the USA – market research activities, reading of CAT scans by doctors in India or "having your own personal remote executive assistant" in India. Friedman noted that India had nearly a quarter-million men and women involved in call centre work; low-wage, low-prestige jobs in America, when shifted to India, became high-wage, high-prestige jobs (Friedman 2005, 24, 31). Offshoring activities of US- and Europe-based multinationals in India cannot belittle the rise of an impressive Indian IT/BPO industry. Industry leaders claim that the spread effects of this development are massive, in terms of both employment and innovation. They claim that India's IT innovations in banking, retail, education, telecom and commodities are creating truly mass access to IT facilities, even in the most remote rural villages, via text messaging including weather forecasts and agricultural information (cf. Nilekani 2008, 110–12). Others maintain that India's IT industry is highly urbancentric and use of IT is confined to large modern organizations. They question whether IT/BPO outsourcing can form the basis for a genuine, sustainable Indian service sector with employment spreading beyond the few cities where international centres are located (cf. Papola 2008; Taylor et al. 2010).

Box 6.2 Indian call centres

Pay is a major issue in Indian call centres. Remuneration tends to be higher for back-office employees than for voice-based agents; MNCs (multinational corporations) tend to pay more than Indian third-party providers, and both considerably more than domestic outsourcers. Work pressure is another hot issue. According to an employee survey, two-thirds of respondents reported that they were either "very" or "quite" pressurized as a result of their work on a normal day; respondents in the domestic segment and women were more likely to report being under pressure. Handling outbound calls was more likely to be a source of pressure. Working times were a prominent issue for employees, too: back-office work is conducted during Indian daytime, while voice processes in international centres are synchronised to customers' times in the various English-speaking geographies served. The North American market accounts for perhaps 70 per cent of Indian BPOs' overseas business; Europe, principally the UK, accounts for around 20 per cent. The result is a multiplicity of shift patterns, which further fragment the construction of BPO work as a unified experience. "In sum, this brief profile indicates that union organising efforts will have to engage with an industry and a workforce that are internally differentiated in important respects" (Taylor et al. 2010, a study undertaken for the Union of Information Technology Enabled Services Professionals (UNITES), a trade union involved in the DFL project).

Health care

For the nine of 14 countries for which data are available, the health care and social work share of female employment varies widely: 0.4 per cent in Malawi, 1.1 per cent in Indonesia, 1.7 per cent in India; four countries (South Africa, Brazil, Azerbaijan and Kazakhstan) have shares between 6 and 7 per cent; Ukraine exceptionally has over 17 per cent of all females employed in health. Not surprisingly, it has also the highest share of females in health and social work (82%), though in Azerbaijan and Kazakhstan (also Brazil) nearly eight in ten health and social workers are women. With nearly six of ten, Indonesia is in the middle. Considering these shares, Indian health care is quite an exception, with less than three in ten employed being female.

A recent study of the health care industry gives insight into wage levels and their distribution among 16 health care occupations in a range of countries, including five of our countries. It shows that those with the highest median wage levels are medical doctors in Brazil, South Africa and India, pharmacists in Belarus and dentists in Ukraine. In the latter two countries health care managers rank second, whereas in the first three they rank much lower, in positions four to eight. Female-dominated occupations are at the bottom of the wage distribution. In Belarus, Ukraine and India nurses rank lowest, whereas in Brazil and South Africa clerical staffers are found there. Community health workers rank next-to-lowest in Brazil, Ukraine and India and only slightly higher in Belarus and South Africa. The wage dispersion across the 16 health care occupations, defined as the ratio of the highest to the lowest median earnings, is highest in Brazil (7.0) and lowest in Belarus (3.3; Tijdens and De Vries 2012).

Public administration and defence

In some developing countries the times are obviously changing, yet public administration and defence are nearly everywhere still a man's world. The public service will not grow to compete with commercial services in the labour market for skilled young women so long as its male-dominated character is preserved. For the time being, in the ten countries where detailed employment figures are available, female shares of public administration and defence remain below total female shares in community, social and personal services. That difference is in most countries considerable, except in Ukraine (67% against 72% for the sector at large) and Mozambique (39% against 40%).

In India and Indonesia in particular, female shares in public administration lag behind equivalent shares in community, social and personal services and in the economy at large. The conclusion is not exaggerated that in these two countries public service remains a male bulwark par excellence. In Indonesia civil service downsizing has been detrimental to women: between 1997 and 2008 their already small share decreased from 22 to 20 per cent (based on ILO Laborsta). Moreover, the female share in the civil service's higher ranks (echelons I-IV) is only 11 per cent (Schech and Mustafa 2010).

In India the low female share in the public sector increased only slightly in the last decade, from 15 per cent in 2000 to 17 per cent in 2007, the last year for which data are available (Government of India 2010). Central government especially remains a male bulwark. The best opportunities for young women applying for jobs as public servants may be in regional and local government, especially where, supported by World Bank and NGOs, rural development and empowerment programs take off. In 2005 regional government staff contained 22 per cent women, local staff 37 per cent (ILO Laborsta).

In Brazil as elsewhere, political decisions on expansion of the public service and appointment of high-ranking public officers may have favoured men in large part. Yet recently the Brazilian public service has shown the potential to absorb many skilled women. In 2007 over 45 per cent (more than 700,000 females) could be found at the three highest occupational levels (based on ILO Laborsta). The expectation seems justified that adoption of equal opportunities legislation by Brazilian public bodies will contribute to many young women's entry into public service in the years to come.

7
Governance, Labour Relations, Union Organization – and the Internet

Introduction

This chapter's focus is the institutional framework important for young women's perspectives on work. It discusses governance and labour market institutions in the 14 countries and strategies and activities for empowering women, including women's rights and labour rights. Labour relations and union organization, including women's position in trade unions, are discussed. With communication and new media, including social media, of growing importance for empowering girls and young women, perspectives on Internet use by them and on their behalf – including the Internet freedom issue – as well as use of print media, TV, radio, mobile phones; mobile Internet and broadband are covered.

The (re)regulation debate

Since its foundation in 1919, the ILO has aimed for a minimum set of labour regulations. Over the past century almost 200 ILO conventions have been agreed. Countries are called on to ratify the conventions and implement them in their national labour regulations. In the early 2000s, following neoclassical views on labour markets, the World Bank started a discussion in favour of deregulation. Its "Doing Business" study quantified and ranked countries' labour regulatory systems. The deregulation narrative concentrated predominantly on setting a minimum wage, which, it was suggested, negatively affected employment growth, and on regulation of working time and employment protection measures, too. The basic argument was that these regulations, favouring "insiders" over "outsiders", hampered young people's entry in the labour market. This study elicited a strong ILO counter-reaction, expressed among others places in its Regulating Decent Work Network (Lee and McCann 2011).

The side of the ILO and researchers cooperating with it argued, first, that the deregulation position did not take ILO's message of setting minimum standards for decent work into account. Second, the position of the World Bank was hardly based on sound empirical research. The bank's research, focused on the minimum wage's impact on employment, leant selectively on outcomes of this research strand. Other relevant topics had been investigated to a far lesser extent, and discussion concerning compliance with national labour regulations had gained little attention. By contrast, within the network the role of the Labour Inspectorates had been discussed extensively (cf. Berg 2011; Pires 2011). Anyway, the re-regulation discourse stimulated discussion on the effectiveness of labour regulation (see Box 7.1), including the limitations of its functioning in low-income countries – an important issue throughout this volume.

Box 7.1 Constraints on Indonesian trade unions

Ratifying ILO's core conventions, as, for example, Indonesia did, does not guarantee labour legislation in which enforcement and compliance are well addressed. The ITUC, as well as Indonesian labour lawyers, remain highly critical of elements of its labour legislation, in particular their enforcement. Critics note that, though private sector workers are by law free to form unions and draw up their own rules, a court can dissolve a trade union if, for instance, its basic principles conflict with the *Pancasila*. In a recent overview of violations of trade union rights, the ITUC concluded that the government of Indonesia continued to undermine worker rights by failing to enforce labour laws effectively. Unions that attempted to enforce their basic contractual or statutory rights by resorting to strikes found that the government ignored the flagrant violations of law by employers and declared the strikes illegal (Suryomenggolo 2008; ITUC 2011c).

Empowering women: activities

In accord with the introductory remarks in on empowerment Chapter 1, let us look at activities of women's organizations in a number of DFL countries, especially in trying to influence government policies and women's political representation – even to change processes on a national scale. Notably in South Africa and Brazil, these activities are embedded in a vivid and continuously developing civil society, while in other countries openly empowering women is still in its infancy and sometimes perceived as suspect by authorities.

In South Africa after the fall of apartheid, many new social movements emerged. They have contributed substantially to the government's shift, in the 2000s, towards pro-poor economic policies (Padayachee and Valodia 2008). Many movements maintain a complex relationship with the nationalist movement's mainstream based on the anti-apartheid struggle; such is definitely true of South Africa's women's movement. Its organizations cover a wide spectrum, from those with limited autonomy within broader struggles against oppression (e.g., the ANC Women's League) to those undertaking more independent action (Hassim 2006). Representation of women in politics is a major issue. The July 2009 general elections raised women's representation in parliament to 43 per cent, up 9 per cent from the 2004 general elections and close to targets set by the Protocol on Gender and Development of the Southern African Development Community (SADC) for achieving 50 per cent in all decision-making areas by 2015. The campaign for the protocol's adoption, ratification and implementation is run by the Southern African Gender Protocol Alliance, a collective of over 40 national and regional gender NGOs in 13 countries (Genderlinks website).

Other southern African countries have also seen the development of a strong civil society in which women's organizations play major roles. They make growing use of the Internet. Mozambique had a forerunner in Forum Mulher, the country's main civil organization connected with women's issues. In 2007 Forum Mulher ran a website with links to sites run by organizations that offered women legal advice (Van den Bergh-Collier 2007, 61). Under the women's movement's pressure, in 2008 Botswana's government and in 2009 Mozambique's government passed laws to protect women from violence, including domestic violence (UNDP 2010b, 30).

Brazil is a highly interesting case of dual influence of organized women. Though women's representation in politics has over the years been rather modest, Brazil has a vibrant women's movement, which uses the participatory governance structure operating in parallel to Brazil's representative democratic system. At each of government's three tiers, sectoral secretariats –for health, education, women, the environment – are obliged to hold regular conferences to engage with civil organizations in shaping and monitoring public policies. These conferences offer significant opportunities for social movements to engage with the state, composed as they are of 50 per cent representatives of organized civil society and 50 per cent state representatives. More than once, many thousands of women have been involved in preparing proposals for legislation (Alcântara 2008).

The position of independent women's organizations seems particularly difficult in Zimbabwe, Azerbaijan and Belarus. Quite often these countries' authorities, to cover up denial of women's rights, use bureaucratic measures and paper declarations. For example, Belarus has signed the optional Protocol referring to the Convention on the Elimination of All Forms of Discrimination against Women. On 3 September 2008 the Council of Ministers approved the National Action Plan for Gender Equality 2008–10. However, funds for execution of the plan were not allocated. Moreover, the Council of Equal Women's Status includes, besides government officials, only one representative of a women's organization. The plan, as a bureaucratic exercise, failed to actually improve women's status. In spite of a considerable female share, the parliament hardly contributed in tackling gender-based discrimination (Mitskevich 2010). Even worse, the repression following the December 2010 protests turned vehemently anti-female. Numerous detained women reported that they were threatened with rape while in custody (US Dept of State 2011c). On the other hand (at least from the outside), progressive politics are no guarantee for a strong representation of women in politics. In "enlightened Botswana" that representation is remarkably weak, with by 31 December 2011 women in parliament numbering fewer than 8 per cent (IPU website) – the lowest share in the 14 countries.

Seizing *and* keeping a role in change processes are complicated affairs for women's organizations. Indonesia poses a clear example. In 1998 protests against the Suharto regime took the form of a broad pro-democracy reform movement *(reformasi)* that led to the president's resignation. The movement consisted of many societal groups, including several women's organizations. Soaring consumer prices brought both poor and middle-class women onto the streets of Jakarta under the shared identity of *Suara Ibu Peduli* (SIP, Voice of Concerned Mothers). They not only responded to rising poverty and violence against women but also raised national and international awareness of the problems women workers faced (Ford and Parker 2008; Schech and Mustafa 2010). Yet the decade that followed made clear that *reformasi* was an unfinished project, not least concerning the position of women at various levels. As for political representation, the Electoral Law passed in February 2003 suggested a quota system, calling on parties to select women for at least 30 per cent of the candidate slots. However, in December 2008 the Indonesian Constitutional Court effectively abolished the party ranking list. The court's verdict did not legally abolish the quota system but rendered it virtually useless (Ardani and Kanadi 2009). In spite of this setback, women's share in the House of Representatives grew from under 9 per cent after the reform era's first general elections (1999) to 18.2 per cent in the 2009 elections.

Women's rights

The past decades have seen a global consensus that women's rights concern equal rights for men and women and that these are an essential part of human rights. In 1979 the UN General Assembly adopted the Convention on the Elimination of All Forms of Discrimination against Women (CEDAW), often described as an international bill of rights for women. It defines what constitutes discrimination against women and sets up an agenda for national action to end it. In 1995 the UN Fourth World Conference on Women in Beijing reaffirmed that rights for women and girls were human rights and that they should be respected by all international institutions, national governments and civil society. The Beijing conference developed a groundbreaking analysis of the impact of the many economic and social factors that result in the disempowerment and poverty of women throughout the world (ITUC 2009b).

The ILO Core Labour Standards are a set of four fundamental rights, universal and indivisibly human, ensuring freedom of association and protection of the right to organize, freedom from forced labour, freedom from child labour and freedom from discrimination at work. These standards are regarded as human rights by all other parts of the United Nations. All four are important for women, but particularly the fourth. In addition to the standards, representatives of governments, employers and workers in the ILO draw up conventions. These are important because they set a global reference frame for national labour laws. Once a convention is agreed, countries are expected to adapt their national legislation to accord with it. The main ILO conventions that provide instruments for promoting gender equality relate to equal remuneration, discrimination (employment and occupation), workers with family responsibilities and maternity protection at work. As shown in Table 7.1, by early 2012 all 14 DFL countries had ratified conventions 100 and 111, but only two did so for conventions 156 (ratified by Azerbaijan and Ukraine), and 183 (by Azerbaijan and Belarus; see Table 7.2).

Table 7.1 Ratification of ILO conventions by March 2012

Convention no.	100	111	117	156	171	175	177	183
Title	**Equal remuneration**	**Discrimination**	**Social policy**	**Workers with family response.**	**Night work**	**Part-time work**	**Home work**	**Maternity protection**
Year	**1950**	**1958**	**1962**	**1981**	**1990**	**1994**	**1996**	**2000**
Angola	1976	1976	–	–	–	–	–	–
Azerbaijan	1992	1992	–	2010	–	–	–	2010
Belarus	1956	1961	–	–	–	–	–	2004
Botswana	1997	1997	–	–	–	–	–	–
Brazil	1957	1965	1969	–	2002	–	–	–
India	1958	1960	–	–	–	–	–	–
Indonesia	1958	1999	–	–	–	–	–	–
Kazakhstan	2001	1999	–	–	–	–	–	–
Malawi	1965	1965	–	–	–	–	–	–
Mozambique	1977	1977	–	–	–	–	–	–
South Africa	2000	1997	–	–	–	–	–	–
Ukraine	1956	1961	–	2000	–	–	–	–
Zambia	1972	1979	1964		–	–	–	–
Zimbabwe	1989	1999	–	–	–	–	–	–

Source: ILO website, ILOLEX database, last accessed 10 March 2012.

Table 7.2 Ratification year of the four ILO conventions important to women

	Conv. 100: Equal remuneration (1950)	**Conv. 111: Discrimination convention (1958)**	**Conv. 156: Workers with family responsibilities (1981)**	**Conv. 183: Maternity protection (2000)**
Angola	1976	1976	–	–
Azerbaijan	1992	1992	2010	2010
Belarus	1956	1961	–	2004
Botswana	1997	1997	–	–
Brazil	1957	1965		–
India	1958	1960	–	–
Indonesia	1958	1999	–	–
Kazakhstan	2001	1999	–	–
Malawi	1965	1965	–	–
Mozambique	1977	1977	–	–
South Africa	2000	1997	–	–
Ukraine	1956	1961	2000	–
Zambia	1972	1979		–
Zimbabwe	1989	1999	–	–

Source: ILO website, ILOLEX database; last accessed 27 January 2012.

Union organization

At least two requirements have to be met if trade unions are to be able to adequately defend workers' rights and interests: first, a minimum level of trade union organization, or union density, in the country, industry or company in question; second, a solid union building where internal democracy rules and the various layers of members are well represented. For the first aspect, union densities in the 14 countries are studied. Next follows a snapshot of debates on women's position in the unions before going into successes in unions' internal and external operations linked with the DFL project.

Based on the ITUC's March 2011 registration concerning membership of their affiliates and non-affiliates, union densities for the 14 countries can be calculated (Table 7.3). Given that trade unions predominantly organize workers in formal employment, density is computed for the formal labour force; its rate varies from 18 per cent in Botswana and Brazil to 70 per cent in Zambia. For seven countries the table's last column shows female union density rates, revealing it as 60 to 90 per cent of the overall density – notably excepting Botswana, where female density seems higher than the total rate.

Table 7.3 Trade union membership (2010–11) and density (most recent years)

	Members of ITUC-affiliated trade unions (× 1,000)	Members of non-ITUC-affiliated trade unions (× 1,000)	Total membership (× 1,000)	Total TU density (formal labour) (%)	Female TU density (%)
Mozambique	90	100	190	20	17
Angola	267	30	300	28	20
South Africa	2,470	300	3,300	24	20
Zambia	400	0	400	70	54
Botswana	56	0	56	18	22
Malawi	200	10	210	25	15
Zimbabwe	242	0	242	40	?
Ukraine	9,098	0	9,100	55	?
Azerbaijan	735	0	735	37	?
Kazakhstan	–	2,400	2,400	45	?
Belarus	10	?	?	4*	?
Brazil	10,915	200	11,000	18	16
India	15,246	15,800	31,000	60	?
Indonesia	1,339	8,700	10,000	30	?

Note: * independent union.

Source: ITUC (March 2011; × 1,000 members); Van Klaveren et al. 2009a, b, c, d, e, f, g; Muneku and Phiri 2011; Lentsie 2011; Chinguwo 2011.

For some countries detailed union densities by gender, industry or occupational group are available. In South Africa the female union density has stayed 6 to 7 percentage points behind the male rate. Organized women, including black women, are relatively highly educated. In 2003 nearly half of unionized African women were teachers or nurses (Casale and Posel 2009), though these occupational groups contribute only about 13 per cent to the female workforce. Notably, unions affiliated with the COSATU confederation have made efforts to organize women in low-skilled, often informal jobs, as in clothing production, retail, security and contract cleaning. In 2009 and 2010 waves of strikes took place in public services, including hospitals and schools, as well as in retail firms (ITUC 2011c). Reaching out to informal workers and retaining them as union members clearly continues to be a hard task. Partly this has to do with self-imposed policy limitations: South African mainstream unions do not organize self-employed workers (Ordor 2011). Estimates for 2010, based on dispersed union information, showed the union density in the formal sector at 30 per cent, against about 4 per cent in the informal sector.

In Brazil the union density pattern by industry – including informal workers – partly confirms the international pattern, with utilities (2007, 35%), education and social services (29%) and public administration (26%) relatively well organized. Surprisingly high are densities among agricultural wage earners (25% in 2007) and among transport and communication workers (24%). By contrast, union density in commerce was less than 11 per cent (IBGE 2008). Based on various sources the estimate for women's union density is, at 15 to 16 per cent, slightly lower than the overall 18 per cent.

In several of the countries selected for the DFL campaign, trade unions encounter a hostile environment when they try to organize. A short anthology may suffice (ITUC 2011c, also for more cases). In Zimbabwe trade unionists face constant harassment, including physical violence and prosecution. In Belarus, too, union leaders are routinely harassed, blackmailed and arrested, and in Ukraine there have been numerous violations of trade union rights in recent years. In Indonesia union rights are not well protected in law and even less so in practice. Many Indian states restrict union rights in law, many employers are explicitly hostile to unions and recent years have seen numerous incidents of police-sponsored violence against trade union officials. Collective bargaining remains low profile in Indonesia, largely by necessity. Nevertheless, over the years there have been successes in organizing women workers and in collective bargaining, particularly for female workers in Indonesia. The hotel sector offers hopeful examples. For example, collective agreements for hotels in Jakarta and Bandung with local unions in the hotel workers' federation affiliated with the IUF global union and negotiated by women's committees include policies regarding sexual harassment and procedures for handling the issue; extension of health insurance to cover husbands or partners and children of women workers; a comprehensive wage scale, bringing transparency concerning equal pay; lactation rooms at the workplace for breastfeeding female employees; flexible working hours for breastfeeding women (IUF website).

Decisions for Life and the position of women in unions

Within the DFL project women's position in trade unions was addressed quite often. Though not an explicit project goal, the problems of organizing women and of organized women in unions elicited continuous discussions in DFL teams, because women felt underrepresented in the trade unions' higher ranks, because they could not influence union decision-making as they would like to and because trajectories for translating demands for women's right into collective bargaining agreements were taking too long. In March 2010 in Maputo, at the DFL midterm meeting of the African and Brazilian project partners, female union officials and activists at union and confederation levels considered the project an opportunity to strengthen their positions. In southern Africa they had promoted the project in such a way that it became part of mainstream union policies within six months of its March 2009 introduction. Paid officials and lay activists alike considered this achievement a unique event in trade union history (see Box 7.2).

The DFL project was not the first to discover the need for strengthening the position of women in trade unions. Gatherings and publications on the subject have piled up (though hardly focusing on the position of *young* women), even for our countries. For example, a study of Indonesia shed light on the generally weak position of women in the unions. If women are represented in union structures, the study showed, they are generally relegated to the "traditional" women's positions: deputy secretaries or treasurers. Women tend to be excluded from major decision-making processes (Ford and Parker 2008). A study of unions in Botswana pointed at underrepresentation of females in the union hierarchy. The Botswana Secondary Teachers Union, for instance, is 67 per cent female but only 27 per cent of the executive committee is female. Similarly, in the 65 per cent female Botswana Teachers Union men hold all five strategic leadership positions (Lentsie 2011).

Box 7.2 Trade union organizing

"It is energizing, stimulating, inspiring and motivating to work with these young women. They have no trade union baggage, they are not fighting for position within. They are what the trade union needs. We mentors are grooming them to take over. If we fail to do this, the position of gender coordinator that I hold lands in the danger zone. You must not forget that union leadership is male dominated. Therefore we must also fight for our own positions within the union if we want to continue helping victimized young women workers." (Patricia Nyman, national gender coordinator SACCAWU, SA service sector trade union, midterm DFL meeting, Maputo, 22–26 March 2010.)

In spite of major difficulties, with unions often functioning under conditions summed up above, the DFL project undertook many initiatives to involve women in trade union work and to organize female workers (see Box 7.3). In Angola the National Women's Committee has been included in the UNTA-CS union confederation. The committee took an active part in the project, using it to strengthen its activities for more (and more decent) women's employment as well as improving legal rights for women in the informal sector, such as domestic workers. In Zimbabwe no less than about 2.1 million of the estimated 3 million-strong informal sector workforce by 2009 had joined the Zimbabwe Chamber of Informal Economy Associations (ZCIEA), created in 2004 by the ZCTU union confederation. ZCTU and ZCIEA have a formal cooperation agreement. ZCIEA's over 100 chapters are spread across Zimbabwe. The associations, representing street vendors, service workers, artists and many more, try to facilitate their work. One of ZCIEA' s primary goals is to make government harassment and brutality of informal workers cease and to show them how to exercise their rights (information ITUC).

In Kazakhstan workers in small and medium-sized trade and catering enterprises founded two grassroots unions. Self-employed market traders, hotel workers and media workers were targeted for training focused primarily on women's and trade union rights. Then women in these areas decided they wanted to create their own unions and organize others (ITUC 2011a). In Indonesia the DFL team improved the position of the Equality Commission at the confederation level. Once they were not consulted on policies; now they make policies. In Belarus self-employed women market traders had tried to create a trade union, Vmeste, but were repeatedly refused recognition by the authorities. The DFL team from the independent confederation BKDP decided it was time to find ways to get round the problem. A campaign team member, along with activists working with about 3,000 women traders in the Gomel region, decided to first register as an NGO in order to legally organize activities for self-employed workers. The plan is to work in stages to turn the NGO into a union. In Brazil the DFL team negotiated 50 new collective agreements with gender-sensitive clauses by the end of the campaign (all cases, ITUC 2011b).

Box 7.3 Decisions for Life organizing

"Decisions for Life has provided a platform to bring victimized girls together for the first time. We organize meetings for maximum 25 girls in a safe environment where they can exchange their embarrassing experiences, bring them out into the open. That in itself is a great relief. Knowing that they are not the only ones boosts their self-confidence. We also hear many domestic violence in this way." (Patricia Nyman, national gender coordinator SACCAWU, SA service sector trade union, midterm DFL meeting, Maputo, 22–26 March 2010)

"Decisions for Life helps women in the trade union to positions of leadership and to mobilize the rank and file. From my position I survey the activities of affiliated unions nationwide. The issues raised by DFL filter down through union officials to shop stewards and the shop floors. Each quarter, after working hours at local confederation offices so-called labour forums are organized to debate conditions at the workplace, sexual harassment, legal protection and combining work with family responsibilities. These are public debates, not just for union members. Such labour forums are held in each of 35 affiliates in different industries." (Fiona Gandiwa Magaya, women and gender coordinator, ZCTU (Zimbabwe Congress of Trade Unions), DFL midterm meeting, Maputo, 22–26 March 2010)

Communication, new media, social media

Adequate modern communication facilities are absolutely essential for a project such as Decisions for Life, which aims to involve girls and young women (see Box 7.4). The term "digital natives" has been coined to describe the generation born after roughly 1980. Its members share a global culture of digital technology, affecting interaction with information technologies and information itself, as well as how they relate to one another, other people and institutions (UNICEF 2011). Obviously, not all young people fall into this category. Lacking access to technologies, electricity and related infrastructure and lacking skills, especially literacy, hampers participation in the Information Technology age. This section discusses traditional media, as well as Internet access, access to mobile phones, broadband subscriptions, the use of social media, and the digital divide.

Box 7.4 Using social media in Brazil

"In the Decisions for Life workshops we have been focusing on explaining the different conditions for men and women in the workplaces[....] Many young women work in the informal sector, and they struggle to get a decent job in the formal sector[....] In Brazil the traditional social media website has been Orkut, but now more and more people are using Facebook, so this is where we will focus our efforts. Orkut is no longer recruiting new members, but Facebook is. I am a member of the Decisions for Life Facebook page, and I can now easily inform myself about what is happening in the campaign. Facebook also has features that don't exist on Orkut, like causes for example. Other social media we use are YouTube, Twitter and MSN." (Jardelia Rodrigues, Training Secretary at the Brazilian trade union confederation CUT, Rio Grande de Sul region, Brazil (Decisions for Life project website))

Print media, TV and radio

For centuries the written word has been the most common medium of communication. Yet as elsewhere, in the DFL countries the written word is rapidly losing importance, especially for our target group. In South Africa, however, print media recently showed some growth. Their reaching out to 52 per cent of the population in 2010 is most likely the highest of the 14 countries (source: South African Advertising Research Foundation). In 2011 Brazilians consumed on average 44 million copies of newspapers a day, a record, equivalent to over 22 per cent of the population (Barbosa 2012). In the other countries print media circulation is much lower.

Television and radio outreach is much larger. In some DFL countries they remain important and influence people's opinions and behaviour. In South Africa, for example, despite the high penetration of the written press, the majority of the population receives news through broadcasts from the government-owned SABC (South African Broadcasting Corporation) and community radio stations. SABC broadcasts in the country's 11 official languages and owns and controls the majority of television and radio outlets. In 2008 the SABC signal reached 92 per cent of the population, with a viewership share of 66 per cent over the age of 16 (US Dept of State 2011k). In Brazil television is an extremely popular amusement and news medium. In 2007 well over nine of ten households (95%) had a TV set, an even higher share than the 88 per cent of households possessing a radio (IBGE 2008). Brazil has over 2,400 radio and about 180 TV stations, most of them commercial (Britannica Online website). In Indonesia 95 per cent of households have TV coverage, but radio is the most popular medium. The country has over 800 radio and 65 TV stations. In India, with more than 312 radio and 562 TV stations (Britannica Online website), the emancipatory force of exposure to cable television is considerable, notably in rural areas. Thorough research on effects of cable TV's introduction into villages shows that it reduces preference for sons and fertility and increases female autonomy and school enrolment – despite there being few explicitly targeted appeals or none, such as socially oriented programming (Jensen and Oster 2006).

Mobile phones

Mobile (or cell) phone use has spread with phenomenal speed both globally and in our 14 countries. Compared with expansion of fixed telephony and the Internet, growth of mobile phone use from 1990

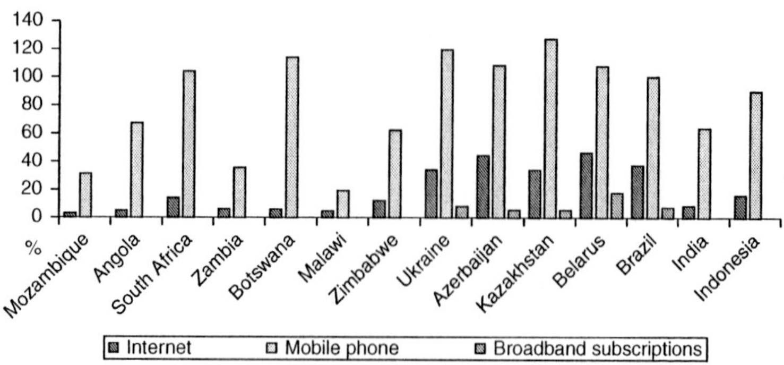

Figure 7.1 Inhabitants (%) with access to the Internet (2010–11), having a mobile phone (2010) and having broadband subscriptions (2010)

Source: ITU 2011, for the Internet and mobile phone; UNCTAD 2011a, for broadband subscriptions.

to 2004 was less hindered by political constraints or high political risks (Andonova and Diaz-Serrano 2009); this pattern is expected to continue. As Figure 7.1 shows, in 2010 the share of the population with a mobile phone varied in the DFL countries: 19 per cent in Malawi, nearly 100 per cent in Brazil, even over 100 per cent (i.e., more than one mobile phone per inhabitant) in South Africa and the CIS countries. Malawi clearly lags here. Even in Mozambique, mobile phone coverage more than doubled, from 3.3 million in 2007 to 7.2 million in 2010, or from nearly one in six to nearly one in three inhabitants. Brazil has been an early adapter and regional leader in the spread of both mobile telephony and the Internet. Between 2003 and 2008 mobile phone use tripled there. Remarkably, though many of Brazil's regional inequalities die hard, the initial advantage of its industrialized Southeast has largely been levelled out: in 2006–7 the North and Northeast showed the largest increases in the percentage of households with access to mobile phone services (IBGE 2008).

In India the number of fixed telephone lines has decreased since the mid-2000s, whereas in the period 2007–10 mobile phone users tripled. Actually, 14 million mobile phones are added each month to India's total. The CIS countries inherited an outdated telecom network requiring modernization at independence from the Soviet Union (1991). In Kazakhstan the initial task was renewing and expanding the fixed telephone network. In this huge country the future focus is on cellular telephone services, though providing the population with mobile cellular networks will be far from easy. In 2010, with 1,274 mobile phone users per 1,000 inhabitants, Kazakhstan had the highest penetration rate of our countries. Worldwide, basic network coverage is hardly a problem: by late 2009 mobile networks covered roughly 89 per cent of the population of low- and middle-income countries (GSMA/ Cherie Blair Foundation 2009, 13).

Besides the availability of network infrastructure, the price basket influences how many people buy access to mobile phones, how often they use them and for how many minutes. In the late 2000s, particularly in developing countries, the market witnessed a trend to seize low-end market segments. In India mobile phone providers discovered the countryside as a huge potential outlet. In rural areas they offer mobile phones for about US$15, and subscriptions start with one-minute calls for US$0.10. Text message (SMS) information can be highly useful in daily life. As noted earlier, one of the largest Indian providers started to offer farmers text message services with weather forecasts, market prices, and other agricultural information. Large numbers of mobile operators compete for low-income customers by decreasing tariffs and offering cheaper handsets. Between 2008 and 2010 the price basket for mobile phones worldwide has fallen from 3.9 to 3.4 per cent of per capita income (ITU 2011). In Mozambique, with prepayment available in amounts as little as US$2.50, cellular phones are now accessible to large parts of the population, including women (Van den Bergh-Collier 2007, 59). Mozambique displayed an example of the use of mobile phone text messaging as a way to foster mobilization during the food protests in September 2010. The authorities reacted by disabling the local mobile phone-texting system and subsequently required all purchasers and owners of prepaid mobile phones to register with the providers (US Dept of State 2011j).

Compared with computers, mobile phones have several advantages. Not needing a regular power supply, they can be used on the street and in other places. They are easily stored and hidden from prying eyes, have low entry and maintenance costs and are an all-in-one communication device, FM radio, camera and calculator. Mobile phones have such non-voice uses as text and picture messaging, Internet access and mobile money transfer (UNCTAD 2011a), but these advanced features are not found in the entry-level mobile handsets widely used in developing countries. Yet with the speed of technological developments, new generations of mobile phones might affordably offer this range of services. Hopefully, poorer households will also be able to afford the Internet data fees.

Mobile phones and the gender gap

The mobile phone adoption rate varies hugely, from country to country, between rural and urban areas, rich and poor, young and old and between the sexes. For the time being, the gender gap in access to and use of mobile phones is worldwide. Millions of women still miss the benefits of mobile phone technology. In low and middle-income countries in 2008 about 300 million fewer females than males were mobile phone subscribers. In South Asia women were 37 per cent less likely to own a mobile phone; in Africa, 23 per cent. Household income, of course, influences women's mobile phone ownership. In low and middle-income countries every additional US$100 of monthly income increases the likelihood of mobile phone ownership by 13 per cent. The other major factor is whether a woman lives in an urban or a rural area; globally, urban women are twice as likely to own a phone as rural women. Girls and young women are keen to use the new technology. Females between 14 and 27 show the highest rates of mobile phone ownership among women; where they do not own a phone, they are prepared to borrow one from someone who does. Also, much more than older women, a majority of them see using a mobile phone as easy or very easy (GSMA/Cherie Blair Foundation 2009).

For young women the mobile phone is an opportunity to get empowered: to feel safer and more secure, to stay in contact with peers and family; to save time with quick communication, to gain access to relevant information, and to improve their value on the labour market. Obviously, without modern technological skills they will often be at a disadvantage in the workplace. Surveys and more scattered evidence demonstrate that these opportunities are not mere castles in the air. According to a 2008 survey in four developing countries (Bolivia, Egypt, India, Kenya), 41 per cent of women 14 to 74 reported increased income and professional opportunities from owning a mobile phone; 85 per cent claimed to feel more independent (GSMA/Cherie Blair Foundation 2009, 21). Quite a few projects of international organizations and NGOs are using the potential of mobile phones, including text messaging, to empower women. A project in Pakistan, for example, used them to regularly send out SMS messages on a variety of topics to help maintain and improve the literacy of 250 young females who completed a basic literacy programme (GSMA/Cherie Blair Foundation 2009, 19). In India one of the objectives of the Self-Employed Women's Association (SEWA) is to achieve livelihood security for its members, with enhancing women's bargaining position one mechanism towards the goal. The mobile phone proves an excellent tool for this purpose. A survey revealed that already in 2009 nearly a third of the 600,000 SEWA members in the Gujarat state owned mobile phones. Said a member from Gujarat SEWA "I can immediately call the wholesale market to inquire about prices and place direct orders. I have eliminated the middleman. I am now recognized as a businesswoman, growing and selling sesame seeds, and not just as somebody's wife or sister" (GSMA/Cherie Blair Foundation 2009, 11, 41).

Mobile internet and broadband

In the past years devices for accessing the Internet have proliferated. The days of a personal computer (PC) being the main Internet access device are clearly numbered. Until recently differences across countries in the penetration of both PCs and the Internet could largely be explained by differences in per capita income and years of education, the latter largely connected with the first. Differences in legal development and urbanization added to that explanation. For the spread of PCs particularly rather large differences persist between high-income and developing countries: the so-called global digital divide (cf. Chinn and Fairlie 2010; Robison and Crenshaw 2010). Concerning Internet usage, these factors may weaken in years to come due to technological developments and related pricing. Mobile devices designed to go online at high-speed, notably smart phones and tablet computers, are increasingly popular. From 2010 on, growth of Internet access has largely stemmed from Internet usage via mobile phone. For example, Opera, a popular browser for low-end Internet-enabled handsets, particularly in developing countries, reported 90 million users in January 2011, up 80 per cent in one year (UNCTAD 2011a).

For fast Internet access broadband is gaining increasing attention. At the end of 2010, there were an estimated 527 million fixed broadband subscriptions worldwide. However, the global digital divide was tangible here, with fewer than one million fixed broadband subscriptions in the least developed countries. In Zambia, for example, no mobile broadband services had been launched by December 2010 (UNCTAD 2011a, Table II.5). In contrast, Belarus is one of three top-performing non-developed economies in this field, with fast-growing fixed broadband connections. Wireless broadband holds significant potential for boosting high-speed Internet access in developing economies (UNCTAD 2011a). In the ITU's (International Telecommunication Union) development index (IDI), one subindex measures use of broadband technologies for 152 countries, including all DFL countries but one (data for Malawi are missing). Comparing the DFL countries, Belarus ranks highest in the index and Mozambique lowest. Between 2008 and 2010 the CIS countries, India, Angola and Mozambique improved their ranking, whereas Brazil, Zambia and Zimbabwe fell and Botswana, South Africa and Indonesia remained the same. The IDI shows that fixed broadband subscriptions are below 0.1 per cent of the population in the African countries (except 1.5% for South Africa), India and Indonesia, whereas it ranges from 5 to 17 per cent in the CIS countries and Brazil. Subscriptions to mobile broadband are at or below 1 per cent in some African countries, Kazakhstan, Azerbaijan and India but range between 4 and 16 per cent in Botswana, Angola, South Africa, Ukraine, Belarus, Brazil and Indonesia. Except in the CIS countries mobile broadband subscriptions are higher than fixed broadband subscriptions (ITU 2011).

Internet use

Worldwide, Internet use is lower than mobile phone use. Population percentages in DFL countries having Internet access range from 2.7 per cent in Mozambique to 46.3 per cent in Belarus, with Internet access rates highest in the CIS countries and lowest in African DFL countries and India (most figures as of June 2010, Figure 7.1). Mozambique lags, also compared with the other African countries, while other than in mobile phone use South Africa is outstripped by the other large countries. In the CIS countries private computers are most commonly used for Internet access, whereas especially in Africa and Latin America Internet cafés are (ITU 2011). For the time being, education, age and urban-rural gaps are much wider in Internet use than mobile telephony. Internet use is higher among people with higher levels of education and among high-income groups. For example, in Botswana only 2 per cent of the lowest 75 per cent of the income distribution access the Internet, against 19 per cent among the top 25 per cent incomes. However, the spread of mobile Internet access and the provision of prepaid Internet services might lower existing income divides in the years to come (ITU 2011).

It is widely recognized that the Internet and related social media (Facebook, Twitter, etc.) can play a forceful role in social mobilization and the emergence and strengthening of civil societies. In this respect one notes the finding of Robison and Crenshaw (2010, 56) that their "state repression indicator" is weakly but positively influential on Internet use. They interpret this peculiar finding cautiously, but it seems a sign of hope that state repression has not been able to frustrate the worldwide expansion of Internet use. Nevertheless, Internet freedom, far from being self-evident, varies across the DFL countries in general relationship with degrees of press freedom, governance, and government surveillance.

For example, in Ukraine in the early 2000s the Kuchma regime aimed at controlling the media, notably at election times. However, in the November 2004 Orange Revolution, independent weeklies, TV and radio stations and Internet sources played a major role, as did text messaging, in sparking social action. Internet sources in particular revealed corruption and related scandals under Kuchma. In the month when Orange started, Internet use in Ukraine grew by nearly 40 per cent (Salnykova 2006). In other DFL countries, too, Internet freedom has been hampered by government, among other means by legal restrictions in South Africa, Zimbabwe, Kazakhstan, Belarus, India and Indonesia. Restrictions vary from limited and targeted ones, as in South Africa, India and Indonesia, to widespread government control and surveillance, blocking of websites regarded as oppositional, and prosecution. The latter policies have had practical effect in Belarus and Kazakhstan in frustrating civil society and opposition groups (see Table 7.5).

Some years ago the European Bank for Reconstruction and Development (EBRD) (2009, 29), calling the Internet "an increasingly vibrant source of news from independent and opposition journalists in Belarus", pointed out Internet penetration rates in Belarus as among the highest in CIS countries (see Box 7.5). How "vibrant" Internet use in Belarus continues to be is questionable. In 2008 and 2009 the government partially restricted Internet access and monitored e-mail and Internet chat rooms. Internet café owners were required to maintain records of customers and submit them to government security services. In April 2009 heavy restrictions on Internet use were formalized in a government decree. From 1 July 2010 going online in an Internet café was possible only after the user was identified. In October 2010 the State Telecommunications Inspectorate of Belarus stated that an (undisclosed) list of restricted websites contained 20 sources that carried "extremist or pornographic" materials. In the course of 2010, the prosecutor opened three defamation cases against the oppositional Charter97 website after the police harassed its female editor and confiscated its equipment. On 16 July 2010 Charter97 reported a cyberattack on its site after posting a documentary critical of President Lukashenko (US Dept of State 2011c; Charter97 website).

Table 7.4 Situation concerning human, women's and labour rights, 2009–10

	Mozambique	Angola	South Africa	Zambia	Botswana	Malawi	Zimbabwe	Ukraine	Azerbaijan	Kazakhstan	Belarus	Brazil	India	Indonesia
Human rights not respected/abuses	x	xx	x	x		x	xx	xx	xx	xx	xx	x	x	xx
Discrimination against women – legislation				x										
Discrimination against women – practice	xx	xx	xx	xx	x	x	x	x	xx	x	x	x	xx	x
Sexual harassment	xx	xx	xx	x	xx	x	xx	x	x	x	x	x	x	x
Societal violence against women, rape	xx	xx	xx	xx	xx	xx	xx	xx	x	x	x		xx	x
Inheritance practices favouring male heirs	x	x	x	xx	x		x		x				xx	x
No access for women to property other than land	x	x		x	x	x	x						x	
Domestic violence, spousal rape	xx	xx	xx	xx	xx	x	xx	xx	xx	xx	xx	xx	xx	xx
Trafficking of women/ girls, forced prostitution	xx	xx	xx	xx	xx	xx	xx	xx	xx	xx	xx	xx	xx	xx
Incidence of child labour (girls' labour)	xx	xx	x	x	x	xx	xx	x	x	x		xx	xx	xx
Restrictions on press freedom – legislation			x				x						x	

Restrictions on press freedom – practice	x	x		x	x	x	xx	x	xx	xx	xx			x
Restrictions on Internet freedom – legislation			x				x			x	x		x	x
Restrictions on Internet freedom – practice										x	x			
Restrictions on freedom of association – legislation				x						x		x	x	
Restrictions on freedom of association – practice	x	x	x	x			xx		x	xx	xx	x	x	x
Restrictions on collective bargaining rights – legislation		x										x	x	
Restrictions on collective bargaining rights – practice	x	x	x	x		x	xx	x	x	xx	xx	x	x	x
TOTAL x scores	18	19	16	19	13	12	23	13	16	17	17	14	22	16

Note: x = limited (0.5 in inheritance practices and no access for women; on governance, x = average 3.0–5.0); xx = widespread (1 in inheritance practices and no access for women, on governance, average < 3.00).

Source: Derived from US Dept of State 2011a–o; ITUC 2011c; OECD 2012.

Table 7.5 Situation concerning governance, 2009

	Mozambique	Angola	South Africa	Zambia	Botswana	Malawi	Zimbabwe	Ukraine	Azerbaijan	Kazakhstan	Belarus	Brazil	India	Indonesia
1. Voice and accountability	5	2	7	4	5	5	1	5	2	2	1	7	7	5
2. Political stability and absence of violence	7	4	5	7	9	5	2	4	4	8	7	6	2	3
3. Government effectiveness	4	2	7	3	7	5	1	3	3	5	2	6	6	5
4. Regulatory quality	5	2	7	4	7	4	1	4	5	5	2	6	5	5
5. Rule of law	4	2	6	4	7	6	1	3	3	4	2	5	6	4
6. Control of corruption	5	1	7	4	8	5	1	2	2	2	3	6	5	3
Average	5.0	2.2	6.5	4.3	7.2	5.0	1.2	3.5	3.2	4.3	2.8	6.0	5.2	4.2

Source: World Bank, Worldwide Governance Indicators (WGI) governance index, 2009, division over 10 deciles (1 = lowest) (World Bank 2012).

Box 7.5 A success story: the Belarusian *WageIndicator*

The *WageIndicator* websites reveal unexpected success stories, showing for example that with almost half a million web visitors between April 2010 and April 2011, a national website can be quite successful in a country like Belarus. The *WageIndicator* website in Belarus, run by Mojazarplata, provides information for young women on salaries, career, rights, work/life balance, promotion options and the like to enable them to make informed choices about their work. It also contains blogs by two young women writing about their experiences after marriage. The website provides interactive tools and checks for a wide audience, with a questionnaire on wages, a tool to calculate your wage, a decent work check, information on bonuses, a partner check and an economic crisis test. During the years 2010–11, almost 1 per cent of the total Belarusian labour force completed the *WageIndicator* web survey, a relatively much higher figure than that of any other *WageIndicator* country. This success was due to a combination of organisational factors including a strong web team, sound international backing, interesting and targeted content and such external factors as the country's large share of high-skilled women and a lack of competing websites (Bandarenka 2011; ITUC 2011a).

Observers in Kazakhstan have reported since 2008 that the government monitors e-mail and Internet activity, blocks or slows access to opposition websites and plants pro-government propaganda in Internet chat rooms. Though the state regulates the country's only two Internet service providers, websites express a variety of views. On 11 July 2009 the president signed amendments to legislation governing the Internet that reclassify all websites, including chat rooms and blogs, as media outlets, thus making them subject to the media law and making it easier to shut them down for violations during electoral periods. In 2010 bloggers reported anecdotally that their sites were periodically blocked. The opposition-oriented website zona.kz reported coordinated cyberattacks on it in February and April and a ten-day attack in May (US Dept of State 2011h).

Girls and women on the internet

As with mobile phone use, women's access to and use of the Internet is lower than men's, but the Internet gender gap varies across countries. Whereas this gap, calculated as the gender pay gap is, was rather marginal in 2009–10 in Brazil (2%), it was substantial in Ukraine (14%) and Belarus (12%), and large in Azerbaijan (34%).

Unfortunately, data for African countries are missing (authors' calculations based on ITU 2011, 117). Older figures point to a considerable gender gap in Internet use in the young generation, too, at least in developing countries. By 2006 Indonesian girls and young women 15 to 24 were half as likely to use the Internet as boys their age (8% versus 16%), though young females were heavier mobile phone users than their male peers (31% versus 22%). Income and education again show up as major factors causing a digital divide. In the mid-2000s in Indonesia, three in five university students (59%) used the Internet, compared with 3 per cent among youth with only a primary education; among those with a monthly household income over 1,250,000 rupees, that share was 29 per cent, versus only 5 per cent among those from households with less than half that income (World Bank 2006a, 202).

Similar results appear for sub-Saharan African countries. Especially there PC and Internet use is a more communal experience than in developed countries. By the time these countries' youth accessed the Internet, they did so predominantly at Internet cafés but hardly ever at schools: data for six Sub-Saharan African countries revealed that fewer than 1 per cent of schools provided Internet access. For some countries there was proof that young women accessed the Internet considerably less often through Internet cafés and other public access points than young men did. They may not feel comfortable or may be restricted from frequenting these points alone. Even at school girls may find it harder to gain access to computers and the Internet. Especially where they are in the minority, they have to compete with boys for scarce computer resources; most (hidden) fights end with boys being in control (cf. World Bank 2006a, 202). These mechanisms have been studied widely in the USA, Australia and other high-income countries, but little evidence on the gender divide comes from classrooms in developing countries. Yet there is little or no reason to assume that, if researched, outcomes would much differ from those in high-income countries (cf. Plan UK/Plan International 2010, 111–17).

Persistence of an Internet gender gap will have serious consequences for the girls and women left out, because being left out online is being left out of something central to many adolescent girls' lives (see Box 7.6). "Even in the rich world, not being part of an online social network can mean missing out not only on what is happening in your peer group, but on opportunities for taking part in a wide range of activities". Plan UK/Plan International (2010, 105–6), from which the citation stems, gives seven reasons why the new communications technologies are important for adolescent girls and can help them achieve the MDG3 goals: to keep in touch with others and reduce isolation; to further their education and acquire new skills; to take an active part in their communities and countries; to have the skills to find work; to build specific skills and knowledge on subjects they might otherwise not know about, such as HIV/AIDS; to build self-esteem through learning to use these technologies; last but definitely not least, to keep safe. The Plan's report builds on research evidence underpinning this enumeration.

Girls and young women increasingly use the latest media outlets. Twitter, used to communicate, share and engage with others, offers possibilities to interact with decision makers and, in a project to amplify girls' voices in the run-up to the G20 meeting in July 2010, take part in global discussions on girls' rights. International organizations also use Twitter to support girls: practitioners can "tweet" about their work in real time, allowing a glimpse into development work (Plan UK/Plan International 2010, 106). Yet listing the advantages of the new communications media may not hide their dark side. That side definitely exists as well. Facebook, MySpace, Craigslist and other social media, apart from offering opportunities for communicating with friends, are misused by traffickers or other perpetrators of abuse to make contact with adolescent girls. These media can bring sexual harassment and exploitation closer to potential victims. Girls in areas that lack decent job prospects, living without adequate family support, are the most vulnerable potential victims. Also, among adolescents in developed countries cyberbullying has become widespread; these

Box 7.6 Decisions for Life: online and offline

The Internet played a major role in the DFL project in reaching the target group of young women. Knowing that Internet access rates are still low in most of the DFL countries, offline practices were adopted in addition to online activities. The offline practices included debates, interviews, essays, theatre and poetry productions, community radio broadcasts and mall committees organised by or in close connection with national trade unions. All work-related information collected for and posted at the national *WageIndicator* websites is designed such that it can easily be printed and handed out at meetings and workplaces. Most web pages are also accessible through mobile phones, multiplying the outreach of the information posted on the websites by tens or even hundreds.

practices do not necessarily stop at a country's borders (Plan UK/Plan International 2010, 119–27). Interestingly, Internet-related US organizations in which girls and young women often play major roles focus on creating safe online spaces for them to interact with their peers (Plan UK/Plan International 2010, 127–8). Such facilities can be included in wider civil society action, among other things aiming at creating safe spaces (physical ones, too) for girls (Levine et al. 2008, 6).

8

Perspectives for Using the Internet on Behalf of Girls and Young Women: The Case of the Statutory Minimum Wage

Introduction

A main part of the Decisions for Life project included the launching of websites with work-related information in the 14 countries. The pages providing information on the statutory minimum wages were among the most popular. This chapter therefore focuses on the case of information dissemination concerning the statutory minimum wage. The level of statutory minimum wages, their potential to reduce women's vulnerability to low pay, their employment effects and their effects on income distribution are discussed. The chapter ends with the role of the *WageIndicator* websites in enforcing minimum wages.

Minimum wages

In the 2000s, developing countries, including Brazil, China and South Africa, relied on minimum wages ever more. Over half of the 108 countries sampled in the ILO's *Global Wage Report 2010/11* chose to increase minimum wages even in 2009. The ILO also noted that minimum wages are applied in about 90 per cent of the world's countries. It estimated that about 35 per cent of these countries set out a single minimum wage with universal coverage, while a majority, 65 per cent, have a set of minimum wages varying by sector, occupation or region (ILO 2010e). In the current crisis there are strong reasons to emphasize statutory minimum wage (SMW) systems' role in maintaining purchasing power and protecting low-paid, vulnerable workers – in particular female workers (ILO 2010a, 64). The ILO concludes that SMWs are more likely to benefit women's pay than men's, arguing that "a growing body of literature [...] points to the important role of minimum wage policies in combating gender-based pay discrimination and addressing the vulnerability of women to becoming trapped in low-paid jobs" (ILO 2010a, 73). The *Global Wage Report 2010/11* refers to recent work of Rubery and Grimshaw; for OECD (high-income) countries they provide support for the argument that institutional arrangements for regulating low-wage work can reduce women's vulnerability to low pay. Rubery and Grimshaw show that countries with a high minimum wage (40% or more of average earnings) had on average the smallest gender pay gap, followed by those with both a high minimum wage and a strong collective bargaining system (with collective bargaining covering at least 80% of the workforce). Countries with weak collective bargaining coverage and a low minimum wage or none had on average the highest gender pay gap. The authors find the same order of country groups concerning the low-pay incidence of women relative to men (Rubery and Grimshaw 2011, 248).

There are good reasons to broaden analyses such as Rubery and Grimshaw's to developing countries. A basic argument is that to the extent that SMWs succeed in influencing wage setting of informal and non-standard work, they are likely to reduce those countries' poverty – which, as noted, hits women more than men (cf. Saget 2001; Devereux 2005). Currently all 14 DFL countries have minimum-wage regulations in place. In most of them trade unions have played a pivotal role in minimum-wage-setting processes and exerting pressure to improve the efficacy of existing arrangements, better compliance and enforcement in particular. Such efforts – documented for Brazil, India, Indonesia, Mozambique (see Box 8.1), South Africa, Zambia and others – have clarified that ensuring compliance with minimum-wage legislation remains a weak spot. Thus, by necessity, it is a major field of ongoing trade union activity. With the *WageIndicator* websites and new social media, the DFL project has made innovative contributions to these activities. The project has pointed out new ways for trade unions to have an active role and for their membership to monitor and enforce minimum-wage regulations.

Box 8.1 Minimum-wage campaign in Mozambique

In 2010 in Mozambique, a minimum-wage campaign of the OTM union confederation, OTM and local union committees were assisted by

WageIndicator, explains Egidio Vaz Raposo from the Regional *WageIndicator* office in Maputo. The campaign has taken the shape of raising awareness among workers on labour law, labour rights and duties, and in particular, on minimum wage and working hours, helped by independent media coverage. It took shape in over ten meetings with workers from various sectors. More than 300 workers attended these offline Decent Work and Labour Law debates, which had substantial impact. They helped to single out the most pressing issues of minimum-wage compliance. Cross-sectoral discussion groups evolved into groups for providing mutual aid. In the cinema sector, for example, the majority of workers were earning less than what the law stipulated. The discussion in the Maputo capital on sector minimum wages helped them claim wages as per the law. The online availability of all relevant information on Meusalario.org, the *WageIndicator* website in Mozambique, has made it the national reference for labour-related issues. In the beginning Meusalario was unknown to the public and the press, but after a year it has become well known. Drawing on earlier experiences and the visibility gained earlier in 2010, by the end of that year *WageIndicator* had begun its Mozambican Minimum Wage and Working Hours Campaign on three fronts; namely, television and radio, printed newspapers and online news portals (Vaz Raposo 2011).

The level of minimum wages

In all 14 countries minimum-wage legislation covers the formal sector, though in South Africa minimum-wage bargaining happens at company or industry level; in addition, administered minimum wages are set by government. Some countries (India, South Africa) have a separate branch of minimum-wage setting targeting the informal sector, though India's central government still excludes domestic workers (Tijdens and Van Klaveren 2011b). In most countries legislation does not rule out informal workers, and Brazil's explicitly includes them. Though across countries a sizeable share of informal wage earners receive almost exactly the minimum wage (the so-called spike in the informal wage distribution; Saget 2006; Freeman 2009), minimum-wage enforcement in the informal sector often undeniably meets problems considerably more serious than the formal sector's.

Table 8.1 provides an overview of the incidence and levels of SMWs in the 14 countries. Six countries turn out to have set one national minimum wage, five others have more than one but a limited number of rates, and India, Indonesia and South Africa each have over a thousand minimum-wage rates. Included, too, are the equivalents in PPP US dollars: this "purchasing power parity" conversion rate implies the purchasing power the dollar has in the USA. In the rightmost column

Table 8.1 Incidence of statutory minimum wage (SMW) by country, 2009–10

	SMW? (2010)	No. of SMWs (2010)	Equivalent in PPP US$ (2009)*	SMW (%) of average wage, formal sector (2009)
Angola	yes	3	94	39
Azerbaijan	yes	1	121	27
Belarus	yes	1	250	23
Botswana	yes	5	159	20
Brazil	yes	1	286	42*
India	yes	over 1,600	65–121	55–90**
Indonesia	yes	over 2,000	71–148	42–87***
Kazakhstan	yes	1	165	23
Malawi	yes	2	53–59	44–49
Mozambique	yes	10	56–103	112–206
South Africa	yes	over 1,800	290–510	31–53
Ukraine	yes	1	311	50
Zambia	yes	1	77	40
Zimbabwe	yes	28	?	7–90

Note:
* median value (= Kaitz index).
** median across states: 72.
*** median across provinces: 65.

Source: Van Klaveren et al. 2009b, d, e, g; 2010a–g; IIM/AIAS/WIF 2011a–e; WageIndicator websites; ILO Conditions of Work and Employment Laws database; ILO Laborsta database; PPP equivalents, ILO 2010a, Table SA2.

are the outcomes of estimations of the ratio of the SMW(s) to the average wage in the formal sector. This measure, mostly close to the Kaitz index, shows the SMW as a percentage of the median wage and is often used to indicate the "bite" of minimum wages at national level. Yet as available statistics did not allow calculation of medians for a majority of countries, averages were used.

Saget, preferring the minimum wage-to-GDP (gross domestic product) per capita per month ratio as central yardstick over the Kaitz index, calculated it for 131 countries. Based on 2002–4 data, she classified countries as in a "mini minimum wage" situation if their SMW/GDP per capita ratio was less than 0.30 (30%) and as in a "maxi minimum wage" situation if their ratio was above 0.60 (60%). As for the DFL countries, following this exercise four – Azerbaijan, Belarus, Botswana, Kazakhstan – had a "mini" minimum wage, and another four – India, Indonesia, Malawi, Mozambique – a "maxi" minimum wage. Five countries – Angola, Brazil, South Africa, Ukraine, Zambia – were in between; data for Zimbabwe were missing (Saget 2008, 29–32). In spite of the different yardsticks used, the classification results of Saget differ only marginally from our outcomes. We agree on the same four mini minimum wage countries and, taking into account the median values calculated for India and Indonesia, except for Malawi the same maxi minimum wage countries as well.

Employment effects

Traditionally, the employment effects of (increases in) the minimum wage have caused a lot of discussion. Employers and their associations worldwide, traditionally supported by economists, have fuelled the fear that SMWs as such would be detrimental for jobs. In 1995 their positions were weakened. The respected US economists Card and Krueger had challenged conventional economic wisdom by concluding, on the basis of a number of US studies, that minimum-wage increases do not decrease employment. Fourteen years later, two other American researchers, extending and advancing Card and Krueger's meta-analysis, concluded that their colleagues' findings still stood: "There never was much accumulated empirical evidence of a negative employment effect from minimum-wage regulation" (Doucouliagos and Stanley 2009, 422). These outcomes were related only to the US labour market. Empirical studies covering European countries found no simple relationship between minimum wages and employment and definitely no clear negative correlation between them (Vaughan-Whitehead 2008; Gautié and Schmitt 2010). Taking into account a multitude of research results from developing countries, Freeman (2009) concludes (to near consensus on the conclusion) that negative employment effects of minimum-wage rises here have been small, even negligible. He found little evidence that the informal sector's high workforce share diminished the effects of minimum-wage setting in developing countries compared with effects in high-income countries.

Nevertheless, going in detail into research outcomes mapping employment effects while covering the position of women is worthwhile. It is a lucky coincidence that there is a body of research available on employment effects of SMWs for countries that in economists' eyes may be "risky": Brazil, with considerable SMW level rises, albeit to a relatively moderate level; and Indonesia, with increases to relatively high minimum levels. The evidence for Brazil largely confirms that for high-income countries. In regard to that country, one should realize that the real value of the statutory minimum wage was first to fall by nearly 50 per cent between 1990 and 1995 before increasing between 1995 and 2009 from year to year (except in 2003). Only in 2004 did its real value surpass the 1990 level (Ferreira et al. 2010). According to the ILO (2008), the substantial rise of the Brazilian SMW "does not seem to have produced any negative effects on employment growth or the level of employment of formalization in the country. To the contrary, both indicators have improved markedly." These claims are supported by research outcomes. The near doubling of the minimum wage in real terms throughout the 2000s did not act as an impediment to employment growth (Berg 2011). Based on 1982–2000 data, Lemos (2007) found no employment effects in the public and private sectors of the minimum-wage hikes, though the hikes strongly compressed wage distribution in both sectors; she had earlier reported small negative long-run employment effects and modest negative effects in the formal and informal sectors (Lemos 2004a, b).

The experience of Indonesia is more equivocal. First of all, much of Indonesia's minimum-wage legislation is open to interpretation; penalties are comparatively small, though enforcement of minimum-wage legislation has increased, in particular in the 1990s. Then, the government's active promotion of minimum-wage policies led to substantial increases in real terms and compared with average wages; the Kaitz index rate rose from 49 in 2001 to 75 in 2009 (varying by province, with a median of 65; Damayanti 2011). Older studies had found hardly any employment effects for Indonesia. Alatas and Cameron (2003), studying the minimum wage's impact on total employment from 1990 to 1996, traced a small negative effect, though hardly significant, dependent on firm size and type. Alisjahbana and Manning (2007) found no clear direction and concluded that employment effects depended on the business cycle, labour market conditions, firm size and sector. Chun and Khor (2010) found in their simulations no significant changes in total employment or unemployment from increases in the minimum wage but a negative impact on the number of workers employed in the formal sector. This negative effect occurred both for low-paid workers (wages less than 90% of the minimum wage) and better-paid workers (earning 1.5 to 2.5 times the minimum). Remarkably, negative effects were concentrated in women: in the formal sector they disproportionally lost work, while male formal jobs stayed the same. Comola and De Mello (2011), using panel data for the period 1996–2004, also found that minimum-wage hikes in Indonesia expanded total informal-sector employment, even more than compensating for job losses in the formal sector, bringing a positive net employment effect. Yet in their outcomes women lost jobs in the formal sector; for them the net employment effect of lifting the SMW was zero.

Effects on income distribution

In Latin America statutory minimum wage increases seem to have had an equalizing effect on income distribution. A study of 19 Latin American countries in the 1997–2001 period showed that minimum wages raised pay at the bottom of the distribution and in most countries (14 of 19) lifted wages in both the formal and informal sectors (Kristensen and Cunningham 2006). It has also been suggested that between 2002 and 2007, this development continued in majority left-of-centre regimes, with wage (formal) employment growing faster than other forms. Also, rising public social expenditure and redistribution efforts helped policies of formalizing employment yield some results (Cornia 2010). The *Global Wage Report 2010/11* seems to paint a less rosy picture. It contains a table with a sample of 27 countries indicating no straightforward statistical relationship between minimum wage levels and the incidence of low pay. The report goes on to conclude, "Thus, while country experiences in Brazil and Chile show that minimum wages have great potential for improving the situation of low-paid workers, the larger picture shows that this potential is often wasted" (ILO 2010a, 70).

The ILO report emphasizes that in practice there are several reasons why the effectiveness of minimum wages may be limited, one obvious factor being enforcement. The labour organization warns that weak implementation machinery –characterized by few labour inspectors, low probability of detection and light sanctions– will often bring large-scale non-compliance. Compliance is already a problem in high-income countries (e.g., the European Union's; cf. Vaughan-Whitehead 2008), let alone developing countries with often weakly developed institutions and small budgets. A second factor limiting the impact of minimum wages may be weak or imperfect coverage, whereby many vulnerable workers are excluded from social protection. Third, the ILO argues, even with broad coverage and genuine enforcement efforts, minimum wages in developing countries will be more effective in the formal than the informal economy.

Finally, the minimum-wage level matters. Very low ("mini") minimum wages, on the one hand, will likely discourage labour-market participation, nor do they help equalize income distribution or prevent a "race to the bottom". Yet very high ("maxi") minimum wages, often originating in situations where collective bargaining is weak or absent, may fuel inflation by making cash money widely available, lead to either non-enforcement or displacement of low-paid workers into unemployment or informal employment and destroy industry competitiveness. It may even endanger collective bargaining as far as it exists (Saget 2008; ILO 2010a). Most likely is the wide ignorance and near-total lack of compliance with a relatively very high minimum wage, as Mozambique's case indicates. With these arguments in mind, outcomes on income distribution effects in four large DFL countries, Brazil, Indonesia, India and South Africa, will be highlighted.

Concerning Brazil, various studies have pointed to the relation between the post-1995 minimum-wage increases and diminishing income inequality. Saboia (2007, cited in ILO 2008), in an analysis of the impact of the SMW on the reduction in wage inequality between 1995 and 2005, finds that 64 per cent of the improvement at household level was due to minimum-wage increases. The findings of Lemos (2004b, 2007) suggest that the SMW redistributes in favour of poorer workers in both the formal and informal sectors, though differently: for the very bottom of the income distribution in the formal sector but more widely for those in the bottom half of the informal sector. Fontes and Pero show that active adjustments in the SMW were one of the critical determining factors allowing Brazilian low-wage earners to move up to higher wages (cited in ILO 2010a, 67). The mechanisms behind these outcomes are that in Brazil SMW hikes are often regarded as signals given to wage setting in the informal sector (the so-called lighthouse effect) and also act as a *numeraire*, with the salaries of higher-paid formal workers expressed in multiples of the minimum wage. Evidence of the lighthouse effect seems rather "hard" (Maloney and Nunez Mendez 2004; Lemos 2004a); obviously Brazilian unions and employers widely use the minimum wage as a point of reference in bargaining processes. Yet in spite of social progress in various fields, risks of being low-paid in Brazil remain considerably higher for female workers than their male colleagues. In 2009, 26.6 per cent of females earned less than two-thirds the national median wage, the international yardstick for "low wage", against 16.7 per cent of males (Fontes et al. 2011).

In Indonesia changes in minimum wages overall correlate negatively with the share of those in low pay, but the effect's size is relatively small, especially given the substantial increases in the Kaitz index since 2004. This can be explained by the fact that the smaller gap between minimum and average wages was driven more by stagnating or even falling real average wages than by increasing minimum wages (ILO 2010a, 70). From 2004 on, the minimum wage's role seems on the way back in Indonesia. Strong increases in minimum-wage levels from 2000 to 2003, when the government sought to accommodate (new) union demands, were "corrected" in the next three years (Manning and Roesad 2007) and continued thus afterwards. Thus, minimum wages may fail to protect large numbers of the country's low-paid and vulnerable workers (Saget 2008, 41). Moreover, in Indonesia, unlike Brazil, positive income effects of a minimum wage in the informal sector seem limited or non-existent. In Indonesia researchers did not univocally point to a lighthouse effect, at least not for males. One research team indeed found rising wages for men in the formal sector combined with higher pay in the informal (Comola and De Mello 2011), but another team found that minimum-wage hikes had no positive effect at all on pay levels of men in the informal sector. Only hours worked seemed to increase significantly. In contrast, the lighthouse effect works for women: minimum-wage rises caused considerable upward pressure on the pay of low-paid women in the informal sector (Chun and Khor 2010).

For India the conclusion is that in practice workers' rights are legally protected only for the small minority of workers in the organized industrial sector (ITUC 2011c; US Dept of State 2011f). In considerable part a lack of transparency is to blame. As the *Global Wage Report 2010/11* puts it, "In India, the Minimum Wage Act of 1948 is considered to be one of the most important pieces of labour legislation; but India's system of minimum wages is also one of the most complex in the world [....] This system has resulted in innumerable minimum-wage rates, which are difficult to monitor and enforce and are not applicable to all workers" (ILO 2010a, 72). Much evidence supports these judgments, as well as that only small shares of employed women earn at least the relevant minimum wage. The Indian National Commission for Enterprises in the Unorganised Sector (NCEUS) computed that 31 per cent of the regular salaried/wage workers did not receive the national minimum wage for 2004–5; at 54 per cent women's share was more than double men's (26%). At the same time large majorities of casual wage workers earned (considerably) below the minimum wage: 74 per cent of males and 95 per cent of all females. Both categories of wage workers earn on average considerably more than the large mass of informal and own-account workers (NCEUS 2007, 2009a). Against this backdrop, that current minimum wages, categorized as "maxi", substantially influence income redistribution and combat (female) poverty is highly unlikely.

Nevertheless, India's situation with the SMW seems gradually improving. There has been recent widespread debate on how a more effective minimum wage system can be realized. A politically disputed floor-level minimum has been declared. Moreover, a new centrally sponsored scheme providing an amount of guaranteed wage employment (and income) has already impacted quality of life in rural India. Also, the MGNREGS (Mahatma Gandhi National Rural Employment Guarantee Scheme) has raised an interesting political debate with regard to jurisdiction of the minimum wage across India. In 2005 the national government initiated the Mahatma Gandhi National Rural Employment Guarantee Act (MGNREGA), an innovative combination of a minimum-wage provision with a public employment rural development scheme. The MGNREGS legally guarantees 100 days of unskilled manual work at statutory minimum wages to each rural household in a year. Many village-level projects, including water conservation, irrigation, rural connectivity and land development, have been undertaken under the scheme. Conditions should be in place to allow women to assume jobs in construction by providing water, care facilities and shade for children; jobs should be within a certain distance from the women's dwellings. In May 2009 the scheme was reaching over 49 million households, and the participation rate of women workers had increased to 47 per cent. An evaluation study in six states showed that the MGNREGS wage has raised the bar for the determination of wages in agriculture. Scheme employment served as a primary wage-earning opportunity for women, with a majority collecting their wages themselves and retaining them (Papola 2008; NCEUS 2009a; Holmes et al. 2010).

In South Africa, in the 2000s job formalization and expansion of the minimum-wage floor to new sectors and occupations have had substantial positive effects. For example, formalization of the position of teachers, nurses and other public sector professionals into the Public Sector Co-ordinating Bargaining Council had a positive effect on females' earnings (Bhorat et al. 2009, 33–6). At the lower end of the labour market, between 2001 and 2005 the monthly median wages of elementary occupations increased by 65 per cent, against an (unweighted) average increase of 18 per cent for all nine occupational groups. This coincided with extension of minimum-wage legislation to industries not previously covered (Hlekiso and Mahlo 2006). In September 2002 roughly a million domestic workers, about 840,000 of them women, were granted formal labour-market protection; subsequently (November 2002) a schedule of minimum wages for domestics went into effect. Jointly the new regulations appear to have raised the relative wages for domestic workers. In September 2003 their average nominal hourly wages were 23 per cent higher than they had been a year earlier; for similar workers in other occupations the nominal increase was less than 5 per cent. Some employment decrease, one not clearly related to the wage increase, occurred. For many low-paid women the minimum wage made a difference (Hertz 2005). Budlender (2010) also found that South African domestic workers' average wages have risen without significant employment loss since minimum wages came into effect, though she notes that their average working hours have decreased.

Enforcement of the minimum wage and the role of the *WageIndicator*

Benassi (2011) addresses several mechanisms through which SMWs are not complied with. Employers may consider the minimum-wage level too high or do not perceive its payment as obligatory. High costs make full coverage of labour inspections impossible; inspectors are at risk of corruption, or fines may be too low. Wage competition may be too strong to enforce minimum wages, or the informal sector's extent may not allow SMW enforcement in developing countries. Importantly, employers do not comply with the SMW because they are not well informed, or workers do not expect to be paid the minimum wage because of lack of information. In both cases raising awareness on the minimum wage is needed, particularly in countries with a complex SMW setting. This is definitely so in India, Indonesia and South Africa, countries with, respectively, over 1,600, 2,000 and 1,800 minimum-wage rates.

Information is key to empowerment, and the *WageIndicator* websites set up by local teams in each country concerned provide the kind of information that young women need to help them make decisions in their lives. National web teams cooperating closely with trade union teams helps ensure that websites meet the needs of the DFL campaign (ITUC 2011a). The websites also contain information about decent work, how to improve career and work/life balance, information on labour law, and minimum wages, as well as articles about the DFL campaign, including interactive sections to allow young women to share experiences. Users of the sites debate online and ask for legal advice via e-mail. Social media are used extensively to communicate with the target group.

Since 2006 minimum-wage information has gradually become a more important part of *WageIndicator* websites, as web visitors expressed interest in this information. For example, when the Indian

WageIndicator team, running the national website, received many minimum-wage-related questions from the public at large, it started chasing Indian state officials for figures. The *WageIndicator* website is now the leading site in India featuring all legal minimum wages, broken down by state and occupation and updated regularly. Civil servants even started asking the Indian team to upload their updated minimum wages (Osse et al. 2012).

In South Africa wide-scale dissemination of both bargained agreements and set minimum wages was often lacking, implying that minimum wages were far from easy to trace. Some rates seemed outdated, or at least publication in the *Government Gazette* was lagging behind decision making on uprating. These practices added considerably to the fact that, as local experts emphasize, non-compliance with minimum wages generally was a large problem. According to the director of Labour Research Services (LRS), Cape Town, widespread ignorance remained on what minimum wage was agreed in a company or sector unless the trade union actively campaigned around the issue (Patel 2011). This situation changed in mid-2010, when the national *WageIndicator* website in South Africa included 13 pages with updated and detailed information about the country's minimum wages. In four months, January to May 2011, these pages attracted 355,037 page views. The South African *WageIndicator* web team explains: "We aim to provide a one-stop shop where young women can find the answers to their questions on maternity leave, what they should be earning, their rights in the workplace and lots more, all at the click of a mouse. We base a lot of our work on the feedback we get from users, as well as trade union feedback, so we have a good idea of what people want to know" (ITUC 2011a).

In Indonesia article 88.1 of the Manpower Law states that "every worker has the right to earn a living that is decent from the viewpoint of humanity", and article 89 of that law sets up that the SMW may consist of provincial or district- or city-based minimum wages or sector-based minimum wages within a given locale. As a result, huge variation in minimum-wage rates shows up even within a province. By establishing a method to collect information about the various minimum wages and posting it on the Indonesian *WageIndicator* website, the site contributes largely to disseminating SMW rates. The availability of this information made the website an instant success (ITUC 2011a).

After its initial success in India, *WageIndicator* started to collect information on statutory minimum wages in a systematic way, build a database with minimum-wage information and post it on all national websites (see *WageIndicator* Minimum Wage website). In many countries these pages are very popular and generate heavy web traffic. In January 2012, for example, South Africa's minimum wage pages registered 13,000 visits, Indonesia's 17,000 and Belarus's even 39,000. All information is downloadable for print. Web visitors participate in online debates and ask for legal advice via e-mail. Increasingly, Facebook and other social media are used to communicate with web visitors. Clearly, *WageIndicator* has become a major promoter of "good practice" in disseminating minimum wages in the countries at stake, thereby contributing to transparency in the labour market (Osse et al. 2012).

References

Acemoglu, D., and Johnson, S. (2009) "Disease and Development: The Effect of Life Expectancy on Economic Growth", in M. Spence and M. Lewis (eds), *Health and Growth*. Washington, DC: Commission on Growth and Development (CGD)/World Bank: 77–129.

Africa Labour Researchers Network (ALRN) (2004) *Trade Unions in Africa*. w.p.

African Development Bank (AfDB) /African Development Fund (ADP) (2008) *Country Gender Profile. Angola*. w.p.

AfDB/Organisation for Economic Co-operation and Development (OECD) (2008) *African Economic Outlook. Zambia*. w.p.

Alatas, V. (2011) "Leaving Poverty Behind. Policy Responses to Help Indonesian Families Overcome Vulnerability to Poverty". *Indonesia 360°* 1(2): 69–81.

Alatas, V., and Cameron, L. (2003) *The Impact of Minimum Wages on Employment in a Low Income Country: An Evaluation using the Differences-in-Differences Approach*. Washington, DC: World Bank, Policy Research Working Papers no. 2985.

Alcântara, A. A. (2008) *Women and Politics: The Brazilian Paradox*. Bahia: Federal University (http://www.opendemocracy.net/article/5050/political_representation_brazil).

Aliber, M. (2003) "Chronic Poverty in South Africa: Incidence, Causes and Policies". *World Development* 31(3): 473–90.

Alisjahbana, A. S., and Manning, C. (2006) "Labour Market Dimensions of Poverty in Indonesia". *Bulletin of Indonesian Economic Studies* 42(2): 235–61.

Alkire, S. (2010) *Human Development: Definitions, Critiques, and Related Concepts*. New York: UNDP, Human Development Research Paper 2010–11.

Allehag, L., De Vylder, S., Durevall, D., and Sjöblom, M. (2006) *The Impact of HIV-AIDS on Livelihoods, Poverty and the Economy of Malawi*. Stockholm: Sida, Sidastudies no. 18.

Amnesty International (AI) (2007) *Zimbabwe: Between a Rock and a Hard Place – Women Human Rights Defenders at Risk*. London: Amnesty International.

Amnesty International (AI) (2008) *Picking Up the Pieces. Women's Experience of Urban Violence in Brazil*. London: Amnesty International.

Anderson, M., Baldwin, T., Lovallo, L., and Pumariega, G. (2012) "Will a Shortage of Qualified Labor Derail the Brazilian Economy?" (posted 3 January on Knowledge – Wharton: http://knowledge.wharton.upenn.edu/article.cfm?articleid=2911).

Andonova, V, and Diaz-Serrano, L. (2009) "Political Institutions and Telecommunications". *Journal of Development Economics* 89: 77–83.

Arcand, J.-L., and D ' Hombres, B. (2004) "Discrimination in the Brazilian Labour Market: Wage, Employment and Segregation Effects". *Journal of International Development* 16(8): 1053–66.

Ardani, A. G., and Kanadi, S. (2009) "Indonesia's Parliamentary Election 2009: Are Women Invited?" (posted 7 April: http://www.awid.org/Library/Indonesia-s-Parliamentary-Election-2009-Are-Women-Invited).

Armstrong, P., Lekezwa, B., and Siebrits, K. (2008) *Poverty in South Africa: A Profile Based on Recent Household Surveys*. Matieland: Stellenbosch Economic Working Paper 04/08.

Asian Development Bank (ADB) (2005) *Azerbaijan. Country Gender Assessment*. Manila: ADB.

ADB (2009) *Millennium Development Goals. Key Indicators for Asia and the Pacific 2009*. New Delhi: ADB.

Badan Pusat Statistik (BPS) (2009) *Perkembangan Beberapa Indikator Utama Sosial-Ekonomi Indonesia. Trends of the Selected Socio-Economic Indicators of Indonesia*. Jakarta: BPS, October.

BPS (2010) "Decent Work – Indonesia" (PowerPoint presentation). Jakarta: BPS.

Bandarenka, T. (2011) "Why Mojarzaplata.by in Belarus Is the Best", in D. Dragstra (ed.), *The Next Decade. 10th Anniversary WageIndicator Foundation*. Amsterdam: WageIndicator Foundation (WIF): 21–4.

Bank Dunia/World Bank (2007) *Investing in Indonesia's Education. Allocation, Equity, and Efficiency of Public Expenditures*. Jakarta: Bank Dunia/World Bank, Poverty Reduction and Economic Management Unit, East Asia and Pacific Region.

Barbosa, M. (2012) "Newspaper Circulation in Brazil Grows 3.5% in 2011", 29 January (http://www1.folha.uol.com.br/internacional/en/finance/1039340-newspaper-circulation-in-brazil-grows-35-in-2011.shtml) Accessed 10 march 2012.

Beegle, K., Filmer, D., Stokes, A., and Tiererova, L. (2010) "Orphanhood and the Living Arrangements of Children in Sub-Saharan Africa", *World Development* 38(12): 1727–46.

Benassi, C. (2011) *The Implementation of Minimum Wage: Challenges and Creative Solutions*. Geneva: ILO, Global Labour University working papers no. 12.

Benner, C., Omar, R., and Lewis, C. (2007) *The South African Call Centre Industry: National Benchmarking Report, Strategy, HR Practices & Performance*. Johannesburg: Sociology of Work Centre/LINK Centre, University of Witwatersrand.

Berg, J. (2011) "Laws or Luck? Understanding Rising Formality in Brazil in the 2000s", in Lee, S., and McCann, D. (eds), *Regulating for Decent Work. New Directions in Labour Market Regulation*. Geneva/Basingstoke: ILO/Palgrave Macmillan: 123–50.

Berquó, E., and Cavenaghi, S. (2005) "Increasing Adolescent and Youth Fertility in Brazil: A New Trend or a One-Time Event?". Paper presented at the Annual Meeting of the Population Association of America, Philadelphia, Pennsylvania, 30 March–2 April.

Bhana, D., and Pattman, R. (2009) "Researching South African Youth, Gender and Sexuality Within the Context of HIV/AIDS". *Development* 52(1): 68–74.

Bhorat, H., Kanbur, R., and Mayet, N. (2010) "Minimum Wage Violation in South Africa". Ithaca, New York: Cornell University. Paper.

Bhorat, H., Van der Westhuizen, C., and Goga, S. (2009) *Analysing Wage Formation in the South African Labour Market: The Role Of Labour Councils*. Cape Town: Development Policy Research Unit Working Paper 09/135.

Biehl, J. G. (2007) "Pharmaceuticalization: AIDS Treatment and Global Health Politics". *Anthropological Quarterly* 80(4): 1083–126.

Bosch, A. (2006) "Determinants of Public and Private-Sector Wages in South Africa". *South African Reserve Bank, Labour Market Frontiers* 8: 17–24.

Bosworth, B., and Collins, S. M. (2007) *Accounting for Growth: Comparing China and India*. Cambridge, Massachusetts: National Bureau of Economic Research (NBER): Working Paper 12943.

Bracking, S., and Sachikonye, L. (2006) *Remittances, Poverty Reduction and the Informalisation of Household Wellbeing in Zimbabwe*. W.p.: Global Poverty Research Group/Economic & Social Research Council.

Brixiová, Z., and Volchok, V. (2005) *Labor Market Trends and Institutions in Belarus*. Ann Arbor, Michigan: William Davidson Institute Working Paper no. 777.

Brouard, P. (2011) "Blog: The 5th Durban AIDS Conference – A Reflection", 23 June (http://www.csa.za.org/blog/item/77-the-5th-durban-aids-conference%E2%80%93a-reflection) Accessed 22 March 2012.

Budlender, D. (2010) *Decent Work for Domestic Workers. Study Prepared for the SERVICES Sector Education and Training Authority*. Johannesburg: Community Agency for Social Enquiry (CASE).

Butler, A. (2005) "South Africa's HIV/AIDS Policy, 1994–2004: How Can It Be Explained?". *African Affairs* 104/417: 591–614.

Buvinic, M., Das Gupta, M., and Casabonne, U. (2009) "Gender, Poverty and Demography: An Overview". *World Bank Economic Review*, Advance Access: 1–23.

Card, D., and Krueger, A. B. (1995) *Myth and Measurement. The New Economics of the Minimum Wage*. Princeton, New Jersey: Princeton University Press.

Cardoso, A. R., and Verner, D. (2006) *School Drop-Out and Push-Out Factors in Brazil: The Role of Early Parenthood, Child Labour, and Poverty*. Bonn: IZA, Discussion Paper no. 2515.

Casale, D. (2004) *What Has the Feminization of the Labour Market "Bought" Women in South Africa? Trends in Labour Force Participation, Employment and Earnings, 1995–2001*. Cape Town: Development Research Policy Unit (DRPU), Working Paper 04/84.

Casale, D., Muller, C., and Posel, D. (2004) "Two Million Net New Jobs. A Reconsideration of the Rise in Employment in South Africa, 1995–2003". Forum Paper African Development and Poverty Reduction: Macro-Micro Linkage, Somerset West, 13–15 October.

Casale, D., and Posel, D. (2009) *Unions and the Gender Wage Gap in South Africa*. Pietermaritzburg: University of Kwazulu-Natal, Working Paper no. 113.

Center Women and Modern World/LGBT Organization Labrys/Sexual Rights Initiative (2009) Fourth Round of the Universal Periodic Review – February 2009. Baku etc. (http://www.gender-az.org/index_En.shtml?id_doc=606) Accessed 15 March 2012.

Central Statistical Office, Zambia (CSO) (2007a) *The Monthly*. Vol. 56. November. Lusaka.

CSO (2007b) *Labour Force Survey Report* (*LFS – 2005*). Lusaka.

CSO (2009) *The Monthly*. Vol. 76. July. Lusaka.

Central Statistical Organisation (CSO) /Government of India (2009) *Millennium Development Goals – India Country Report 2009. Mid-Term Statistical Appraisal*. New Delhi.

Chibba, M. (2011) "The Millennium Development Goals: Key Current Issues and Challenges". *Development Policy Review* 29(1): 75–90.

Chikanda, A. (2005) "Nurse Migration from Zimbabwe: Analysis of Recent Trends and Impacts". *Nursing Inquiry* 12(3): 162–74.

Chinguwo, P. (2011) "Women in Trade Unions in Malawi", in H. Shinondola-Mote, K. N. Otoo, and T. Kalusopa (eds), (2011), *The Status of Women in Trade Unions in Africa. Evidence from 8 Countries*. Accra: African Labour Research Network (ALRN): 107–41.

Chinn, M. D., and Fairlie, R. W. (2010) "ICT Use in the Developing World: An Analysis of Differences in Computer and Internet Penetration". *Review of International Economics* 18(1): 153–67.

Chowdhury, A., Islam, I., and Tadjoeddin, M. Z. (2009) "Indonesia's Employment Challenges: Growth, Structural Change and Labour Market Rigidity". *European Journal of East Asian Studies* 8(1): 31–59.

Chun, N., and Khor, N. (2010) *Minimum Wages and Changing Wage Inequality in Indonesia*. Manila: Asian Development Bank (ADB), Economics Working Paper no. 196.

Clemens, M. A., and Pettersson, G. (2008) "New Data on African Health Professionals Abroad". *Human Resources for Health* 6(1) art. 1.

Commission on Growth and Development (CGD) (2008) *The Growth Report: Strategies for Sustained Growth and Inclusive Development*. Washington, DC: CGD/World Bank.

Comola, M., and De Mello, L. (2011) "How Does Decentralized Minimum Wage Setting Affect Employment and Informality? The Case of Indonesia". *Review of Income and Wealth 57* special series, S79–S99.

Connell, J., Zurn, P., Stilwell, B., Awases, M., and Braichet, J.-M. (2007) "Sub-Saharan Africa: Beyond the Worker Migration Crisis? " *Social Science & Medicine* 64: 1876–91.

Cornia, G. A. (2010) "Income Distribution under Latin America's New Left Regimes". *Journal of Human Development and Capabilities* 11(1): 85–114.

Cornia, G. A. (2007) "Chapter 1. Overview of the Impact and Best Practice Responses in Favour of Children in a World Affected by HIV and AIDS", in G.A. Cornia (ed.), *AIDS, Public Policy and Child Well-Being*. 2nd edn. Florence: UNICEF Innocenti Research Centre: 1–30.

Cosby, K. A., Mustafayev, D., and Vazirova, A. (eds) (2007) *Azerbaijan Human Development Report 2007 Gender Attitudes in Azerbaijan: Trends and Challenges*. Baku: UNDP Azerbaijan/State Committee for Family, Women and Children's Issues of the Republic of Azerbaijan.

Dabash, T., and Perchal, P., Assefa, N., Arruda, S., Babenko, O., and Beatty, S. (2006) *Sexual and Reproductive Health Needs of Women and Adolescent Girls Living with HIV: Research Report on Qualitative Findings from Brazil, Ethiopia and the Ukraine*. New York: Engenderhealth/UNFPA (UN Population Fund).

Damayanti, A. (2011) "Low-Paid Workers in Indonesia". Paper, Second Conference Regulating for Decent Work (RDW): Regulating for a Fair Recovery. Geneva: ILO, 6–8 July.

Das, S., Mukhopadhyay, A., and Ray, T. (2009) "Economic Cost of HIV and AIDS in India", in M. Haacker and M. Claeson (eds), *HIV and AIDS in South Asia: An Economic Development Risk*. Washington, DC: World Bank: 123–54.

De Ruyter, A., Singh, A., Warnecke, T., and Zammit, A. (2009) "Core vs. Non-Core Standards, Gender and Developing Countries: A Review with Recommendations for Policy and Practice". Paper ILO Conference on Regulating for Decent Work (RDW), Geneva, 8–10 July.

De Ruyter, A., and Warnecke, T. (2008) "Gender, Non-standard Work and Development Regimes: A Comparison of the USA and Indonesia". *Journal of Industrial Relations* 50(5): 718–35.

Desai, M. (2010) "Hope in Hard Times: Women's Empowerment and Human Development". New York: UNDP, Human Development Research Paper 2010–14.

Devereux, S. (2005) "Can Minimum Wages Contribute to Poverty Reduction in Poor Countries?". *Journal of International Development* 17: 899–912.

Dewan, S., and Peek, P. (2007) *Beyond the Employment/Unemployment Dichotomy: Measuring the Quality of Employment in Low Income Countries*. Geneva: ILO, Policy Integration and Statistics Department Working Paper.

Dias, R. (2005) "Education and Economic Status in South Africa: Insights from the Labour Force Survey of 2003". Paper presented to the Economic Society of South Africa Biennial Conference, 7–9 September.

Dinka (2007) "Brazil to finance birth control pills", 29 May (http://www.huliq.com/23039/brazil-to-finance-birth-control-pills) Accessed 28 March 2012.

Dinkelman, T., Lam, D., and Leibbrandt, M. (2008) "Linking Poverty and Income Shocks to Risky Sexual Behaviour: Evidence from a Panel Study of Young Adults in Cape Town". *South African Journal of Economics* 76(S1): S52–S74.

Donahue, A. (2010) "Adolescent Girls, Cornerstone of Society: Building Evidence and Policies for Inclusive Societies". Conference Background Paper 5th UNICEF-GPIA International Conference, New York City.

Doucouliagos, H., and Stanley, T. D. (2009) "Publication Selection Bias in Minimum-Wage Research? A Meta-Regression Analysis". *British Journal of Industrial Relations* 47(2): 406–28.

Downie, A. (2011) "On Brazil, Vocational Education Expands to Meet Demands of a Booming Economy". *Chronicle of Higher Education,* 5 July (http://chronicle.com/article/In-Brazil-Vocational/128135/).

Economic Commission for Africa (ECA) /African Union/African Development Bank Group/UNDP (2010) *Assessing Progress in Africa Toward the Millennium Development Goals*. MDG Report 2010. W.p.

European Bank for Reconstruction and Development (EBRD) (2009) "Strategy for Belarus. As Approved by the Board of Directors at its Meeting on 10 December 2009". London: EBRD.

European Training Foundation (ETF) (2010) *Belarus. ETF Country Information Note 2009–11* (update 2010). Torino: ETF.

Eyraud, L. (2009) *Why Isn't South Africa Growing Faster?* Washington, DC: IMF Working Paper no. 09/25.

Ferreira, F. H. G., Leite, P. G., and Ravallion, M. (2010) "Poverty Reduction Without Economic Growth? Explaining Brazil's Poverty Dynamics, 1985–2004". *Journal of Development Economics* 93: 20–36.

Fontana, M. (2004) "Modelling the Effects of Trade on Women, at Work and at Home: Comparative Perspectives". *Economie Internationale* 99: 49–80.

Fontes, A., Pero, V., and Berg, J. (2011) "Low-Paid Employment in Brazil". Paper, Second Conference Regulating for Decent Work (RDW): Regulating for a Fair Recovery. Geneva: ILO, 6–8 July.

Ford, M., and Parker, L. (2008) "Thinking About Indonesian Women and Work", in M. Ford and L. Parker (eds), *Women and Work in Indonesia*. London: Routledge: 1–16.

Forero, J. (2012) "Brazil's Falling Birth Rate: A "New Way of Thinking"", posted 15 January (http://www.npr.org/2012/01/15/145133220/brazils-falling-birth-rate-a-new-way-of-thinking) Accessed 10 March 2012.

Freeman, R. B. (2009) *Labor Regulations, Unions, and Social Protection in Developing Countries: Market Distortions or Effective Institutions?* Cambridge, Massachusetts: NBER, Working Paper 14789.

Friedman, T. L. (2005) *The World Is Flat. A Brief History of the Globalized World in the Twenty-first Century.* London: Allen Lane.

Gautié, J., and Schmitt, J. (eds) (2010) *Low-Wage Work in the Wealthy World.* New York: Russell Sage Foundation.

Gaye, A., Klugman, J., Kovacevic, M., Twigg, S., and Zambrano, E. (2010) *Measuring Key Disparities in Human Development: The Gender Inequality Index.* New York: UNDP, Human Development Research Paper 2010–46.

Government of Botswana (2009) *The Millennium Development Goals (MDGs). Second Progress Report 2009.* Gaborone.

Government of India (2010) *Government Budget. Economic Survey 2009/2010.* New Delhi.

Government of Malawi (2010) *2010 Malawi Millennium Development Goals Report.* Lilongwe.

Government of the Republic of Belarus (2005) *National Report of the Republic of Belarus. Status of Achieving the Millennium Development Goals.* Minsk.

Government of Zimbabwe (2009) *Zimbabwe Millennium Development Goals. 2000–2007 Mid-Term Progress Report. A report of the Government of Zimbabwe to the United Nations.* Harare, August.

Greene, M. E., Cardinal, L., and Goldstein-Siegel, E. (2009) *Girls Speak. A New Voice in International Development. A Girls Count Report on Adolescent Girls.* New York: International Center for Research on Women (ICRW).

GSMA Development Fund/Cherie Blair Foundation (2009) *Women & Mobile: A Global Opportunity. A Study on the Mobile Phone Gender Gap in Low and Middle-Income Countries.* London.

Gupta, P., Hasan, R., and Kumar, U. (2008) *What Constrains Indian Manufacturing?* Manila: Asian Development Bank (ADB) Working Paper Series no. 119.

Guzi, M. (2011) "Potential for Global Wage Comparisons", in D. Dragstra (ed.), *The Next Decade. 10th Anniversary WageIndicator Foundation.* Amsterdam: WIF: 31–3.

Hanlon, J. (2007) "Is Poverty Decreasing in Mozambique?" Paper Inaugural Conference of the Instituto de Estudos Sociais e Económicos (IESE). Maputo, 19 September.

Hassim, S. (2006) *Women's Organizations and Democracy in South Africa: Contesting Authority.* Madison, Wisconsin: University of Wisconsin Press.

Heintz, J. (2006) *Globalization, Economic Policy and Employment: Poverty and Gender Implications.* Geneva: ILO, Employment Strategy Papers 2006/3.

Hertz, T. (2005) *The Effect of Minimum Wages on the Employment and Earnings of South Africa's Domestic Service Workers.* Washington, DC: American University, Department of Economics, Working Paper Series no. 2005–04.

Hervish, A., and Feldman-Jacobs, C. (2011) *Who Speaks for Me? Ending Child Marriage.* Washington, DC: Population Reference Bureau, Policy Brief, April.

Hlekiso, T., and Mahlo, N. (2006) "Wage Trends and Inequality in South Africa: A Comparative Analysis, in South African Reserve Bank". *Labour Market Frontiers,* October, no. 8: 9–16.

Holmes, R., Hagen-Zanker, J., and Vandemoortele, M. (2011) *Social Protection in Brazil: Impacts on Poverty, Inequality and Growth*. London: ODI.

Holmes, R., Sadana, N., and Rath, S. (2010) *Gendered Risks, Poverty and Vulnerability in India. Case Study of the Indian National Rural Employment Guarantee Act (Madhya Pradesh)*. London/New Delhi: ODI/Indian Institute of Dalit Studies.

Hoogeveen, J. G., and Özler, B. (2005) *Not Separate, Not Equal: Poverty and Inequality in Post-Apartheid South Africa*. Madison, Wisconsin: William Davidson Institute Working Paper no. 739.

Hossain, N., and Eyben, R. (2009) *Accounts of Crisis: Poor People's Experiences of the Food, Fuel and Financial Crises in Five Countries. Report on a pilot study in Bangladesh, Indonesia, Jamaica, Kenya and Zambia, January–March 2009*. Brighton: Institute of Development Studies (IDS).

Huisman, J., and Smits, J. (2009) "Effects of District- and Household-Level Factors on Primary School Enrollment in 30 Developing Countries". *World Development* 37(1): 179–93.

Human Sciences Resource Council (HSRC) (2009) *South African National HIV Prevalence, Incidence, Behaviour and Communication Survey, 2008. A Turning Tide among Teenagers?* Cape Town: HSRC Press.

IIM (Indian Institute of Management) /AIAS/WIF (WageIndicator Foundation) (2011a) *Minimum Wage 2010–2011 Report. India*. Ahmedabad/Amsterdam (www.paycheck.in).

IIM (Indian Institute of Management) /AIAS/WIF (2011b) *Minimum Wage 2010–2011 Report. Indonesia*. Ahmedabad/Amsterdam (www.gajimu.com).

IIM (Indian Institute of Management) /AIAS/WIF (2011c) *Minimum Wage 2010–2011 Report. South Africa*. Ahmedabad/Amsterdam (www.mywage.co.za).

IIM (Indian Institute of Management) /AIAS/WIF (WageIndicator Foundation) (2011d) *Minimum Wage Report. Malawi*. Ahmedabad / Amsterdam (www.mywage.com).

IIM (Indian Institute of Management) /AIAS/WIF (2011e) *Minimum Wage Report. Mozambique*. Ahmedabad/Amsterdam (www.meusalario.org/mocambique).

Instituto Brasileiro de Geografia e Estatística (IBGE) (2008) *Pesquisa Nacional por Amostra de Domicílios – PNAD 2007*. Brasilia DF: IBGE.

International Institute for Population Sciences (IIPS) /Macro International (2007) *The National Family Health Survey-3, 2005–06. India* (Vol. I). Mumbai: IIPS and Macro International.

International Labour Organization (ILO) (2009a) *Labour and Social Trends in Indonesia 2009: Recovery and Beyond Through Decent Work*. Jakarta: ILO Office for Indonesia.

ILO (2009b) *Implications of the Global Economic Crisis for Tourism Employment: Case Study for Indonesia*. Jakarta: ILO Office for Indonesia.

ILO (2010a) *Global Wage Report 2010/11: Wage policies in times of crisis*. Geneva: ILO.

ILO (2010b) *Global Employment Trends for Youth. Special Issue on the Impact of the Global Economic Crisis on Youth*. Geneva: ILO, August.

ILO (2010c) *Global Employment Trends*. Geneva.

ILO (2011a) *Global Employment Trends for Youth: 2011 Update*. Geneva: ILO, October.

ILO (2011b) *ILO Estimates and Projections of the Economically Active Population: 1990 2020* (6th edn). *Methodological Description*. Geneva: ILO, October.

ILO (2011c) *Indonesia: Reinforcing Domestic Demand in Times of Crisis. Studies on Growth with Equity.* Geneva: ILO.

ILO (2012) *Global Employment Trends 2012. Preventing a deeper jobs crisis.* Geneva: ILO.

ILO/IILS (International Institute for Labour Studies) (2012) *World of Work Report 2012. Better Jobs for a Better Economy.* Geneva: ILO, April.

ILO Labour Force Surveys website, last accessed 20 February 2012 (http://www.ilo.org/dyn/lfsurvey/lfsurvey.home).

International Monetary Fund (IMF) (2007) *Malawi: Poverty Reduction Strategy Paper – Growth and Development Strategy.* IMF Country Report no. 07/55. Washington, DC, February.

International Planned Parenthood Association (IPPF) /UNFPA/Young Positives (IPPF 2007a) *Change, Choice and Power: Young Women, Livelihoods and HIV Prevention. Literature Review and Case Study Analysis.* London/New York/Amsterdam.

IPPF/UNFPA/Young Positives/The Global Coalition on Women and AIDS (IPPF 2007b) *Ending Child Marriage. A Guide for Global Policy Action.* London, November 2007 edn.

International Telecommunications Union (ITU) (2011) *Measuring the Information Society 2011.* Geneva: ITU.

International Trade Union Confederation (ITUC) (2009a) *Gender (in)equality in the labour market: An overview of global trends and developments.* Brussels: ITUC, 8 March.

ITUC (2009b) *ITUC Report. 1st World Women's Conference. The Decent Work agenda: A gender work perspective.* Brussels: 19–21 October.

ITUC (2011a) *Living with Economic Insecurity: Women in Precarious Work.* Brussels: ITUC, March.

ITUC (2011b) *Decisions for Life. Empowering Young Women Workers.* Brussels: ITUC, brochure, May.

ITUC (2011c) *Annual Survey of Violation of Trade Union Rights 2011.* Brussels: ITUC (http://survey.ituc-csi.org/) Accessed 10 March 2012.

IRINnews (2009) "South Africa: Child Labour Ban Increases Poverty, but Raises Hope", 20 May (http://www.irinnews.org/Report/84470/SOUTH-AFRICA-Child-labour-ban-increases-poverty-but-raises-hope) Accessed 22 April 2012.

IRINnews (2010) "Zimbabwe: Mining industry attracts child labour as economy picks up", 14 October (http://www.irinnews.org/Report/90770/ZIMBABWE-Mining-industry-attracts-child-labour-as-economy-picks-up) Accessed 15 March 2012.

Jejeebhoy, S. J. (1998) "Adolescent Sexual and Reproductive Behavior: A Review of the Evidence from India". *Social Science & Medicine* 46(10): 1275–90.

Jensen, R., and Oster, E. (2007) *The Power of TV: Cable Television and Women's Status in India.* Washington, DC: National Bureau of Economic Research, NBER Working Paper no. 13305.

Jha, P., Kumar, R., Vasa, P., Dhingra, N., Thiruchelvam, D., and Moineddin, R. (2006) "Low Male-to-Female Sex Ratio of Children Born in India: National Survey of 1.1 Million Households. " *The Lancet* 367: 211–18.

Kateta, M. (2009) "Sexual Harassment in the Workplace in Malawi" (http://www.mywage.com/main/women-and-work/no-sex-no-job.-sexual-harassment-in-the-workplace, last accessed 21 March 2012).

Katz, E. (2008) *Programs Promoting Young Women's Employment: What Works?* Washington, DC: Adolescent Girls Initiative/World Bank.

Kingdon, G. G., and Knight, J. (2007) "Unemployment in South Africa, 1995–2003: Causes, Problems and Policies". *Journal of African Economics* 16(5): 813–48.

Krishna, A. (2007) "Escaping Poverty and Becoming Poor in Three States of India, with Additional Evidence from Kenya, Uganda, and Peru", in D. Narayan and P. Petesch (eds), *Moving out of Poverty.* Vol. 1. *Cross-Disciplinary Perspectives on Mobility.* Washington, DC/Basingstoke: World Bank/Palgrave Macmillan: 165–98.

Kristensen, N., and Cunningham, W. (2006) *Do Minimum Wages in Latin America and the Caribbean Matter? Evidence from 19 Countries.* Washington, DC: World Bank, Policy Research Working Papers no. 3870.

Kundu, A., and Sarangi, N. (2009) "Chapter 5. Inclusive Growth and Economic Inequality in India under Globalization. Causes, Consequences and Policy Responses", in *Country Policy Dialogues on Inequality.* Colombo: UNDP Regional Office: 97–138.

Kyle, S. (2007) *Oil, Growth and Political Development in Angola.* Ithaca, New York: Staff paper, Department of Applied Economics and Management, Cornell University.

Lake, H. (2008) *Analysis of Human Resource Management Practices. Indonesia's Labour-Intensive Light Manufacturing Industries.* Jakarta: USAID/SENADA – Indonesia Competitiveness Program.

Lancet, The (2009) "Health in South Africa. An Executive Summary for *The Lancet* Series", 24 August (http://download.thelancet.com/flatcontentassets/series/sa/sa_Execsum.pdf) Accessed 10 March 2012.

Lee, S. (2012) *Working Conditions in Mozambique.* Dublin: European Foundation for the Improvement of Living and Working Conditions.

Lee, S., and McCann, D. (2011) "New Directions in Labour Regulation Research", in S. Lee and D. McCann (eds), *Regulating for Decent Work. New Directions in Labour Market Regulation.* Geneva/Basingstoke: ILO/Palgrave Macmillan: 1–30.

Lehmann, H., and Pignatti, N. (2007) *Informal Employment Relationships and Labor Market Segmentation in Transition Economies: Evidence from Ukraine.* Bonn: IZA, IZA Discussion Paper no. 326.

Leibbrandt, M., Levinsohn, J., and McCrary, J. (2005) *Incomes in South Africa since the Fall of Apartheid.* Cambridge, Massachusetts: National Bureau of Economic Research, NBER Working Paper 11384.

Leibbrandt, M., Woolard, I., Finn, A., and Argent, J. (2010) *Trends in South African Income Distribution and Poverty since the Fall of Apartheid.* Paris: OECD, Social, Employment and Migration Working Paper 101.

Lemos, S. (2004a) "Minimum Wage Policy and Employment Effects: Evidence from Brazil". *Economia*, Fall 2004: 219–66.

Lemos, S. (2004b) *The Effects of the Minimum Wage in the Formal and Informal Sectors in Brazil.* Bonn: IZA, Discussion Paper no. 1089.

Lemos, S. (2007) "Minimum Wage Effects across the Private and Public Sectors in Brazil". *Journal of Development Studies* 43(4): 700–20.

Lentsie, L. (2011) "Women in Trade Unions in Botswana", in H. Shinondola-Mote, K. N. Otoo, and T. Kalusopa (eds), (2011) *The Status of Women in Trade Unions in Africa. Evidence from 8 Countries*. Accra: African Labour Research Network (ALRN): 17–48.

Levine, D. I., and Ames, M. (2003) "Gender Bias and the Indonesian Financial Crisis: Were Girls Hit Hardest?". Berkeley, California: Center for International and Development Economics Research (CIDER), Working Paper no. C03-130.

Levine, R., Lloyd, C. B., Greene, M., and Grown, C. (2008) *Girls Count. A Global Investment & Action Agenda. A Girls Count report on adolescent girls*. Washington, DC: Center for Global Development.

Lipsey, R. E., and Sjöholm, F. (2004) "Foreign Direct Investment, Education and Wages in Indonesian Manufacturing". *Journal of Development Economics* 73(1): 415–22.

Lloyd, C. B. (2007) *Poverty, Gender and Youth. The Role of Schools in Promoting Sexual and Reproductive Health among Adolescents in Developing Countries*. New York: Population Council, Working Paper no. 6.

Lloyd, C. B., and Hewett, P.C. (2009) "Educational Inequalities in the Midst of Persistent Poverty: Diversity across Africa in Educational Outcomes". *Journal of International Development* 21(8): 1137–51.

Lloyd, C. B., and Mensch, B. S. (2008) "Marriage and Childbirth as Factors in School Exit: An Analysis of DHS Data from Sub-Saharan Africa". *Population Studies* 62(1): 1–13.

Lloyd, C. B., with Young, J. (2009) *New Lessons. The Power of Educating Adolescent Girls. A Girls Count Report on Adolescent Girls*. New York: Population Council.

Lopez, N. (2008) "Urban and Rural Disparities in Latin America: Their Implications for Education Access". Paper commissioned for the EFA Global Monitoring Report 2008, "Education for All by 2015: Will we make it?". Buenos Aires: UNESCO.

Lovell, P. A. (2006) "Race, Gender, and Work in Sâo Paolo, Brazil, 1960–2000". *Latin American Research Review* 41(3): 63–87.

Luke, N., and Munshi, K. (2011) "Women as Agents of Change: Female Income and Mobility in India". *Journal of Development Economics* 94: 1–17.

Mahmud, S., Shah, N. M., and Becker, S. (2012) "Measurement of Women's Empowerment in Rural Bangladesh". *World Development* 40(3): 610–19.

Maloney, W. F., and Nunez Mendez, J. (2004) "Measuring the Impact of Minimum Wages: Evidence from Latin America", in J. Heckman and C. Pagés (eds), *Law and Employment: Lessons from Latin America and the Caribbean*. Cambridge, Massachusetts: National Bureau of Economic Research (NBER)/University of Chicago.

Manning, C., and Roesad, K. (2007) "The Manpower Law of 2003 and its Implementing Regulations: Genesis, Key Articles and Potential Impact". *Bulletin of Indonesian Economic Studies* 43(1): 59–86.

Mishra, S. C. (2009) *Economic Inequality in Indonesia. Trends, Causes and Policy Response*. Colombo: UNDP Regional Office: Strategic Asia.

Mitskevich, Y. (2010) *Equal Chances Remain a Declaration. Women's Status in Belarus*. Warsaw: Heinrich Boell Stiftung.

Mookodi, G. (2004) "The Dynamics of Domestic Violence against Women in Botswana". *Pula: Botswana Journal of African Studies* 18(1): 55–64.

Moore, A. M., Singh, S., Ram, U., Remez, L., and Audam, S. (2009) *Adolescent Marriage and Childbearing in India: Current Situation and Recent Trends*. New York/Washington, DC: Guttmacher Institute.

Morrison, A., and Sabarwal, S. (2008) *The Economic Participation of Adolescent Girls and Young Women: Why Does It Matter?* Washington, DC: World Bank /Adolescent Girls Initiative.

Mugoni, P. (2005) ´Southern African News Features. A Step Closer to Reducing Poverty – Botswana and Namibia Achieve Goal Three" (http://www.sardc.net /Editorial/Newsfeature/120302.htm, accessed 23 June 2010).

Muneku, A., and Phiri, A. (2011) "Women in Trade Unions in Zambia", in H. Shinondola-Mote, K. N. Otoo, and T. Kalusopa (eds), (2011) *The Status of Women in Trade Unions in Africa. Evidence from 8 Countries.* Accra: African Labour Research Network (ALRN): 217–43.

Narayan, D., and Petesch, P. (2007) (eds) *Moving out of Poverty.* Vol. 1. *Cross-Disciplinary Perspectives on Mobility.* Washington, DC/Basingstoke: World Bank/Palgrave Macmillan.

National Commission for Enterprises in the Unorganised Sector (NCEUS) (2007) *Report on Conditions of Work and Promotion of Livelihoods in the Unorganised Sector.* New Delhi: Government of India.

National Commission for Enterprises in the Unorganised Sector NCEUS (2009a) *The Challenge of Employment in India. An Informal Economy Perspective.* Vol. I. *Main Report.* New Delhi: Government of India.

NCEUS (2009b) *Skill Formation and Employment Assurance in the Unorganised Sector.* New Delhi: Government of India.

National Labour and Economic Development Institute (NALEDI) (2008) "The Annual Report on Bargaining 2008. Bargaining for a Living Wage". Report for COSATU's CEC. 26 February 2008. Johannesburg.

National Statistical Office (NSO) (2006) *Welfare Monitoring Survey (WMS) 2006.* Zomba: Republic of Malawi.

NSO/UNICEF (2006) *Malawi Multiple Indicator Cluster Survey 2006 (MICS). Preliminary Report.* Zomba: NSO; Lilongwe: UNICEF.

Ndungu, S. K. (2007) "Report. National Collective Bargaining Workshop, 16–17 May 2007, Barayi Training Centre, Yeoville, Johannesburg". Johannesburg: NALEDI/Friedrich Ebert Stiftung.

Ndungu, S. K. (2008) *Collective Bargaining. Wage and Non-Wage Settlement Trends in the South African Labour Market.* Johannesburg: NALEDI.

Neumayer, E., and De Soysa, I. (2011) "Globalization and the Empowerment of Women: An Analysis of Spatial Dependence via Trade and Foreign Direct Investment". *World Development* 39(7): 1065–75.

Nijssen, A. J., and Grijpstra, D. H. (2006) *Project: Tertiary Education Assessment Ukraine.* Leyden: Research voor Beleid.

Nilekani, N. (2008) *Imagining India. Ideas for the New Century.* London: Allen Lane.

Office of the High Commissioner for Human Rights (OHCHR) /UNFPA/UNICEF /UN Women and WHO (2011) *Preventing Gender-Biased Sex Selection.* Geneva: WHO.

Ordor, A. (2011) "Exploring Civil Society Partnerships in Enforcing Decent Work in South Africa". Paper, Second Conference Regulating for Decent Work, ILO, Geneva, 6–8 July.

Organisation for Economic Cooperation and Development (OECD) (2008) "Briefing Note for Brazil", in *Education at a Glance 2008.* Paris: OECD.

OECD (2012) *Gender, Institutions and Development Database 2009* (GID-DB). Paris: OECD (http://stats.oecd.org/Index.aspx?DatasetCode=GID2, last accessed 28 March 2012).

Osse, P., Tijdens, K. G., and Van Klaveren, M. (2012) "Publish What They Preach. Wage Indicator Applies Minimum Wage Research both Online And Offline". *International Journal of Labour Research* (in press).

Padayachee, V., and Valodia, I. (2008) "Economic Reform in South Africa: The Role of Social Movements". Paper, 8th International Conference for Third Sector Research, University of Barcelona, 9–12 July.

Pakpahan, Y. M., Suryadarma, D., Suryahadi, A. (2009) *Destined for Destitution: Intergenerational Poverty Persistence in Indonesia*. Jakarta: SMERU Research Institute, Working Paper.

Pandin, M. R. L. (2009) "The Portrait of Retail Business in Indonesia: Modern Market". *Economic Review*, no. 215, March.

Papola, T. S. (2008) *Employment Challenge and Strategies in India*. New Delhi: ILO Subregional Office for South Asia, ILO Asia-Pacific Working Paper Series.

Pastore, F., and Verashchagina, A. (2007) *When Does Transition Increase the Gender Wage Gap? An Application to Belarus*. Bonn: IZA, Discussion Papers no. 2796.

Patel, R. (2010) "Mozambique's Food Riots – The True Face of Global Warming". *The Observer*, 5 September (http://www.guardian.co.uk/commentisfree/2010/sep/05/mozambique-food-riots-patel) Accessed 15 March 2012.

Patel, S. (2011) "The Effect of Collective Bargaining Data Online", in D. Dragstra (ed.), *The Next Decade. 10th Anniversary WageIndicator Foundation*. Amsterdam: WIF: 45–6.

Perlman, J. E. (2007) "Elusive Pathways Out of Poverty: Intra- and Intergenerational Mobility in the Favelas of Rio de Janeiro", in D. Narayan and P. Petesch (eds), *Moving Out of Poverty*. Vol. 1. *Cross-Disciplinary Perspectives on Mobility*. Washington, DC/Basingstoke: World Bank/Palgrave Macmillan: 227–71.

Phorano, O., Nthomang, K., and Ntseane, D. (2005) "Alcohol Abuse, Gender-Biased Violence and HIV/AIDS in Botswana: Establishing the Link based on Empirical Evidence". *Journal of Social Aspects of HIV/AIDS* 2(1): 188–202.

Pignatti, N. (2010) *Labor Market Segmentation and the Gender Wage Gap in Ukraine*. Berlin: ESCIRRU/DIW Berlin, ESCIRRU Working Paper no. 17.

Pires, R. R. (2011) "Governing Regulatory Discretion: Innovation and Accountability in Two Models of Labour Inspection Work", in Lee and McCann (2011) op. cit., 313–38.

Plan International (2011) *Because They Are Girls. Mapping Plan's Experience in Improving the Lives of Girls*. Woking.

Planning Commission (India) (2007) "Report of Sub-group on Gender and Agriculture". Submitted to the Working Group on Gender Issues, Panchayat Raj Institutions, Public Private Partnership, Innovative Finance and Micro Finance in Agriculture for the Eleventh Five Year Plan (2007–2012). Delhi.

Plan UK (2011) *Breaking Vows. Early and Forced Marriage and Girls' Education*. London.

Plan UK / Plan International (2007) *Because I Am a Girl. The State of the World's Girls 2007.* London/Woking.

Plan UK/Plan International (2010) *Because I Am a Girl. The State of the World's Girls 2010. Digital and Urban Frontiers: Girls in a Changing Landscape.* London /Woking.

Pulerwitz, J., Michaelis, A., and Weiss, E. (2010) "Looking Back, Moving Forward: Promoting Gender Equity to fight HIV". Washington, DC: Population Council, Horizon Synthesis Background Paper.

Rachmawati, R., and De Ruyter, A. (2007) "Multinationals and Unionism in Indonesia". *South East Asian Journal of Management* 1(1): 3–15.

Rajput, J. S. (2009) "Chapter 25. India: Policy Perspectives and Challenges Ahead", in J. Fien, R. Maclean and M.-G. Park (eds), *Work, Learning and Sustainable Development*. New York: Springer: 343–59.

Ranis, G., Stewart, F., and Samman, E. (2006) "Human Development: Beyond the Human Development Index". *Journal of Human Development and Capabilities* 7(4): 323–58.

Ravallion, M. (2009) *A Comparative Perspective on Poverty Reduction in Brazil, China and India*. Washington, DC: World Bank Development Research Group, Policy Research Working Paper 5080.

Ravallion, M., and Lokshin, M. (2007) "Lasting Impacts of Indonesia's Financial Crisis". *Economic Development and Cultural Change* 56: 27–56.

Republic of Mozambique (2010) *Report on the Millennium Development Goals*. Maputo: Republic of Mozambique.

Republic of Zimbabwe (2010a) *National Migration Management and Diaspora Policy*. Draft. Harare.

Republic of Zimbabwe (2010b) *2010 Millennium Development Goals Status Report*. Harare.

Richardson, E., Boerma, W., Malakhova, I., Rusovich, V., and Fomenko, A. (2008) "Belarus: Health System Review". *Health Systems in Transition* 10(6): 1–118.

Robison, K. K., and Crenshaw, E. M. (2010) "Reevaluating the Global Digital Divide: Socio-Demographic and Conflict Barriers to the Internet Revolution". *Sociological Inquiry*, 80(1): 34–62.

Robson, E., Ansell, N., Huber, U. S., Gould, W. T. S., and Van Blerk, L. (2006) "Young Caregivers in the Context of the HIV/AIDS Pandemic in Sub-Saharan Africa". *Population, Space and Place* 12: 93–111.

Rowbottom, S. (2007) *Giving Girls Today & Tomorrow. Breaking the Cycle of Adolescent Pregnancy*. New York: UNFPA.

Rubery, J., and Grimshaw, D. (2011) "Gender and the Minimum Wage", in S. Lee and D. McCann (eds), op. cit.: 226–54.

Saget, C. (2001) "Poverty Reduction and Decent Work in Developing Countries: Do Minimum Wages Help?". *International Labour Review* 140(3): 237–69.

Saget, C. (2006) *Wage Fixing in the Informal Economy: Evidence from Brazil, India, Indonesia and South Africa*. Geneva: International Labour Office, Conditions of Work and Employment Series no. 16.

Saget, C. (2008) "Fixing Minimum Wage Levels in Developing Countries: Common Failures and Remedies". *International Labour Review* 147(1): 25–42.

Salinas, G., and Haacker, M. (2006) *HIV/AIDS: The Impact on Poverty and Inequality*. W.p.: IMF Working Paper WP/06/126, African Department.

Salnykova, A. (2006) *The Orange Revolution: A Case Study of Democratic Transition in Ukraine*. Burnaby, BC: Simon Fraser University, MA thesis.

Santhya, K. G., and Erulkar, A. (2011) "Supporting Married Girls: Calling Attention to a Neglected Group". Population Council Transitions to Adulthood Brief no. 3, February.

Schech, S., and Mustafa, M. (2010) "The Politics of Gender Mainstreaming Poverty Reduction: An Indonesian Case Study". *Social Politics* 17(1): 111–35.

Self-Employed Women's Association (SEWA) (2009) *Financial Crisis Based on Experiences of SEWA*. Gujarat: SEWA.

Sen, A. (2003) "Missing Women – Revisited. Reduction in Female Mortality has been Counterbalanced by Sex Selective Abortions". *British Medical Journal* 327: 1297–8.

Simonovsky, Y., and Luebker, M. (2011) *Global and Regional Estimates on Domestic Workers*. Geneva, ILO: Domestic Work Policy Brief no. 4.

Situmorang, A. (2003) *Adolescent Reproductive Health in Indonesia. Consultancy Report*. Jakarta: STARH Program.

Statistics Agency of Kazakhstan (SAK) (2009) *Preliminary results of the March 2009 Census*. Astana.

Statistics South Africa (SSA) (2005) *Quarterly Labour Force Survey*. Pretoria: SSA, September.

SSA (2009a) *Quarterly Labour Force Survey. Quarter 2, 2009*. Pretoria: SSA, July.

SSA (2009b) *Labour Force Survey. Historical Revision September Series 2000 to 2007*. Pretoria: SSA, March.

SSA (2010) *Millennium Development Goals. Third Progress Report South Africa*. Pretoria: Republic of South Africa/UNDP.

SSA (2011) *Quarterly Labour Force Survey. Quarter 3, 2011*. Pretoria: SSA, November.

Suryadarma, D., Poesoro, A., Budiyati, S., Akhmadi, and Rosfadhila, M. (2007) *Impact of Supermarkets on Traditional Markets and Retailers in Indonesia's Urban Centers*. Jakarta: SMERU Research Institute, Research Report.

Suryadarma, D., Suryahadi, A., and Sumarto, S. (2006) [Suryadarma et al. 2006a] *Causes of Low Secondary School Enrollment in Indonesia*. Jakarta: SMERU Research Institute, Working Paper.

Suryadarma, D., Widyanti, W., Suryahadi, A., and Sumarto, S. (2006) [Suryadarma et al. 2006b] *From Access to Income: Regional and Ethnic Inequality in Indonesia*. Jakarta: SMERU Research Institute, Working Paper.

Suryomenggolo, J. (2008) "Labour, Politics and the Law. A Legal-Political Analysis of Indonesia's Labour Law Reform Program". *Labour and Management in Development* 9.

Taylor, P., Scholarios, D., Noronha, E., and D ' Cruz, P. (2010) *Union Formation in Indian Call Centres/BPO – The Attitudes and Experiences of UNITES Members*. Glasgow: Strathclyde Business School; Ahmedabad: Indian Institute of Management.

Temin, M., and Levine, R. (2009) *Start with a Girl: A New Agenda for Global Health*. Washington, DC: Coalition for Global Development.

Thomas, D., and Frankenberg, E. (2007) "Household Responses to the Financial Crisis in Indonesia. Longitudinal Evidence on Poverty, Resources, and Well-Being", in A. Harrison (ed.), *Globalization and Poverty*. Chicago: University of Chicago Press, 517–560.

Tijdens, K. G., and De Vries, D. (2012) "Health Workforce Remuneration: Comparing Wage Levels, Ranking and Dispersion of 16 Occupational Groups in 20 Countries using Survey Data". *Human Resources for Health*, submitted for publication.

Tijdens, K. G., and Van Klaveren, M. (2011a) *Young Women in Service Sector Occupations. Bookkeepers, Call Centre Operators, Receptionists, Housekeepers, IT-Programmers, Sales Persons, Secretaries, Travel Agency Clerks.* Amsterdam: WageIndicator data report, June.

Tijdens, K. G., and Van Klaveren, M. (2011b) *Domestic Workers. Their Wages and Work in 12 Countries.* Amsterdam: WageIndicator data report, October.

Tijdens, K. G., and Van Klaveren, M. (2012) *Frozen in Time: Gender Pay Gap Unchanged for 10 years.* Brussels: ITUC.

United Nations (UN) (2005) *South Africa. Millenium Development Goals Country Report. 2005.* New York.

UN (2008) *The 2007 Malawi Millennium Development Goal Report.* Lilongwe.

UN (2011) *The Millennium Development Goals Report 2011.* New York.

UNAIDS (Joint UN Programme on HIV/AIDS) (2010) *Global Report: UNAIDS Report on the Global AIDS Epidemic 2010.* Geneva.

UNAIDS (2011) *AIDS at 30. Nations at the Crossroads.* Geneva.

UNAIDS/World Health Organization (WHO) (2008) *07 AIDS Epidemic Update.* Geneva.

UNAIDS/WHO (2009) *09 AIDS Epidemic Update.* Geneva.

UN Children' s Fund (UNICEF) (2005) *Children out of School: Measuring Exclusion from Primary Education.* Montreal: UIS.

UNICEF (2011) *The State of the World's Children 2011. Adolescence. An Age of Opportunity.* New York.

UNICEF (2012) *The State of the World's Children 2012. Children in an Urban World.* New York.

UN Conference on Trade and Development (UNCTAD) (2010) *World Investment Review 2010. Investing in a Low-Carbon Economy.* New York and Geneva.

UNCTAD (2011a) *Information Economy Report 2011.* New York and Geneva.

UNCTAD (2011b) *Trade and Development Report 2011.* New York and Geneva.

UNCTAD (2011c) *World Investment Report 2011. Non-Equity Modes of International Production and Development.* New York and Geneva.

UN Data (2012) Demographics. Table 10. Live births by age of mother and sex of child 2000–2009; Table 23. Marriages by age of groom and by age of bride 2000–2009 (http://unstats.un.org/unsd/demographic/products/dyb/dyb2009-2010.htm, last accessed 19 March 2012).

UN Dept of Economic and Social Affairs (UNDESA) (2010) *The World's Women 2010. Trends and Statistics.* New York.

UNDESA (2011a) *World Fertility Policies 2011* (leaflet). New York.

UNDESA (2011b) *The Millennium Development Goals Report 2011.* New York.

UN Development Group (UNDG) (2010a) *Thematic Papers on MDG3: Promote Gender Equality and Empower Women.* New York.

UNDG (2010b) *MDG Good Practices.* Chapter 1. "Poverty, Employment and Hunger". New York.

UNDG (2010c) *MDG Good Practices.* Chapter 2. "Achieve Universal Primary Education/Gender Equality and Empowerment of Women". New York.

UNDG (2010d) *MDG Good Practices.* Chapter 3. "Child Mortality. Maternal Health. Combating Diseases". New York.

UNDP (2007a) *National Human Development Report 2007 – Mozambique. Challenges and Opportunities. The Response to HIV and AIDS.* Maputo.
UNDP (2007b) *Zambia Human Development Report. Enhancing Household Capacity to Respond to HIV and AIDS.* Youth-friendly version. Lusaka.
UNDP (2007c) *Country Programme Document for Brazil (2007–2011).* W.p.
UNDP (2008) *2007/2008 Human Development Report. Country Factsheet Zambia* (http://hdrstats.undp.org/countries/data_sheets/cty_ds_ZMB.html) Accessed 10 March 2012.
UNDP (2009) *Human Development Report 2009. Overcoming barriers: Overcoming mobility and development.* New York.
UNDP (2010a) *Human Development Report 2010. The Real Wealth of Nations: Pathways to Human Development.* New York.
UNDP (2010b) *Asia-Pacific Human Development Report. Power, Voice and Rights. A Turning Point for Gender Equality in Asia and the Pacific.* Delhi: Macmillan, for UNDP.
UNDP (2011) *Human Development Report 2011. Sustainability and Equity: A Better Future for All.* New York: UNDP.
UN Educational, Scientific and Cultural Organisation (UNESCO) (2006) *EFA Global Monitoring Report 2006. Literacy for Life.* Paris: UNESCO.
UNESCO (2011) *EFA Global Monitoring Report 2011. The Hidden Conflict: Armed Conflict and Education.* Paris: UNESCO.
UNESCO Institute for Statistics (UIS) (2011) *Global Education Digest 2011. Comparing Education Statistics Across the World. Focus on Secondary Education.* Montreal: UIS.
UN Girls' Education Initiative (UNGEI) (2011) *Education for All Global Monitoring Report 2011. A Gender Review.* Working Paper. New Work: UNICEF Education Section.
UN Population Fund (UNFPA) /WHO/UNICEF (2003) *Adolescents: Profiles in Empowerment.* New York.
UNFPA (2011) *State of the World Population 2011.* New York: UNFPA.
UN System in Angola (2002) *Angola. The Post-War Challenges. Common Country Assessment 2002.* Luanda.
US Dept of State, Bureau of Democracy, Human Rights, and Labor (2009) *2008 Human Rights Report: India.* Washington, DC.
US Dept of State, Bureau of Democracy, Human Rights, and Labor (2011a) *2010 Human Rights Report: Angola.* Washington, DC.
US Dept of State, Bureau of Democracy, Human Rights, and Labor (2011b) *2010 Human Rights Report: Azerbaijan.* Washington, DC.
US Dept of State, Bureau of Democracy, Human Rights, and Labor (2011c) *2010 Human Rights Report: Belarus.* Washington, DC.
US Dept of State, Bureau of Democracy, Human Rights, and Labor (2011d) *2010 Human Rights Report: Botswana.* Washington, DC.
US Dept of State, Bureau of Democracy, Human Rights, and Labor (2011e) *2010 Human Rights Report: Brazil.* Washington, DC.
US Dept of State, Bureau of Democracy, Human Rights, and Labor (2011f) *2010 Human Rights Report: India.* Washington, DC.
US Dept of State, Bureau of Democracy, Human Rights, and Labor (2011g) *2010 Human Rights Report: Indonesia.* Washington, DC.
US Dept of State, Bureau of Democracy, Human Rights, and Labor (2011h) *2010 Human Rights Report: Kazakhstan.* Washington, DC.

US Dept of State, Bureau of Democracy, Human Rights, and Labor (2011i) *2010 Human Rights Report: Malawi*. Washington, DC.

US Dept of State, Bureau of Democracy, Human Rights, and Labor (2011j) *2010 Human Rights Report: Mozambique*. Washington, DC.

US Dept of State, Bureau of Democracy, Human Rights, and Labor (2011k) *2010 Human Rights Report: South Africa*. Washington, DC.

US Dept of State, Bureau of Democracy, Human Rights, and Labor (2011l) *2010 Human Rights Report: Ukraine*. Washington, DC.

US Dept of State, Bureau of Democracy, Human Rights, and Labor (2011m) *2010 Human Rights Report: Zambia*. Washington, DC.

US Dept of State, Bureau of Democracy, Human Rights, and Labor (2011n) *2010 Human Rights Report: Zimbabwe*. Washington, DC.

VandeMoortele, J. (2011) "The MDG Story: Intention Denied". *Development and Change* 42(1): 1–21.

Van den Bergh-Collier, E. (2007) *Towards Gender Equality in Mozambique. A Profile on Gender Relations – Update 2006*. Maputo: Swedish International Development Cooperation Agency (SIDA).

Van der Hoeven, R. (2010) "Income Inequality and Employment Revisited: Can One Make Sense of Economic Policy?". *Journal of Human Development and Capabilities* 11(1): 67–84.

Van Klaveren, M., and Tijdens, K. (eds) (2008) *Bargaining Issues in Europe: Comparing Countries and Industries*. Brussels: ETUI-REHS/AIAS-University of Amsterdam/WageIndicator.

Van Klaveren, M., and Tijdens, K. G. (2011) *Minimum Wages and Women's Work*. Amsterdam: WageIndicator data report, December.

Van Klaveren, M., Tijdens, K., Hughie-Williams, M., and Ramos Martin, N. (2009a) *An Overview of Women's Work and Employment in Mozambique*. Amsterdam: AIAS Working Paper 09–77.

Van Klaveren, M., Tijdens, K., Hughie-Williams, M., and Ramos Martin, N. (2009b) *An Overview of Women's Work and Employment in Angola*. Amsterdam: AIAS Working Paper 09–78.

Van Klaveren, M., Tijdens, K., Hughie-Williams, M., and Ramos Martin, N. (2009c) *An Overview of Women's Work and Employment in South Africa*. Amsterdam: AIAS Working Paper 09–79.

Van Klaveren, M., Tijdens, K., Hughie-Williams, M., and Ramos Martin, N. (2009d) *An Overview of Women's Work and Employment in Zambia*. Amsterdam: AIAS Working Paper 09–80.

Van Klaveren, M., Tijdens, K., Hughie-Williams, M., and Ramos Martin, N. (2009e) *An Overview of Women's Work and Employment in Botswana*. Amsterdam: AIAS Working Paper 09–81.

Van Klaveren, M., Tijdens, K., Hughie-Williams, M., and Ramos Martin, N. (2009f) *An Overview of Women's Work and Employment in Malawi*. Amsterdam: AIAS Working Paper 09–82.

Van Klaveren, M., Tijdens, K., Hughie-Williams, M., and Ramos Martin, N. (2009g) *An Overview of Women's Work and Employment in Brazil*. Amsterdam: AIAS Working Paper 09–83.

Van Klaveren, M., Tijdens, K., Hughie-Williams, M., and Ramos Martin, N. (2010a) *An Overview of Women's Work and Employment in India*. Amsterdam: AIAS Working Paper 10–90.

Van Klaveren, M., Tijdens, K., Hughie-Williams, M., and Ramos Martin, N. (2010b) *An Overview of Women's Work and Employment in Indonesia*. Amsterdam: AIAS Working Paper 10–91.

Van Klaveren, M., Tijdens, K., Hughie-Williams, M., and Ramos Martin, N. (2010c) *An Overview of Women's Work and Employment in Azerbaijan*. Amsterdam: AIAS Working Paper 10–92.

Van Klaveren, M., Tijdens, K., Hughie-Williams, M., and Ramos Martin, N. (2010d) *An Overview of Women's Work and Employment in Kazakhstan*. Amsterdam: AIAS Working Paper 10–93.

Van Klaveren, M., Tijdens, K., Hughie-Williams, M., and Ramos Martin, N. (2010e) *An Overview of Women's Work and Employment in Ukraine*. Amsterdam: AIAS Working Paper 10–94.

Van Klaveren, M., Tijdens, K., Hughie-Williams, M., and Ramos Martin, N. (2010f) *An Overview of Women's Work and Employment in Belarus*. Amsterdam: AIAS Working Paper 10–96.

Van Klaveren, M., Tijdens, K., Hughie-Williams, M., and Ramos Martin, N. (2010g) *An Overview of Women's Work and Employment in Zimbabwe*. Amsterdam: AIAS Working Paper 10–97.

Vargas da Cruz, M. J., Porcile, G., Nakabashi, L., and Dória Scatolin, F. (2008) *Structural Change and the Service Sector in Brazil*. Paraná: Universidade Federal do Paraná, Department of Economics, Working Paper 75.

Vaz Raposo, E. G. (2011) "The Meusalario.org Campaign: Debates and Publicity", in D. Dragstra (ed.), *The Next Decade. 10th Anniversary WageIndicator Foundation*. Amsterdam: WIF: 41–2.

Vaughan-Whitehead, D. (ed.) (2008) *The Minimum Wage Revisited in the Enlarged EU*. Geneva: ILO.

Vij, V. (2010) "Economic Participation of Adolescent Girls in India: The Hidden Potential to Transform the Economy" (http://www.paycheck.in/main/career-tips/women-paycheck/articles/economic-participation-of-adolescent-girls-in-india-the-hidden-potential-to-transform-the-economy) Accessed 15 March 2012.

Von Holdt, K., and Webster, E. (2008) "Organising on the Periphery: New Sources of Power in the South African Workplace". *Employee Relations* 30(4): 333–54.

Wilkinson, R., and Pickett, K. (2009) *The Spirit Level. Why More Equal Societies Almost Always Do Better*. London: Allen Lane.

Winters, P., De la O, A. P., Hertz, T., Davis, B., Zezza, A., and Carletto, G. (2008) *A Comparison of Rural Wage Employment in Ghana, Malawi and Nigeria with Other Developing Countries*. Washington, DC: World Bank, paper.

Wodon, Q., and Beegle, K. (2006) "Labor Shortages despite Underemployment? Seasonality in Time Use in Malawi", in M. Blackden and Q. Wodon (eds), *Gender, Time Use, and Poverty in Sub-Saharan Africa*. Washington, DC: World Bank: 97–116.

Worku-Yergou Belay, S. (2007) "Marriage Markets and Fertility in South Africa with Comparisons to Britain and Sweden". PhD diss., Amsterdam: Tinbergen Institute.

World Bank (2004) *Kazakhstan – Dimensions of Poverty in Kazakhstan*. Vol. I: *Policy Briefing*. Report no. 30294-KZ. W.p.

World Bank (2006a) *World Development Report 2007. Development and the Next Generation*. Washington, DC.

World Bank (2006b) *India Development Policy Review: Inclusive Growth and Service Delivery: Building on India's Success. Overview.* New Delhi: Macmillan India.
World Bank (2008) *Beating the Odds: Sustaining Inclusion in a Growing Economy – A Mozambique Poverty, Gender, and Social Assessment.* Vol. I. Washington, DC: World Bank Report no. 40048-MZ.
World Bank (2009a) *An Avoidable Tragedy: Combating Ukraine's Health Crisis. Lessons from Europe.* Washington, DC: World Bank/Verso 04.
World Bank (2009b) *Ukraine Labor Demand Study.* Washington, DC.
World Bank (2011a) *World Development Indicators 2010. Update.* Washington, DC.
World Bank (2011b) *World Development 2012. Gender Equality and Development.* Washington, DC.
World Bank (2011c) *Migration and Remittances Factbook 2011.* 2nd edn. Washington, DC.
World Bank (2011d) *Gender and Climate Change: Three Things You Should Know.* Washington, DC.
World Bank (2012) *Governance Matters 2012. Worldwide Governance Indicators, 1996–2010. Country Data Report for [country].* Washington, DC.
World Health Organization (WHO) (2011) *World Health Statistics 2011.* Geneva.
World Travel & Tourism Council (WTTC) (2012) *Travel and Tourism. Economic Impact 2012. Ukraine.* London: WTTC.
World Vision US (2008) *Before She's Ready. Fifteen Places Girls Marry by 15.* Federal Way, Washington.

Websites

Belstat (http://www.belstat.gov.by/homep/en/main.html, last accessed 28 March 2012).
Brittanica Online Encyclopaedia / Broadcasting (http://www.britannica.com/EBchecked/topic/80543/broadcasting/25228/Brazil, last accessed 28 March 2012).
Charter 97 (*Belarus human rights group*) (last accessed 21 December 2010) (http://www.charter97.org/en/news).
CRY (*Child Rights and You*) (last accessed 25 March 2012) (http://www.cry.org/index.html) website *Decisions for Life Project* (http://dfl.wageindicator.org/home, last accessed 15 March 2012).
eLearning Africa (www.elearning-africa.com, last accessed 10 March 2012).
Genderlinks (http://www.genderlinks.org.za/, last accessed 10 March 2012).
ILO ILOLEX Database (http://www.ilo.org/ilolex/english/index.htm, last accessed 10 March 2012).
ILO LABORSTA Database (http://laborsta.ilo.org, last accessed 22 April 2012).
Internetworldstats (http://www.internetworldstats.com, last accessed 28 February 2012).
International Telecommunications Union (*ITU*) */ statistics* (http://www.itu.int/ITU-D/ict/, last accessed 7 March 2012).
Inter-Parliamentary Union (*IPU*) *Women in national parliaments* (http://www.ipu.org/wmn-e/classif.htm, last accessed 28 February 2012).

IUF /Asia Pacific (Asian Food Worker) (http://asianfoodworker.net/?p=1525, last accessed 14 April 2012).

MDG3 (http://www.micahchallenge.org/beinformed/mdgs/mdg3-gender-equality, last accessed 28 February 2012).

OECD-SIGI (*Gender Equality and Social Institutions*) / *Country Profiles* (http://genderindex.org/countries, last accessed 30 March 2012).

ProLiteracy (http://www.proliteracy.org/page.aspx?pid=370, last accessed 15 April 2012).

Rural Poverty portal / Brazil (http://www.ruralpovertyportal.org/web/guest/country/home/tags/brazil last accessed 28 March 2012).

SOMO (*Centre for Research on Multinational Corporations, Amsterdam*) (http://somo.nl/about-somo/successes/garments, last accessed 15 April 2012).

Statistics Ukraine (http://www.ukrstat.gov.ua/, last accessed 23 March 2012).

UNAIDS (http://www.unaids.org/en/, last accessed 13 March 2012).

UN Data (http://data.un.org, last accessed 14 March 2012).

UNDP (http://www.undp.org/content/undp/en/home.html, last accessed 14 March 2012).

UNFPA, Adolescent Data Guides (http://www.unfpa.org/youth/dhs_adolescent_guides.html, last accessed 28 March 2012).

UNGEI, "Education project in Rajasthan", posted in 2009 (http://www.ungei.org/news/india_2294.html, last accessed 22 March 2012).

UNICEF, Country statistics (http://www.unicef.org/infobycountry/, last accessed 28 March 2012).

UN Millennium Development Goals (*MDG*) *indicators* (*statistics*) (http://mdgs.un.org/unsd/mdg/Default.aspx, last accessed 9 March 2012).

UN Office for the Coordination of Humanitarian Affairs (*OCHA*) / *Zimbabwe* (http://ochaonline.un.org/Default.aspx?alias=ochaonline.un.org/zimbabwe, last accessed 28 March 2012).

WageIndicator Minimum Wage (http://www.wageindicator.org/main/minimum-wages, last accessed 25 March 2012).

WHO (*World Health Organization*) *Malawi* (http://www.who.int/countries/mwi/en/, last accessed 25 March 2012).

WTTC (*World Travel and Tourism Council*) (http://www.wttc.org/eng, last accessed 5 April 2012).

Index

Printed and bound in the United States of America